U.S. Policy
Toward Africa

edited by
Frederick S. Arkhurst

Published in cooperation with the
Phelps-Stokes Fund

The Praeger Special Studies program—
utilizing the most modern and efficient book
production techniques and a selective
worldwide distribution network—makes
available to the academic, government, and
business communities significant, timely
research in U.S. and international economic, social, and political development.

U.S. Policy Toward Africa.

PRAEGER SPECIAL STUDIES IN INTERNATIONAL POLITICS AND GOVERNMENT

Praeger Publishers New York Washington London

Library of Congress Cataloging in Publication Data
Main entry under title:

U. S. policy toward Africa.

(Praeger special studies in international politics and government)
"Published in cooperation with the Phelps-Stokes Fund. "
Includes bibliographical references and index.
1. Africa—Foreign relations—United States.
2. United States—Foreign relations—Africa.
I. Arkhurst, Frederick S. , 1920-   II. Phelps-Stokes Fund.
DT38. U59   1975   327. 73'06   74-33028
ISBN 0-275-05330-X

PRAEGER PUBLISHERS
111 Fourth Avenue, New York, N.Y. 10003, U.S.A.

Published in the United States of America in 1975
by Praeger Publishers, Inc.

Printed in the United States of America

FOREWORD
Franklin H. Williams

Historically, American interest in Africa has been
exercised by proxy through the colonial powers that controlled Africa. During the 1950s and 1960s, when African
independence was in flood, American interest in Africa
became more direct even though in certain official circles
there was a tendency to subsume African interest to those
of the former colonial powers.

Nevertheless there has been considerable and genuine
American popular interest in Africa, which has been reinforced by the successes of the civil rights movement in
the 1960s. An index of American interest in Africa was
the enthusiasm with which various arrangements developed
for the education and training of African students in the
United States. The featuring of African issues in the
American press was also a frequent occurrence and African
politicians, diplomats, and other public officials tra-
versed the United States on a regular basis. African-
American relations showed signs of fruitful development
for the mutual benefit of the peoples of the two continents.

A decade later African-American relations are at the
nadir of their fortunes. Official American attitude is
at best one of marginal interest, and at worst a tendency
to defer to white racist regimes in Africa. General public interest seems to have evaporated together with those
public and private programs that ten years ago were pro-
liferating to offer assistance of various kinds to Africa.
The only redeeming feature of the current period is the
resurgence of black American interest in Africa.

America, with a population of some 25 million citizens of African origin, should need no persuasion to recognize the importance of African-American goodwill.
There is no doubt that the role of Afro-Americans is going to increase in importance and, like other ethnic and
racial groups that make up the American population, Afro-
Americans will be concerned about relations with their
roots. The development of mutually beneficial relations
between Africans and Americans is a major concern of the
Phelps-Stokes Fund and our African programs have emphasized this concern in the form of exchanges at various
levels. In addition the Phelps-Stokes seminars on
African-American relations have sought to explore in

depth various aspects of African-American relations and
to make recommendations for their improvement.

This book--U.S. Policy Toward Africa--is a collection
of papers presented at one of these seminars and is published in the hope that they will throw additional light on
a crucial aspect of African-American relations--governmental
relations. The papers that have been assembled in this
volume are frank and uninhibited, and I hope that they will
be of some use to decision makers both in Africa and in the
United States.

The Phelps-Stokes Fund is the oldest American philanthropic foundation operating in Africa, and for the past
63 years the fund has been stimulating human talent and
potential both in the United States and in Africa. The
fund's primary interest has been the improvement of educational opportunities for black people on both continents.

Founded in 1911 by an endowment under the will of
Caroline Phelps Stokes, some of the fund's earliest proj-
ects were its surveys of African education conducted in
1922 and 1924, the reports of which are still considered
classic prescriptions for African educational development.
Among its other activities the fund founded the Booker T.
Washington Agricultural and Industrial Institute of
Liberia and, in 1961, cosponsored with the United Nations
Economic Commission for Africa a survey of manpower needs
in ten African countries.

The thrust of the fund's current programs relative
to Africa is the development of contact points between
Africans and Americans as the basis for mutual understanding and the improvement of African-American relations. These programs were made possible by a grant from
the Ford Foundation.

The chairman of the fund's Board of Trustees is
Isaac Newton Phelps-Stokes, a grandnephew of the founder.

CONTENTS

LIST OF TABLES

xi

Map courtesy of <u>Africa Report</u> magazine, a publication of the African-American Institute, 833 United Nations Plaza, New York, New York 10017.

INTRODUCTION
Frederick S. Arkhurst

The relatively substantial economic and military
strength of the United States in the contemporary world
makes the development of U.S. policy, and even the perception of such policy, of vast importance to every region of the world. American policy has a considerable
impact even on peripheral states that are not major actors in world power politics, as these nations are affected in a significant way by American attitudes on various issues of international relations. Africa, no less
than the other developing regions of the world, has been
continually preoccupied with American policy toward major
African issues, because American policy toward these issues has often appeared unpredictable; this has been the
cause of serious anxiety in Africa. Furthermore the fact
that U.S. foreign policy is often derivative of major
domestic concerns of the American people makes the assessment and prediction of American foreign policy a difficult
undertaking.

From the African perspective the epitome of U.S. policy toward Africa is the American stance on Southern Africa. This is so because, besides the issue of African
economic and social development, the issue of white dominance and racism in the southern part of Africa is a major
preoccupation of all the African states. On this issue
Africa can seem to make no compromise, and yet it does not
appear that the United States is sufficiently sensitive to
this preoccupation. It is apparent that American policy
toward Southern Africa has been a combination of pious
pronouncements, to allay the anxieties of Africans, and
massive economic and diplomatic support in terms of U.S.
foreign investments and technical assistance and cooperation with the white-minority regimes of Southern Africa.

With regard to Portugal's African territories American
assistance has involved military and logistical support
given ostensibly to further certain objectives of the
North Atlantic Treaty Organization (NATO). In these circumstances American policy has predictably been interpreted on one hand simply as support of racist regimes in
Africa, made inevitable by the racism inherent in the
United States itself, and on the other hand in terms of
the achievement of strategic objectives. This latter interpretation is based on the presumption that the United
States and its North Atlantic allies are anxious to secure
the South Atlantic and the Indian oceans in the event of
future hostilities in these areas. In light of this
knowledgeable observers have insisted that NATO policy,
and particularly American policy, has been geared to prevent the littoral states of Southern Africa from coming
under non-Western influence--in effect to ensure that control of the area remains with the white regimes of Southern
Africa. The coup d'etat in Portugal in April 1974 and its
repercussions on Portuguese African territories have, to
all intents and purposes, frustrated this objective; with
the dismantling of Portugal's African empire, Western control of two of the most important littoral states of Southern Africa (Angola and Mozambique) has been lost. The implications of these developments for U.S. policy in Southern Africa will be momentous. However, before dealing
with American policy it will be useful to analyze the implications of independence in the Portuguese territories
for the white-minority regimes in Rhodesia and South
Africa.

RHODESIA

     Insurgency in Rhodesia has escalated since the an-
nouncement of independence for the above mentioned Portuguese African territories effective in 1975; and nationalist guerrillas have been operating within striking distance of the Rhodesian capital of Salisbury. With the independence of Mozambique, Rhodesia is confronted with a
hostile eastern frontier of almost indefensible length.
Because of a shortage of manpower 50 percent of Rhodesia's
5,000-man army already is black--obviously a risky state
of affairs. On the economic front the situation is bound
to be even more dismal; the probable closing of two ports
in Mozambique--Beira and Lourenco Marques--to Rhodesian
exports and imports could prove catastrophic--South African

ports will be no help to Rhodesia since these ports are facing problems of acute congestion. To make matters more discouraging there is no guarantee of continued South African support for Rhodesia in these changed circumstances. South Africa's Prime Minister, John Vorster, has been reported to have urged Ian Smith, Rhodesia's Prime Minister, to reach a settlement with the African majority in Southern Rhodesia, and in spite of the solidarity that has existed between South Africa and Rhodesia, it is most unlikely that the South Africans will risk possible international military intervention in South Africa by its own overt military actions in Rhodesia.

The release by Smith of both Joshua Nkomo, leader of the Zimbabwe African Peoples' Union (ZAPU), and Ndabaningi Sithole, leader of the Zimbabwe African National Union (ZANU), in December 1974 as a concession to help initiate talks to resolve the constitutional deadlock that has existed between whites and nonwhites in Rhodesia (Zimbabwe) since 1965 is a sign that at long last the white settlers in Rhodesia are beginning to understand the writing on the wall--the inevitability of majority rule in Zimbabwe.

The acceptance of a cease-fire, at least in principle, by both sides not only attests to the success of the December 1974 contacts between these groups held in Lusaka, but is also an indication of the importance of unity between the two African political groups and an index of the untenable long-term political and military situation in which the white settlers have found themselves. The fact that the South African government played a significant role in bringing about the contacts between both groups of Rhodesian protagonists is indicative of the seriousness with which the South Africans view the overall situation in Southern Africa following the recession of Portuguese colonialism in that part of the continent.

The negotiation of a Rhodesian settlement will undoubtedly be long and difficult, but the events of December 1974 signify an erosion of the hitherto unrealistic and rigid position of the whites in regard to majority rule; it is clear that, from the point of view of African nationalists, this is the principle around which any negotiated settlement in Zimbabwe must revolve.

SOUTH AFRICA

The implications for South Africa of the abdication of empire by Portugal are more complex. From the military standpoint the independence of Angola and Mozambique poses for South Africa a logistics and defense problem of huge proportions. No longer will South Africa enjoy the cordon sanitaire provided by the Portuguese territories; it will have to defend an interminable hostile frontier controlled by revolutionary black African governments. In addition the success of African nationalist movements to the north will provide a tremendous fillip to domestic insurgency in South Africa. South African and Namibian freedom fighters will have secure sanctuaries across the borders of Angola and Mozambique, and incursions into South Africa will very likely escalate to the point of posing real difficulties for the South African defense establishment.

The impact on the South African economy could be equally disconcerting for the South Africans. For years the major South African ports have been facing problems of congestion and, under an agreement with Portugal, Lourenco Marques (in Mozambique) has handled 50 percent of traffic for the Transvaal, South Africa's major industrial region. The denial of the use of these port facilities by South Africa, which is quite likely under the revolutionary government of an independent Mozambique, could lead to serious problems for South African trade.

The giant Cabora Bassa dam in northern Mozambique was conceived on the basis of the export to South Africa of a significant portion of the power generated by the project. (The Cabora Bassa dam is the fourth largest hydroelectric generating plant in the world, its nine turbines together having a capacity of 3,600,000 kilowatt hours.) In fact it has been projected that two of the three turbines that first go into operation at the dam will generate power for South African industry. Clearly this projection becomes a very chancy one under an African majority government in Mozambique. Even assuming that from economic necessity the government of Mozambique undertakes to supply power to South Africa, can the South Africans dispel the nagging uneasiness of their long-term dependence on such a source for a large portion of their industrial power?

SOUTH AFRICAN OPTIONS

Unquestionably the eclipse of the Portuguese empire in Africa presents some difficult choices for South Africa. Three options are open to the South Africans: accommodation with the independent black states to the north; subversion of these new governments in Angola and Mozambique to bring them under control; and preemptive military intervention with an inevitable racial confrontation in Southern Africa.

Accommodation between South Africa and the new governments of Angola and Mozambique is hardly conceivable unless it were accompanied by an easement of the racist policies of South Africa's government toward the black majority of that country. On August 30, 1974, Vorster told the South African parliament that a black government in Mozambique was inevitable and that he would

> take the earliest opportunity to establish
> contact with it and to come to an under-
> standing with it. The Prime Minister,
> however, seemed to offer no possibility of
> the "urgent and meaningful change" in
> South Africa's rigid policies of white
> racial supremacy that opposition politi-
> cians urged him to adopt to prevent black
> insurgency.[1]

Clearly this uncompromising attitude on the part of South Africa can rule out the possibility of an easy accommodation in the long term. No African government, particularly a seasoned cadre that has come to power through revolutionary warfare, can be expected to accept racism as the basis of its international intercourse. Furthermore the success of black nationalism in neighboring countries will feed the frustrations of the black majority in South Africa, leading to an escalation of black insurgency that will obviously receive, at the very least, moral and material support from across the borders. A combination of such circumstances could lead South Africa to its second option--the subversion of neighboring African governments.

Subversion would have very little success in Mozambique because of the unity and discipline of Mozambique's revolutionary leadership. It would, however, have some effect in creating confusion in Angola because of the fragmentation of the Angolan nationalist movement, which developed through diverse factions under antagonistic leaders. However, it is not clear that in such an eventuality the control of Angola or parts of it would go to South Africa or to elements sympathetic to the South Africans. It is more likely that a chaotic situation reminiscent of the 1960 "Congo situation" would emerge with no clearly defined authority in control. The opportunities for intervention inherent in such a situation are limitless and could extend to secessionist movements in the north. A state of affairs of this sort could conceivably tempt a nervous South Africa--probably laboring under the paranoia of an extreme laager syndrome--to launch a preemptive military action in Angola. The limiting factor to such a move is, of course, that the South Africans have always been conscious of the need to avoid the creation of any situation for which they could be indicted on a breach of international peace and security; such an indictment could lead to the application of Chapter 7 of the U.N. Charter, providing for the imposition of international sanctions and possible U.N. military action.

In any event the scenario mapped out above could result in a racial confrontation in Southern Africa. In addition racial conflict in this area would not be confined to the African continent but would have repercussions throughout the world that could not be ignored by any government, particularly the United States. All indications seem to suggest that the South African government is very conscious of the inevitable disaster that racial conflict can bring to Southern Africa. The efforts of the South African government in helping to promote the contacts between the white settlers and the African nationalists in Lusaka in December 1974 is an augury of South Africa's groping for some kind of viable accommodation between her and her neighboring African countries; but it is inconceivable that such an agreement can come about without the amelioration of the apartheid policy of the South African government.

Here again the progression from a rigid position to one of accommodation will no doubt be slow and complicated. But as in the case of Rhodesia the rulers of South Africa must have at long last recognized the inevitable: that peaceful coexistence based on multiracial rights and responsibilities is preferable to the real possibility of racial conflict.

IMPLICATIONS FOR AMERICAN POLICY

The events of December 1974 in Southern Africa have made the choices for American policy much simpler than they have been in a long time. With the momentum of these events seemingly moving in desirable directions, American pressure on South Africa can be exerted without

the inhibition of offending white sensibilities--the white
minorities are beginning to realize that there is only one
way to go and pressure in that direction should lead to
meaningful results. In this connection it is notable that
on December 12, 1974, a statement issued by the U.S. Department of State emphasized the need for pressure to be
exerted on Rhodesia, in the light of the events of December 1974, to move toward a peaceful settlement.[2] However,
American policy will have to demonstrate a decided shift
away from the prescriptions of the National Security Council's Memorandum 39 before American policy can become
credible to the African states.[3]

U.S. policy toward Africa is in a state of flux and
thus provides a unique opportunity for the African states
to develop initiatives and a joint policy that would bring
their influence to bear on American policy in the interest
of the primary aspirations of Africa. This will require
concerted action on the part of the African nations--clear
definition of their objectives, resolute planning, and
prompt action. Regrettably the diplomacy of the African
states in Western countries, and particularly in the United States, has been relatively ineffectual. A major
weakness of African diplomacy in the United States has
been a misunderstanding of the workings of the American
power structure. At variance with European practice, the
American Department of State has very limited room for
maneuvering vis-a-vis the Congress; thus it is absolutely
essential that African governments, through their representatives in Washington, develop appropriate and judicious links with the sources of power in the American
legislature. Equally important is the need for African
diplomats to develop contacts with the leaders of the
black community, Africa's natural constituency in the
United States. With black political power growing steadily, and with the upsurge of communitywide identification
with Africa, black political leaders will seek increasingly to influence American policy relative to Africa;
African identification with this power is indispensable
to any effort by Africans to influence American policy.

Another weakness of African diplomacy in the United
States has been the virtual absence of any real and concerted attempt to tell the African story--particularly in
relation to Southern Africa--to the American people in an
effort to mobilize American understanding and commitment,
both of which are essential in influencing American policy.
Africa has yet to make any expenditure of collective resources on such essential public relations in the United

States; alone the South African government spends at least $44 million a year in promoting its image in America.

In the last analysis U.S. policy toward Africa will be determined by the perceived interests of America in Africa; but American policy can be influenced by the earnestness and consistency of Africa's advocacy at the centers of American power.

SUMMARY OF CHAPTERS

Immanuel Wallerstein, in Chapter 2, "Africa, the United States, and the World Economy: The Historical Bases of American Policy," examines U.S. policy within the context of the fluctuations of the world economy. Since Africa had been a peripheral area without direct linkages with the U.S. economy, it did not hold a major interest for the United States before the decolonization of the African countries; thus before 1960 American policy toward Africa was one of "indifference" arising from America's "relative satisfaction" with the status quo in Africa under the management of the European colonial powers. As most of Africa became independent not only did U.S. policy seek to establish direct diplomatic relations with African states, but American interest in Africa became direct and active; this occurred within the context of the Cold War, since U.S. economic interests in Africa were still marginal. Wallerstein describes U.S. intervention in Zaire and its aftermath as the "opening salvo of U.S. involvement in Southern Africa generally," noting that "I believe it was brought on by an emerging world economic crisis whose early signs were appearing precisely around 1960." Wallerstein concludes by speculating on two scenarios of possible U.S. policy in Southern Africa. The first of these would involve pressure on South Africa to concede Namibian independence under a government with the political complexion of Botswana; the restoration of Zimbabwe to the path of decolonization along the lines of the Kenyan experience; a split in the Nationalist party in South Africa and a U.S.-fostered coalition government of verligtes and the United party, granting independence to some of the Bantustans; and a Southern African common market linked in various ways to the United States. The alternative scenario is predicated on the Rhodesian white minority balking at African majority rule; the French and the Soviets combining to frustrate U.S. maneuvers in the region; and the regeneration of an "African revolutionary

movement inside South Africa in opposition to the racist
regime." Wallerstein speculates that a Southern African
common market could eventually emerge "that would resemble
in tone and outlook the China of today. In which case,
some worthy successor of Mr. [Henry] Kissinger may also
fly to Johannesburg."

Herbert Spiro presents in Chapter 3 an official over-
view of U.S. policy and reflects on the realities that
will influence both future U.S. policy and African-
American relations. According to Spiro, these realities
include the decline of U.S. aid and relative public indifference to African issues--"a lack of a popular American constituency is already reflected in such congressional
actions as the defeat of the International Development
Association replenishment resolution, the passage of the
Byrd Amendment and Senator Fulbright's resolution to end
A.I.D., the Sahelian drought, and the most important reality, the limits of U.S. power." Spiro notes that Americans have little control over the development of various
situations of interest to Africans and that there is little
value in rhetorical resolutions that can only exacerbate
already difficult problems. He notes that Americans can,
however, be realistic in recognizing the limits of their
power to influence others to do things they do not want to
do. They can keep their priorities straight, recognizing
that they will not always accord with those of the Africans but that it is worth searching for areas of agreement.

Chapter 4, "U.S. Policy and Southern Africa," is a
comprehensive study by George Houser of American policy as
it relates to the problems of Southern Africa. The chapter begins by stating Houser's view that U.S. policy has
been much more dynamically keyed to the forces attempting
to maintain the status quo in Southern Africa than to the
forces of change. Houser than details the major issues,
attitudes, and policies that lead to this conclusion. He
points out the necessity for a unitary approach to the
problems of Southern Africa. His critique of U.S. policy
is well documented and the theme is that "whatever the
events of the future, they will not eradicate the record
of the past nor invalidate the thesis presented in this
study: that U.S. policy in Southern Africa, up to the
time of this writing has been one of support for the dominant white minority and colonial regimes." Houser concludes that a basic change in U.S. policy toward Southern
Africa will be difficult to achieve without some basic
changes within America itself, but that a new policy that
meets the urgent demand for change in Southern Africa
will be a positive departure.

Chapter 5, "Conflicting Economic Interests of Africa and the United States," by Eleanora West and Robert West, begins with a detailed survey of African-American economic relations. It discusses areas of potential economic conflict, including foreign aid, food supplies, the impact of higher oil prices both on the African and American economies, African raw materials, and U.S. foreign investments. The authors provide a wealth of statistical data. They suggest that the consideration of issues of possible conflict is "much less important than the perceptions of such a danger by an excited and sullen public and its harassed government." They note that in the period of change and uncertainty in the 1970s and 1980s, during which an international economic order is constructed, "the greatest danger of perceived conflicting interests of Africa and the United States may derive from the fear of change itself."

In Chapter 6, "Conflicting Political Interests of Africa and the United States," Wentworth B. Ofuatey-Kodjoe postulates a "Balkanized" conception of Africa, at least to the extent that Africa features some of "the same interpenetration of factors such as governmental instability, economic insufficiency, ethnic and racial animosities and conflicting ideologies that characterized the Balkans during the latter part of the nineteenth century." The author describes the nature of American interest in Africa as mainly strategic and "cultural," defined in relation to U.S. conceptions of world order and to how the world should be organized in order to insure the safety and integrity of the American way of life. The African interest is viewed by the author in terms of goals, expressed primarily in the United Nations, that envisage both the eradication of colonialism and racism and the promotion of human rights in general. The areas of potential African-American political conflict, Ofuatey-Kodjoe suggests, revolve around the issues of colonialism, racism, and nonalignment--as articulated by the African states and the U.S. conception of world order based on "the principles of international peace and security, anticommunism and the assimilation of non-Western cultures to the norms and values of Western society."

NOTES

1. New York _Times_, August 31, 1974.
2. New York _Times_, December 13, 1974.
3. _Washington Afro-American_, October 15, 1974; Washington _Post_, October 22, 1974; _Christian Science Monitor_, October 22, 1974.

10

CHAPTER

2

AFRICA, THE
UNITED STATES, AND
THE WORLD ECONOMY:
THE HISTORICAL BASES
OF AMERICAN POLICY
Immanuel Wallerstein

We normally define the "foreign policy" of a "state"
as that set of short- and middle-run objectives vis-a-vis
the world polity that are seen as serving the "interests"
of the "state." However, there are hidden in such an in-
nocuous definition all sorts of assumptions and debatable
points.

One such assumption is that state policy (decisions
taken by political leaders and bureaucrats) can have an
impact on some institutions (primarily, but certainly not
exclusively, other governments) that will significantly
affect the allocation of power and hence the distribution
of reward in the world system. This is no doubt true to
some extent, but clearly it is infinitely more true of
core-states of the world economy (such as the United
States) than it is of states considered in the economic
periphery (as for example probably all African independent states are today).

A second assumption is that "states" have "interests"; this is more debatable. Lenin spoke of the state
as the "executive committee of the ruling class," and
this is perfectly acceptable as a rough approximation,
provided several points are noted: "executive committees"
are not absolute monarchs but operate within constraints;
groups with differing interests located within the framework of the state have some access to political power,
albeit considerably unequal access; groups outside the
state often have access to power within that state's political machinery; and the extent to which a "ruling
class" is homogeneous and united varies over time and
space.

A third assumption is that since a state's interests are relatively continuous, the foreign policy of a state will survive minor (and perhaps even major) perturbations of regime.

A fourth assumption is that one can locate these interests somewhere. Their usual location is internal to the state. But insofar as interests refer to shares in the distribution of profit, they must relate to the economic framework within which profit is distributed. And this framework in the modern world system is not a national one but that of the world economy, which therefore means that the primary interest of a state is to obtain or retain an optional position within this world economy—to be in its core rather than its periphery or semiperiphery. Since, however, this study is concerned with relational concepts—core, periphery, etc.—by definition it is not possible for all states to have an optional position.

Since in addition the history of the system shows that it is possible to shift position,[1] all states must be in a situation of perpetual insecurity, from which it follows that foreign policies are never benign, always assertive (or aggressive if one wants to be pejorative), and never ultimately bound by formalities. This viewpoint, essentially espoused by such different personalities as Machiavelli, Henry John Palmerston, Lenin, and Hans Morgenthau, is occasionally deprecated as "cynical"; but such deprecation is ideological rhetoric. The view is rather a simple description of one of the primary mechanisms of a capitalist world economy—the use of state machineries not to facilitate but to distort the law of supply and demand in the world market as the primary determinant of prices, and hence of profits; the rest is commentary.

The point of this is that if one wants to understand the bases of American foreign policy toward Africa, one has to place both America and Africa in their historical relationship to the evolving world economy.

HISTORICAL DEVELOPMENTS

The historical development of America's role in the world economy is well known, certainly in its gross outlines. From the American Revolution to the Civil War there were two somewhat contradictory trends in American economic growth. On the one hand there was an industrial sector that sought to use the federal government in classic mercantilist ways—increasing barriers to external trade, both by investment in infrastructure and removal of domestic barriers, and protecting American industry against the then world hegemonic power, Great Britain, by means of a tariff. And on the other hand there was an expanding cash-crop exporting sector that developed ever-increasing ties of dependence to Britain.[2] For whatever reasons adduced,[3] this internal conflict of interest led to the North's victory in the Civil War and to the enactment of the series of measures (from railway construction to the Homestead Act, to high tariffs) that permitted the remarkable industrial surge in America during the late nineteenth century.

As British economic hegemony became increasingly precarious, in a virtually steady decline from 1873 to the First World War,[4] the United States emerged as a more effective challenger to Britain than Germany or France; the United States closed off its own market to Britain and then began to compete as an exporter, primarily to Latin America, the Far East, and Europe. This situation was climaxed by the acute differentials in U.S. and British growth patterns brought about by the First World War. The United States replaced Britain as the world's leading economic power as of that time, but held unquestioned hegemony only in the period from 1945 to 1965, during which time the United States came to be faced with the same kind of challenges from Western Europe and Japan that Great Britain had faced from the United States and Germany as of 1873.

The history of Africa's involvement in the world economy was quite different from that of the United States. One can date Africa's incorporation into the capitalist world economy at about 1750,[5] the time of the upturn of the European world economy from its century-long relative contraction. Africa subsequently went through three stages of development--informal empire, colonial rule, and decolonization--that mark three points on a curve of ever-deepening involvement in the world economy.

Africa's informal empire, which ran roughly from 1750 to 1885, marks the early phase of limited cash-crop exports, including in the first 75 years or so the transformation of slave export from the "luxury" trade it had once been to the bulk staple it then became. Slavery as a staple coming from a peripheral area of the world economy is ultimately uneconomic[6] and was replaced in West Africa by "legitimate commerce," as in the case of the famous palm oil for soap. Essentially, however, during this period Africa was a minor producer for the world economy and a minor importer.

It was the world economic contraction beginning in 1873 that ultimately got the "scramble for Africa" going in the sense that it led France and Germany to push toward "pre-emptive colonization" of Africa and Britain to react defensively by emulation.[7] European conquest of Africa was a process in which it took 20 years to achieve even the primary "pacification." But this was just in time for the world economic upturn at the beginning of the twentieth century; the expanded world market created a demand for the launching of the cultivation of the series of African cash crops that colonial agricultural and tax policies now enforced, as well as for the exploitation of African mineral resources.

The initial African expansion soon reached a relatively stable plateau,[8] in part because of the limitations of production given the mode of social organization, and in part because the world saw another agricultural depression from 1921 to the Second World War. The post-World War II rise in world demand for African primary resources coincided with both the rise of African nationalist movements and the conversion of European powers to decolonization—with the exception of course of Portugal, which was too weak to neocolonize.[9]

What decolonization did was to create in Africa the social framework in which it would be possible to convert the totality of agricultural land to cash-cropping (which would represent a considerable increase in land area used to this end), expand to a maximum the exploitation of mineral resources, and encourage the development of a limited sector of primary transformation industries (thereby reinforcing world demand for the machinery exports of core countries). Widespread expropriation of underproductive food-growing regions would politically have been extremely expensive in a colonial structure but it was perfectly feasible for independent African states to take such action, whether by decree or by the free play of the market, especially in the wake of what have been ever more frequent droughts.

Thus far in this discussion the U.S. role in the world economy has been described without mentioning Africa and Africa's role without mentioning the United States. This is no accident because thus far the economic histories of the two regions have had virtually no direct linkage, although of course both histories are the consequence of the workings of the same world economic system and hence each presupposed what was happening in the other region.

Without direct linkage between two regions there would normally be very little place for the overt appearance of diplomacy. Normally an absence of diplomatic initiatives by a core nation vis-a-vis a peripheral area of the world economy would be designated as a foreign policy of "indifference." And it would not be grievously off-base to so characterize U.S. foreign policy toward Africa from 1789 to 1960, and quite possibly to today.[10]

But "indifference" is far too neutral a term. In fact in general it is the case that from her perspective the United States was perfectly content with what was happening in Africa and therefore seldom felt any need to intervene in a significant way. However, a review of U.S. attitudes toward the main political issues of Africa since 1945 may reveal the possible pattern for the future. For we may expect that the U.S. foreign policy of "indifference," or perhaps it should be called "relative satisfaction," is now coming to an end.

The primary political issue in Africa since the Second World War has been the struggle for national independence, led by nationalist movements in the various units of colonial administration. This struggle has had two phases. The first was the so-called downward sweep of African liberation, which involved proclamations of independence beginning in 1956, climaxing in the cascade of independences won in 1960, and more or less petering out in 1964 when Zambia became the last major country to achieve independence in this wave. The wave included virtually all colonies that had belonged to Britain, France, Belgium, and Italy.

The second phase--now at an end--was the struggle for national liberation in Portuguese and Southern Africa. In this phase African nationalists have faced a far stronger opposition to decolonization (or its equivalent, majority rule) from Portugal and the white African settlers (in Angola, Mozambique, and Rhodesia).

The demands of the nationalist movements in both phases have been essentially identical in each territory. The movements have utilized virtually the same moral and pragmatic arguments to win adherence to their cause, both from their own populations and from the outside world. In every instance the movements initially engaged in political activities to obtain their objectives, and in virtually every instance there have been moments of disorder and rioting. In all cases except Portuguese and Southern Africa, the colonial power responded by first deprecating the strength and legitimacy of the nationalist movement but later negotiating a transfer of power, usually to the

very same nationalist movement. In those cases where the
willingness to negotiate came relatively late--for example
in Kenya or Algeria, where the presence of settler communities retarded this development--the movement for independence took the form of armed struggle, as it is doing today in Portuguese and Southern Africa.

Throughout this whole development U.S. foreign policy
has been remarkably consistent; John Foster Dulles set the
tone for it on June 1, 1953, and there has been no substantial deviation from his proclaimed policy in the subsequent years. In a speech to the American nation following a trip to the Near East and Southern Asia, Dulles made
the following remarks regarding the issue of colonialism:

> Most of the peoples of the Near East and
> Southern Asia are deeply concerned about
> political independence for themselves and
> others. They are suspicious of the colo-
> nial powers. The United States too is
> suspect because, it is reasoned, our NATO
> alliances with France and Britain require
> us to try to preserve or restore the old
> colonial interests of our allies.
> I am convinced that United States
> policy has been unnecessarily ambiguous in
> this matter. The leaders of the countries
> I visited fully recognize that it would be
> a disaster if there were any break between
> the United States and Great Britain and
> France. They don't want this to happen.
> However, without breaking from the frame-
> work of Western unity, we can pursue our
> traditional dedication to political liberty.
> In reality, the Western powers can gain,
> rather than lose, from an orderly develop-
> ment of self-government.
> I emphasize, however, the word "or-
> derly." Let none forget that the Kremlin
> uses extreme nationalism to bait the trap
> by which it seeks to capture the dependent
> peoples.[11]

U.S. POLICY IN THE COLONIAL PERIOD

The essential elements of U.S. policy in the colonial
period are (1) the priority of world political alliances
for the United States, (2) the urging of the wisdom of

decolonization on Europe, and (3) the opposing of any political "radicalism" in Africa. Within the framework of these premises there has been some disagreement about pace; the conservative viewpoint has differed from the liberal viewpoint in the assessment of how strongly and how publicly one might "urge the wisdom" of decolonization, and how seriously to take the radical rhetoric of particular African leaders or movements.

Thus for example in 1955 Dulles said that Goa was a "province" of Portugal and not a "colony,"[12] while the then U.S. representative to the United Nations, Henry Cabot Lodge, said that Algeria was "administratively an integral part of the French Republic," and that it would be a "grave danger to the future of the United Nations [if it took up] questions whose consideration would conflict with the provisions of Article 2, paragraph 7 [of the U.N. Charter]."[13]

A different viewpoint was expressed by the then Senator John F. Kennedy, at that time chairman of the Subcommittee on Africa of the Senate Foreign Relations Committee. Kennedy introduced Senate Resolution 153 (85th Congress) on July 2, 1957, which urged the U.S. government to

> place the influence of the United States
> behind efforts . . . to achieve a solution
> that will recognize the independent per-
> sonality of Algeria and establish the
> basis for a settlement interdependent with
> the French neighboring states. [The Reso-
> lution further provided that if no progress
> were shown by the following General Assem-
> bly of the United Nations, the United
> States should] support an international
> effort to derive for Algeria the basis for
> an orderly achievement of independence.[14]

Dulles commented the same day that the "problem of Algeria is one of exceptional difficulty," noting that "if anyone is interested in going after colonialism, there are a lot better places to go after it than in the case of France"; he cited Latvia, East Germany, and Hungary.[15]

No doubt under President Kennedy the United States was willing to be slightly more open in its position, occasionally voting in the United Nations in favor of resolutions critical of Portuguese colonialism. On the occasion of a resolution on the situation in Angola, Adlai Stevenson, the U.S. representative to the United Nations, on March 15, 1961, told the Security Council:

17

The United States would be remiss in its
duties as a friend of Portugal if it failed
to express honestly its conviction that
step-by-step planning within Portuguese
territories and its acceleration is now imperative for the successful political and
economic and social advancement of all inhabitants under Portuguese administration--
advancement, in brief, toward full self-
determination.[16]

Stevenson's principal argument was the danger that if Portugal did not engage in "step-by-step planning," the result would be similar to the situation in the Congo, then
in turmoil:

I do not think it would be straining the
truth to conclude that much of the Congo's
problems result from the fact that the
pressure of nationalism rapidly overtook
the preparation of the necessary foundation essential to the peaceful and effective exercise of sovereign self-government.
The important thing for us, then, is to insure that similar conditions do not exist
for the Angola of tomorrow.[17]

But except for the minor nuance of voting for a few
U.N. resolutions on Portugal and on South Africa, U.S.
attitudes toward nationalism in as yet nonindependent African states were substantially the same under Presidents
Kennedy and Johnson as under President Eisenhower; the
United States still argued that primary initiative lay
and should lie with Europe. Thus it never supported any
U.N. resolution on Southern Rhodesia that was opposed by
the United Kingdom. And on March 18, 1965, then Assistant
Secretary of State for African Affairs G. Mennen Williams
included in his "five pillars" of U.S. policy one that
urged "encouragement of other countries of the world, particularly the former European metropoles, to recognize
their continuing responsibilities toward Africa."[18]
Thus it was only in the continuing logic of these
basic premises that under President Nixon, Assistant Secretary of State for African Affairs David Newsom stated
U.S. Policy toward Southern Africa in this fashion on
September 21, 1971:

> Our differences with the African independent nations are essentially over how change in southern Africa will be achieved . . . not whether. . . . We believe change will come in southern Africa. Economic and demographic pressures make this inevitable. . . . We can understand the impatience which leads to demands for the use of force. Nevertheless, we see little prospect for its effective use in bringing change in southern Africa, and we cannot favor its use.[19]

Thus basically on the political issue that for Africans has taken priority ever since the Second World War--decolonization--U.S. policy has been quite consistent. It has adhered to a position that was characterized by M'hamed Yazid, when he was the Algerian National Liberation Front's (FLN) representative at the United Nations during Algeria's War of Independence, as "anti-colonialism de dimanche."

This however did not preclude behind-the-scenes U.S. pressure on slow-moving colonial authorities, as is said to have occurred vis-a-vis Belgium in 1960 and vis-a-vis Portugal during the Kennedy era. But neither at the other end of the continuum did it preclude backing up the efforts of a colonial power to contain an overly radical nationalist movement by the tactic of ceding power to a friendlier group, as in the U.S. support for France's manipulation in Cameroun just prior to Cameroun's independence in 1960. This U.S. support for France took the form of opposition within the United Nations to a U.N.-supervised preindependence election in Cameroun that would have tested the true strength of the nationalist movement in question, the Union Populaire du Cameroun (UPC).

However, on the whole the United States relied on the steady workings of the various forces present on the African scene to bring about results that in general were in the U.S. interest. For the United States operated in the confident expectation that direct U.S. involvement was not necessary to bring about the dual U.S. objective: an expansion of African involvement in the world economy, and a relative open door for U.S. investment and trade. Both the continuation of direct colonial rule and the coming to power of revolutionary regimes might threaten this, but the "wind of change" was both strong enough and gentle enough to make both unlikely (except possibly in Southern Africa).

U.S. POLICY IN THE ERA OF INDEPENDENCE

Once independence began to be achieved the United
States moved quickly to increase its direct diplomatic
links with the various African states. The then Vice
President Nixon, heading the U.S. delegation for the cele-
bration of the independence of Ghana on March 6, 1957,
proceeded to make a tour of the various independent states
(few in number at the time); and in his report of April 7,
1957, to President Eisenhower he recommended the creation
within the U.S. Department of State of a Bureau of African
Affairs.[20] Such a bureau was in fact created on August
20, 1958. When a whole series of African states became
independent in 1960, the Eisenhower administration hesitated to name separate ambassadors to each state, especially in the former French territories. This was partly
out of deference to French sensibilities. One of the
first measures of the Kennedy administration was to decide
that each African state would have its own ambassador.
This symbolic move was followed by a further gesture:
President Kennedy sought to arrange meetings with as many
African heads of state as possible. He named presumably
"sympathetic" ambassadors to Guinea[21] and to the United
Arab Republic (UAR),[22] two African countries with whom
U.S. relations had been somewhat strained.

The concrete meaning of these symbols has to be measured in two arenas: forms and degree of U.S. economic
transfers to African governments; and reactions to, and
involvement in, internal upheavals in African independent
states.

If one looks at U.S. economic involvement in Africa,
whether via private enterprise or government assistance,
the overall figures are small. Taking 1965 as an optimal
year (after most African states had achieved independence
and before the recent perturbations in the world market
had set in), one finds in the following figures that Africa represents a total of about 4 percent of both U.S.
exports and imports, of which South Africa represents
about a third (the figures are in $ million):

Exports		Imports	
Worldwide	$27,346.2	Worldwide	$21,366.4
Africa, total	1,224.1	Africa, total	875.1
South Africa	437.8	South Africa	225.1

Source: Survey of Current Business 46, no. 12
(December 1966).

In fact the pattern, going back to the period beginning after the Second World War and continuing to now, has remained fairly steady.

Looking at the book value of U.S. investment abroad, it is notable that despite a fairly continuous worldwide increase, South Africa has continuously represented about 1 percent of the total (see Table 1). The rest of Africa represented another 1 percent up to about 1960, when it jumped to about 3 percent.

TABLE 1

Book Value of U.S. Investment Abroad
($ million)

	All Regions	Africa	South Africa	Rest of Africa
1929	7,527	130	77	53
1936	6,690	120	55	65
1943	7,861	131	50	81
1950	11,788	287	140	147
1957	25,262	664	301	363
1965	49,328	1,918	529	1,390
1971	86,000	3,833	964	2,869

Note: Figures for "Rest of Africa" in 1929 and 1936 include French Oceania, Indochina, and Thailand.

Source: Figures are drawn from the following issues of Survey of Current Business: vol. 32, no. 2, December 1952, Table 1, p. 8; vol. 40, no. 9, September 1960, Table 1, p. 20; vol. 47, no. 9, September 1967, Table 3, p. 42; vol. 52, no. 11, November 1972, Table 7a, pp. 28-29.

A look at U.S. trade relations with African countries other than South Africa reveals that for 1965 only four of these countries exported more than $50 million worth of goods to the United States (Ethiopia, Ghana, Liberia, and Nigeria) and only six imported more than $50 million from the United States (Egypt, Liberia, Libya, Morocco, Nigeria, and Zaire). This represents the absolute importance of these countries as U.S. trading partners. However, it can also be discerned how relatively important the United States was to each of them by seeing how the United States ranked as a trading partner compared to other countries:

the United States was the main recipient of exports for
only four of these African countries--Ethiopia (which sent
the United States about three-quarters of its total exports), and Guinea, Liberia, and Uganda (each of which
sent the United States less than half but more than a
third of its exports). The United States was the main
country from which goods were imported only in the case
of Guinea (about half) and that of Liberia (about two-
thirds).

Figures for total U.S. aid (all forms) to African nations for the period from 1946 to 1967 are shown in Table
2; since U.S. aid has been drastically reduced in the
years since 1967 these figures can be taken as a reasonable base from which to draw various inferences.

Those African countries for whom overall U.S. aid
figures are relatively high (defining "high" generously),
either in absolute terms (over $100 million) or on a per
capita basis (over $10) or in both cases, fall into five
categories, as shown in Table 3.

Each of these categories merits brief attention. In
the first category, Liberia of course is the historic
"semicolony" of the United States, and a country with significant U.S. investments; Libya and Morocco were the
sites of two major U.S. air bases, both now discontinued.
The nations in the second category--Algeria, Guinea,
Tunisia, and Zaire--show fluctuating figures over the
years, almost directly correlated with the relations these
countries had with France (and in the case of Zaire with
Belgium). For example over half of all U.S. aid to Algeria was given in the two years immediately following
Algerian independence when relations with France were at
a nadir. The nations in the third category are all in
northeast Africa, strategically overlapping with the Arab
world. Three of these countries--Egypt, Somalia, and
Sudan--are Moslem and notoriously "neutralist" in their
foreign policy, receiving considerable aid over time from
Russia as well as from the United States; the fourth,
Ethiopia, has come to be in many ways a second (after
Liberia) U.S. "historic" interest, with key U.S. military
communications installations and the largest single amount
of U.S. military aid ($124.1 million).

These three categories suggest that the United States
has paid primary attention to those countries in which it
had direct military interests and those countries in which
it could not rely on its European allies to oversee the
political and economic "needs" of the regimes in power.

From this point of view both the fourth and fifth
categories may seem to be anomalies, but they are anomalies

TABLE 2

U.S. Aid to African Nations, 1946-67

Nation	Total Aid ($ million, including--in parentheses--military aid)	1967 Population (in millions)	Per Capita Aid (rounded)
Algeria	193.2	12.4	16
Botswana	5.1	0.6	1
Burundi	6.8	3.3	2
Cameroun	28.3 (0.2)	5.5	6
Central African Republic	4.4	1.4	3
Chad	7.4	3.4	2
Congo (Brazzaville)	2.1	0.9	2
Dahomey	10.5 (0.1)	2.5	4
Ethiopia	222.3 (124.1)	23.4	10
Egypt	1,038.9	30.9	34
Gabon	7.0	0.5	18
Gambia	1.0	0.3	3
Ghana	209.9	8.4	25
Guinea	71.4 (1.0)	3.7	19
Ivory Coast	32.8 (1.1)	4.0	8
Kenya	59.7	9.9	6
Lesotho	2.1	0.9	2
Liberia	243.2 (6.9)	1.1	221
Libya	208.5 (16.5)	1.7	123
Malagasy Republic	12.5	6.9	2
Malawi	14.0	4.1	3
Mali	18.6 (2.8)	4.8	4
Mauritania	3.4	1.1	3
Mauritius	0.5	0.8	1
Morocco	586.7 (54.0)	14.2	41
Niger	12.9 (0.1)	3.5	4
Nigeria	207.2 (1.5)	44.5	5
Rwanda	6.1	3.3	2
Senegal	27.8 (2.8)	3.7	8
Sierra Leone	36.2	2.4	16
Somali Republic	68.5	2.7	25
Southern Rhodesia	7.0	4.5	2
Sudan	127.4 (2.2)	14.3	9
Swaziland	0.1	0.4	*
Tanzania	56.4	10.9	5
Togo	13.2	1.7	8
Tunisia	521.1 (24.9)	4.5	116
Uganda	27.9	7.9	3
Upper Volta	9.6 (0.1)	5.1	2
Zaire	372.8 (20.9)	16.7	22
Zambia	49.2	4.0	12

*Less than half a dollar.

Source: Compiled by author from figures of U.S. Agency for International Development, in AID Economic Data Book--Africa (PB 180-910) and AID Economic Book--Near East and South Asia (PB 180-909).

TABLE 3

Major U.S. Aid Recipients among
African Nations, 1946-67

Category of African Nations	Total Aid (in $ millions)	Per Capita Aid (rounded)
Direct U.S. interests		
Liberia	243.2	221
Libya	208.5	123
Morocco	586.7	41
Quarreled with European ex-metropole		
Algeria	193.2	16
Guinea	71.4	19
Tunisia	521.1	116
Zaire	372.8	22
No obvious metropole		
Egypt	1,038.9	34
Ethiopia	222.3	10
Somalia	68.5	25
Sudan	127.4	9
Ex-British West Africa		
Ghana	209.9	25
Nigeria	207.2	5
Sierra Leone	36.2	16
Other		
Gabon	7.0	18
Zambia	49.2	12

Source: Compiled by author from figures of Agency for International Development, in AID Economic Data Book--Africa (PB 180-910).

easily explained. The fourth category--Ghana, Nigeria, and Sierra Leone, which comprise ex-British West Africa-- received extra U.S. attention for several reasons: (1) the British objected to U.S. ties less than the French did because of the so-called special relationship Britain developed with the United States in the period after 1945; (2) insofar as blacks in the United States served as an interested pressure group, the primary historical orientation had been to only a few countries--Liberia, Ethiopia, South Africa, and British West Africa; (3) the former British territories offered no linguistic barrier; and (4) Ghana was the "first" black African state to obtain independence, and Nigeria was the largest in population. As for Gabon and Zambia, which comprise the fifth category of major U.S. aid recipients in Africa, they are both countries with rich natural resources and relatively small population. Hence even a standard percentage of U.S. aid, if given in relation to the overall level of U.S. contribution to the world market, appears as high in the per capita calculations.

Thus the aid figures tend to confirm the analysis that the U.S. "interest" in Africa was expressed primarily and preferably through the agency of Western European intermediaries. It was only when this was not possible, either because of some direct pressures originating within the United States or because of an absence or a breakdown (even temporary) of Western European political capabilities, that the United States moved in directly. And even then on the whole it was scarcely massive intervention, although massive intervention generally was not necessary.

U.S. INTERVENTION

This then raises the question of whether there have in fact been situations in Africa in which massive intervention might have been seen by the United States as "necessary." There was clearly no African situation similar to that in Vietnam, where the nationalist movement was led by a Communist party in a country bordering a state governed by a Communist party. Nor was there a situation similar to that either in the Dominican Republic or in Cuba, which were both geographically close to the United States and where the United States had long since renounced the idea of using European intermediaries for its own imperial interests. The situation in most of Africa was not even comparable to that in the Middle East, which involved not only a strategic commodity (oil) but geographical proximity to the USSR, and a U.S. commitment to Israel based in part on domestic political considerations.

Still for a world hegemonic power, which the United States certainly has been since 1945 (and probably since 1918), all natural resources are important, all political upheavals potentially dangerous, and all unfriendly regimes at least minor thorns. Considering the number of coups d'etat, attempted coups, and civil wars in Africa since 1960, it is noteworthy that only one country, Zaire, has been the scene of massive direct U.S. involvement; in all others the U.S. involvement has been indirect and/or discreet. Three questions should therefore be discussed: what accounted for U.S. involvement in Zaire; what accounted for U.S. "indirection" and/or "discretion" elsewhere; and whether the historical conditions that explain both of these phenomena are likely to continue?

Zaire (formerly the Congo) became an independent state on January 30, 1960: within ten days the army had rebelled, the government of the richest province in Zaire had proclaimed its secession, Belgian troops had invaded the country, and the central government had appealed for military and economic assistance from the United Nations. Subsequently there was a civil war in Zaire in 1963-64, and a rebellion/invasion in 1967; since that time, however, internal turmoil has been minimal.

Politically Zaire has gone through a number of regimes. It was first governed by a parliamentary coalition led by a radical nationalist, Prime Minister Patrice Lumumba, in 1960. There followed a period of almost a year in which there were two regimes--one headed by Lumumba and the other by President Joseph Kasavubu--both claiming to be the country's legitimate central government. A secession movement in Katanga province, led by Moise Tshombe, was finally overcome by U.N. forces in December 1962. In 1965 Kasavubu suspended parliament; and in December of that year there was a military coup d'etat led by General Joseph Mobutu, who has since ruled the country as president.

American massive intervention can be seen at various points in this history. The United States gave full support not merely to U.N. assistance in the 1960-65 period but also to the arrogation by U.N. personnel of a degree of direct intervention in the Congo's internal affairs that was contested by many Congolese, in particular by Lumumba; several of the key U.N. Secretariat officials involved were U.S. citizens. The United States also lent its support (certainly after the event and quite probably before it) to the ouster of Lumumba by Kasavubu in 1961. It was this ouster (of dubious legality) that led to the crisis of legitimacy mentioned above. Following this the United States took the lead within the U.N. General Assembly for a credentials vote that ultimately favored Kasavubu over Lumumba.

Once the crisis of legitimacy was momentarily resolved, the United States gave active political and economic support to the new prime minister, Cyrille Adoula, who was considered by most observers to be the Congolese political leader most favorable to close political cooperation with the United States. After much hesitation the United States threw its weight behind the abovementioned U.N. military intervention that ended the secession in Katanga. During the civil war in 1964 the United States gave direct logistical support to the use of Belgian paratroopers to give a crucial military edge to the central government (by then headed by Tshombe) against the forces of the Congolese National Liberation Council. When Mobutu overthrew the Kasavubu government in 1965 the United States responded to this action with active sympathy and perhaps covert assistance. When the Mobutu government was faced with a mercenary rebellion in 1967, crucial military assistance was given to the central government by the United States, both directly and through the intermediary of the Ethiopian government. Throughout this period and afterward the U.S. ambassador was generally considered to be the most influential diplomat in Kinshasa, Zaire.

What was it about Zaire that occasioned such massive activity on the part of the United States, unparalleled elsewhere on the African continent? There are certain obvious and elementary facts. Zaire is a large country centrally located. Its former metropole, Belgium, was by and large unable to maintain a steady patronage relationship with Zaire, partly because of the collapse of good relations at the time of independence and partly because Belgium was ultimately too weak herself, both militarily and economically. In addition Zaire is a wealthy country in terms of natural resources and industrial potential. The breakdown of internal order immediately after independence seemed intolerably great, and Zaire was also plagued by an acute shortage of personnel trained for higher bureaucratic positions as a result of Belgium's policies during the colonial era.

But all of this seems insufficient to account for both the degree and persistence of U.S. intervention in

Zaire. Therefore was there anything else that made the Congo crisis seem to call for such a massive response by the United States? This observer thinks there was, but to uncover this one has to place the Congo crisis in the larger context of the evolving U.S. and African roles in the world economy. U.S. intervention in the Congo was the opening salvo of more general U.S. involvement in Southern Africa and it was brought on by an emerging world economic crisis whose early signs began appearing precisely around 1960.

It is still a bit early to sketch with any definitiveness what has been happening in the world economy since 1945, but one can see the broad outlines of this situation: there has been a fairly steady inflation of prices and a fairly steady expansion of total world production; and there has of course been a fairly steady population rise. But the crucial problem is the relation of total production to effective demand. The world has been moving into a crisis in effective demand, presaging a downturn in total production and hence an acute competition for markets for manufactured goods and an acute concern for "export" unemployment.

The problem is that effective demand can only really be measured inferentially. In 1945 U.S. production was unrivaled because of the destruction of European plants by wartime devastation. The imbalance, however, was so great that although the socially expressed demand for goods was higher than world production, financial liquidity was low (the so-called dollar crisis) and hence credit had to be drastically expanded. The Marshall Plan served to restore European financial liquidity and the Korean War created a sharp rise in demand for imports from the economic periphery, including Africa. This rise in demand for peripheral primary production led to a rapid rise in net government income but also to a decline in real wages that fed the fires of anticolonial nationalism.[23] This accounted for an initial thrust toward decolonization that was reinforced by cold war competition and a desire to expand total productivity in the periphery; thus the so-called downward thrust of African liberation, which found its first major stumbling block and ultimate brake in the Congo crisis.[24]

The "reconstruction" of Western Europe (as well as of Japan) was fairly well completed by 1955 or 1960 at the latest, and the United States began to feel real competition in the world export market about this time. This accounts for two major developments: (1) the first steps

28

toward detente, initiated by Eisenhower and Nikolai Bulganin in 1955, confirmed by the test ban agreement reached by Kennedy and Nikita Khrushchev in 1963, and made more concrete by the meetings of Nixon and Leonid Brezhnev in 1973; and (2) the beginning of a political disengagement of Western Europe from the United States, launched and still principally sponsored by France, furthered by Willy Brandt's Ostpolitik, and yet to reach its apogee.

One of the critical factors in this overall situation has been the prospective patterns of world trade. The USSR wanted technological support to become a competitive exporter of manufactured goods, while both the United States and Western Europe wanted ultimate access to the vast and potentially very lucrative Soviet internal market. And all three groups began to worry about peripheral areas both as prospective markets and as sources of the ever-expanding world demand for primary resources.

After the spiraling inflation launched by the credit expansion during the Vietnam War and the consequent U.S. balance-of-payments dilemmas; after the continuing infighting on the world currency scene; after the abandonment by the United States (in 1971) of its free-trade stance and the political truce with China; and after the so-called energy crisis and its effective reallocation of world income primarily at the expense of Western Europe and Japan, to talk of a current crisis in effective demand may not seem very daring. But the turning points on the various curves all began somewhere between 1955 and 1960.

In this kind of competitive squeeze there are the competitors (the United States, Western Europe, the USSR, and Japan); the areas that are relatively insignificant economically; and the areas that are arenas of competition because they are not only strong enough in resources, developed enough in infrastructure, and large enough in size to be significant suppliers and markets but also large enough to make a difference during a long-term world cyclical downturn. There are a number of these latter areas: China, Southeast Asia (especially Indonesia), the Indian subcontinent, the Arab world, Southern Africa, Brazil, and probably Canada. Each of these areas may be seen as an arena of world politico-economic struggle in which of course one major element are the forces indigenous to the area.

In regard to Africa it is quite clear that it is no longer a viable policy for the United States to pursue its interests in so crucial an arena as Southern Africa via European intermediaries since it is far from clear that

29

U.S. and Western European interests are identical, and since it is clear that internal political struggles will crucially affect the economic ties of Southern Africa with the rest of the world in the coming 25 years.

U.S. involvement in Zaire was the launching pad of this new U.S. attitude toward Southern Africa; Zaire was the first part of Southern Africa to flirt with the idea of drastic political realignments, and 1960 was the point where U.S. policy first became actively aware that there was a need to be concerned with Southern Africa in view of long-term economic trends.

EXPLOSIVENESS OF THE CONGO CRISIS

There were two extremely explosive aspects to the Congo crisis. One was the political volatility of the Congo itself, which was the result of a combination of factors: a thinness of the layer of trained cadres (who elsewhere in Africa had tended to play a conservatizing role after independence); a lack of time for the Movement National Congolais (MNC), the potential movement of national control, to establish real dominance before independence (which meant the risk that it would use appeals to radical mobilizing techniques after independence to achieve this dominance); the populist style of Lumumba, the leading Congolese politician; and the relative wealth of the Congo, which put great resources at the disposal of the political leadership. Many of these were transitory phenomena, as time indeed has shown, but they meant that as of 1960 there was a clear possibility that a radical nationalist regime could in fact consolidate power.

While that in itself was quite probably enough for many to cast anathema upon it, the Congo situation was aggravated by the beginnings of the nationalist revolution in Angola. It is rather clear that a Lumumba government securely in power would have given extensive support to an Angolan national liberation movement (indeed such support was already in evidence immediately in the wake of Congolese independence). The potential of such support to Angola is analogous to what Tanzania later gave to the Mozambique Liberation Front (FRELIMO), with two differences: it would have come much earlier on, when the Portuguese were far less prepared for it, and the Western world less certain of its immediate stance; and it would have come from a country--the Congo--with far more resources to throw into the fray. It could have made a considerable difference to the whole history of liberation movements in Southern Africa. Portugal might have crumbled, Rhodesia might never have been able to proclaim a Unilateral Declaration of Independence (UDI), and South Africa might have found itself without buffers. The Congo crisis gave the white forces of Southern Africa crucial time in which to consolidate their defensive structure.

It is not that all outside forces wanted to preserve a political status quo in Zaire; it is that various forces each wanted certain kinds of very "contained" change. The United States wanted what it eventually got: a politically stable, economically conservative regime in Zaire whose only true interest in Angola is to help establish there a regime of exactly the same variety. Translated into the terms of the Angolan liberation movements, this has meant obstruction of the Popular Movement for the Liberation of Angola (MPLA), considered a "dangerous" movement.

Britain was basically interested in the same outcome in Zaire as the United States sought. The British would probably have had a slight preference for a "Kenya" solution in Southern Rhodesia, but ultimately UDI represented only a minor annoyance. France would have preferred a regime in Zaire less tied to the United States but the French have been aware all along that by themselves they can only be marginally competitive; they have kept their options open in Zaire without investing much in the arena.

The same can ultimately be said of the USSR, which has played a continually passive role, responding to demands for aid--from Lumumba and from national liberation movements--by granting it but never excessively. For the USSR knew all along that the possibilities of detente and hence of technological assistance from the West were dependent on Soviet willingness to take part in the various areas of competition as a member of the "club" of the rich (which had its rules) rather than as an ally of indigenous radical forces. This is made very clear in a recent semi-official statement by Herbert J. Spiro, a member of the Planning and Coordination Staff of the U.S. Department of State. In a study of the implications for Africa of U.S.-Soviet detente, Spiro noted:

> The first--and the last--threat of a major
> Soviet-American confrontation in Africa
> occurred shortly after the Belgian Congo
> received its independence, and no real con-
> frontation took place. . . . This is not
> to say that issues of substance have

31

> evaporated, either between the U.S. and
> the USSR, or among other states. . . .
> However, both sides evidently recognize
> that neither the nuclear nor the ideologi-
> cal issues can be resolved at present, so
> that everyone--and especially those to
> whom enormous power has given special
> global responsibilities--will have to
> learn to live with the postponment (in
> the Hegelian sense, <u>Aufhebung</u>) of their
> resolution.[25]

Finally the African white settlers wanted time, and
that they got. They also wanted an active ally in Zaire,
which probably would have made possible the overthrow of
both Kenneth Kaunda in Zambia and Julius Nyerere in Tanzania, but that they did not get--thanks to the United
States. This points up the difference of interests between the United States and the white settlers, at least
as it has thus far been demonstrated.

The white settlers basically hope to construct a new
industrial nexus in the world economy and thereby use the
current world economic contraction to bargain for far better trade terms than they presently have by profiting from
the competition among the core states (including eventually even the USSR). Had their maneuvers in Zaire in the
1960s succeeded they might have been able to proceed to
establish an economic common market that would have included both Zaire and Zambia as well as Angola, Mozambique,
and Rhodesia--a group that would have been a truly powerful political instrument. This clearly ran counter to
long-term U.S. interests, which is no doubt why France has
flirted with assisting in the construction of the common
market in Southern Africa (both by its policy in Zaire
and by its policy vis-a-vis South Africa).

Therefore apart from Zaire why did the United States
not intervene on a massive scale elsewhere in Africa? The
simple answer, already indicated, is that she did not need
to; indeed such intervention would have been counterpro-
ductive.

From an economic point of view access to trade in
areas other than Southern Africa seemed and still seems
marginally important to the United States. In any case
the major obstacle to such trade, if there has been one,
has been the resistance at various times and places to
U.S. intrusion by the French government. And in the
larger context of differences between the United States

and France this issue has been a very minor one. On the
affirmative side the most significant U.S. assistance was
support for Ghana's Volta Dam project and for Guinea's
FRIA aluminum development operations. In both cases U.S.
firms were directly interested and in both cases it was
hoped to gain political mileage out of such assistance.
In the case of Ghana, Great Britain offered no objection.
And in the case of Guinea, France's attitude was precisely the motive for the assistance. In both cases failure
to assist would have been regarded as greater "interference" than the assistance, and might have led ultimately
to Soviet aid, as in the 1960 Aswan Dam project.

From a political point of view U.S. intervention
might have been occasioned by the existence of persistent-
ly unfriendly or unstable governments, either of which
could possibly have resulted in consequences that the
United States would have been unhappy about. But was
this actually the case? Of the so-called radical governments almost all were very careful not to offend the United States on crucial matters; for example both Algeria
(under Ahmed Ben Bella) and Guinea refused refueling
rights to Soviet military transport during the Cuban confrontation of 1962. The only exceptions to this rule
were the aforementioned Congo government of Lumumba and
possibly Kwame Nkrumah's Ghana in the last years of his
regime. There is no doubt that the United States assisted
in world economic sanctions against Ghana in 1964-65 by
being most unsympathetic to Ghana's balance-of-payments
dilemmas, and that this international freeze contributed
directly to Nkrumah's inability to satisfy internal complaints against the regime. The United States certainly
treated Nkrumah's successor, General Ankrah, in a more
sympathetic manner (just as it did with General Suharto
after President Sukarno in Indonesia or with Augusto
Pinochet after Salvador Allende in Chile).

Did Nkrumah therefore do anything to warrant an extra
ingredient of U.S. hostility, as compared to Sekou Toure,
Nyerere, Modibo Keita, or Ben Bella? No doubt yes; it was
Nkrumah's combination of very active involvement in Southern African internal affairs plus his active "subversion"
of neighboring conservative regimes that ultimately seemed
an intolerable perturbation of a relatively delicate
status quo. It was probably the unpredictability and
volatility of Nkrumah's intervention mechanisms combined
with their persistence that aroused wrath and fear. When
all is said and done, however, it is quite possible that
even had the United States been studiously neutral in

Ghanaian politics, Nkrumah might have had difficulty surviving. He had burned many internal bridges and stirred enmity among other governments in the region, so that the African forces arrayed against his regime were impressively strong.

As for the question of unstable governments in Africa there have been only a few instances of continued internal disorder. In the cases of the Sudan, Rwanda, and Burundi the issues remained local and never acquired an international dimension. In the cases of Cameroun and Chad there were French troops to aid the governments in putting down rebellions of groups with leftist orientations. And in the major civil war of Nigeria, there was the strange alignment of Britain and the USSR in support of the federal government and France and Portugal in support of Biafra. Thus in all these cases it was easy for the United States to take the stance of mild and passive support for the reigning government; the situations were all in hand.

CONCLUSION

Historically, given Africa's role in the world economy and given a fundamentally expanding world economy in the twentieth century, the United States has had little reason to have more than the mildest interest in Africa. It has been content to leave Africa as a chasse-gardee of Western Europe, occasionally prodding the Europeans to extend some timely political concessions to African elites and occasionally stepping in to fill gaps left by the European powers.

The only significant exception has been the U.S. policy toward Zaire in the years since Congolese independence in 1960. As noted above, this active concern for Zaire stems primarily from Zaire's key role in the emerging politics of Southern Africa; moreover the United States is now in the process of becoming actively involved in the internal politics of Southern Africa because of the long-term cyclical downturn of the world economy. As a result of this downturn Southern Africa has become a key arena of economic competition among the core powers of the world economy.

This downturn was presaged around 1960, became widely visible in 1971, and as of this writing has not halted. It is clear that in view of this one can expect a massive political intervention by the United States in Southern

Africa in the coming years, even with the drastically
changed conditions following the coup d'etat in Portugal.

But with whom will the United States ally itself
politically? Clearly not with the African governments
that are emerging in the area, whose policies are yet to
be defined. And quite possibly not always with the white
settler governments, with whom the relationship is bound
to be ambiguous, given the contradictory nature of some
of the interests involved. No doubt the optimal objective for U.S. interests to pursue is the erection of politically stable, economically friendly African-controlled
regimes, of which Mobutu's Zaire stands as a model. Can
this be achieved? Such a question goes beyond the framework of this study. However, among the possible scenarios
that are within the realm of the conceivable for Africa
over the next 10 to 20 years, one might consist of American pressure on South Africa to concede the independence
of Namibia, with the establishment in Namibia of a government having the political complexion of Botswana; the
restoration of Zimbabwe to the path of decolonization
a la Kenya, as the British originally envisaged it; a
split in the Nationalist party in South Africa and a U.S.-
encouraged regime of the verligtes and the United party,
combined with some of the Bantustans moving forward to independence; and a Southern African common market going
south from Zaire and Zambia and linked in various ways
economically to the United States. None of this is beyond Henry Kissinger's fertile imagination.

Of course alternative scenarios are possible. For
example the Rhodesian settlers might refuse to be sacri-
ficed to the larger interests of the United States and
the South African whites. The French and the Russians
might combine forces to forestall various U.S. maneuvers.
Revolutionary nationalist upheaval might be strong enough
and simultaneous enough throughout the world so that the
capacity of the United States to intervene in Southern
Africa would be seriously circumscribed. The possible
regeneration of an African revolutionary movement inside
South Africa might suddenly produce a militarily relevant
internal opposition to the regime. In that case after 30
years or so one might emerge with a Southern African "common market" that would resemble in tone and outlook the
China of today; in which case some worthy successor to
Kissinger may also fly to Johannesburg.

Of the two scenarios which better serves the interests of the people of Southern Africa? And which better
serves the interests of the United States? The answer

is obvious for both Southern Africans and Americans: it
depends on how you define those interests, in terms of
which groups within both areas; it is for each of them to
choose.

NOTES

1. Immanuel Wallerstein, "Dependence and an Interdependent World: The Limited Possibilities of Transformation Within the Capitalist World Economy," African Studies
Review (April 1974).

2. See Stuart Bruchey, The Roots of American Economic Growth, 1607-1861 (New York: Harper and Row, 1968).

3. These conflicting trends are explained by Barring-
ton Moore, Jr. in The Social Origins of Democracy and Dictatorship (Boston: Beacon Press, 1966), chap. 3.

4. Whether this decline dates from the 1870s or the
1890s is a debatable subject; see E. H. Phelps-Brown and
S. J. Handfield-Jones, "The Climacteric of the 1890's,"
Oxford Economic Papers n.s., vol. 4, no. 3 (October 1952):
279-89, and D. J. Coppock, "The Climacteric of the 1870's,"
Manchester School of Economic and Social Science 24, no. 1
(January 1956): 21-31.

5. "Africa in a Capitalist World," Issues 2, no. 3
(Fall 1973): 1-11.

6. Wallerstein, "The Rise and Future Demise of the
Capitalist World System: Concepts for Comparative Analysis," Comparative Studies in Society and History (forthcoming).

7. See "The Colonial Era in Africa: Changes in the
Social Structure," in Colonialism in Africa, 1870-1960,
vol. 2, The History and Politics of Colonialism, 1914-
1960, ed. L. H. Gann and Peter Duignan (Cambridge: Cambridge University Press, 1970), pp. 399-421.

8. Evidence of this in the Gold Coast is given in
R. Szereszewski, Structural Changes in the Economy of
Ghana, 1891-1911 (London: Weidenfeld and Nicolson, 1965).

9. Address delivered by the late Amilcar Cabral,
October 20, 1971, Finland, published in M. Amilcar Cabral
a Visite la Finlande les 19-22 octobre 1971.

10. For example if one looks at the collection of
basic documents of American foreign policy in the 1940s
one finds not a single reference to Africa; see U.S.
Congress, 81st Cong., 1st sess., Senate doc. no. 23, A
Decade of American Foreign Policy: Basic Documents,
1941-1949 (Washington: U.S. Government Printing Office,

1950). A similar collection for 1950–55 shows a reference only to Libya, with whom the United States signed an agreement for the use of defense facilities on September 9, 1954; see U.S. Department of State, American Foreign Policy: Basic Documents, 1950-1955 (New York: Arno Press, 1971), vol. 2, pp. 2207-23.

11. U.S. Department of State, American Foreign Policy: Basic Documents, 1950-1955, op. cit., pp. 2173-74.

12. Ibid., pp. 2294-95.

13. Ibid., p. 2301.

14. U.S. Department of State, American Foreign Policy: Current Documents, 1957 (New York: Arno Press, 1971), p. 1071 n.

15. Ibid., pp. 1071-72.

16. U.S. Department of State, American Foreign Policy: Current Documents, 1961 (New York: Arno Press, 1971), p. 884.

17. Ibid.

18. U.S. Department of State, American Foreign Policy: Current Documents, 1965, Publication 8372 (Washington: U.S. Government Printing Office, 1968), p. 628.

19. Department of State Bulletin, October 11, 1971, pp. 6-7.

20. See U.S. Department of State, American Foreign Policy: Current Documents, 1957, op. cit., p. 1066.

21. See William Attwood, The Reds and the Blacks (New York: Harper and Row, 1967).

22. See John S. Badeau, "U.S.A. and U.A.R.: A Crisis in Confidence," Foreign Affairs 43, no. 2 (January 1965): 281-96.

23. Elliot J. Berg, "Real Income Trends in West Africa, 1939-1960," in Economic Transition in Africa, ed. Melville J. Herskovits and Mitchell Harwitz (Evanston: Northwestern University Press, 1964), pp. 199-238.

24. For further discussion see Africa: The Politics of Unity (New York: Random House, 1967).

25. Herbert J. Spiro, "United States-Soviet Detente: Implications for Africa," paper delivered at Third International Congress of Africanists, Addis Ababa, December 9-19, 1973, pp. 3, 11.

While this observer shares much in common with
Wallerstein's analysis, there are important differences
between his use of economic determinism and my interpretation that places economic interests within transnational
cultural-racial systems. The history of American policy
toward Africa is best understood within the overall context of the rise and decline of the Western racial imperialism of which it is an integral part.

Whenever foreign policy is discussed certain concepts
have to be defined; foreign policy is generally considered
to be the official positions of government, whereas foreign relations are the total relationships of one society
with another society. The contributions of James Rosenau
and Ken Waltz to this broader view are well known in comparative politics.[1] Joseph Nye's view that our "traditional conceptual nets" may give us the mistaken impression that nothing new is happening summarizes our need for
new means for grasping the transnational pattern of relationships between major powers and the new states in a
region such as Africa.[2]

Despite the centralization of American life in other
ways, we have become increasingly pluralistic as a people
both in terms of ethnic/racial groups and class. Government itself falls under this influence and American foreign policy has become both a reflection of these internal
political realities and a response to the changing realities in the outside world.

The major actors historically and in the contemporary
period are basically the same, but their strength and influence have changed in response to America's changing internal and external environment. Very generally these
actors in foreign relations and their interests can be
categorized as economic, ethnic, racial, religious, and
military-political-bureaucratic (there are many other
categories that can be established to make the analysis
more precise, but they represent only subcategories of
these five).

The economic actors represent a wide range of corporate, investment, financial resource, and trading interests; their motives cover profits, business expansion,
raw material supply, etc. Not only corporate directors
and stockholders but also trade unions and white-collar

workers are affected. And to the extent that the individual's income is tied to investments in areas like
South Africa, as is the case in the United Kingdom, a
class economic interest exists.

Ethnic/racial and religious actors are often put
into one category, but it is important to distinguish
them in any thorough foreign relations analysis of an
area like Africa. For example the interests of foreign
missions of various churches have until the late 1960s
been a reinforcement of colonial and settler interests
while racial groups have supported or opposed colonialism
from their black or white perspective. Even within religious groups this has been the case, though indifference
has characterized the majority. Independent black American missions like the African Methodist Episcopal Church
were, however, always a major opponent of white supremacy.[3]
Military-bureaucratic-and-political actors are closely related as well, but the considerations for each are important to distinguish in varied situations.

Conflicting interest groups and linkages characterize
U.S. relations with Africa and become especially apparent
in the case of Southern Africa. Corporate financial and
ideological interests as well as racial linkages are major
determinants of U.S. relations with Southern Africa. The
rapid growth of American investments in the new industries
of Southern Africa simply cannot be ignored; the oil of
Angola and the mineral industry of Namibia are prime examples. And alongside of this must be placed the enormous
racial, ethnic, and ideological affinity between American
Anglo-Saxons and the Anglo-Saxons and Afrikaners of South
Africa. The racial identification of American blacks with
independent black Africa and with the oppressed blacks of
Southern Africa is also important. Most of these interests
operate independently of U.S. government policy, although
the State Department, the White House, and the Central Intelligence Agency, among others, try to influence them.

In certain areas of the world nongovernmental influences have been more determinative of American relations
with those areas than has official policy; they have in
fact shaped American policy toward Africa and especially
Southern Africa. For example the policies and interests
of American churches in their missionary role over the
past century have been a much greater point of contact
with most areas of Africa than has the U.S. government.
The latter until the late 1950s operated through colonial
offices in Europe, whereas American missions had direct
day-to-day contact with Africans as well as with colonial

officials. The policy of these churches frequently paralleled government policy because both shared an interest in
African stability and had the same paternalistic perspectives. The humanization of colonialism by church educational policies did not alter their historic role in legitimizing the subjection of Africans and therefore the
European empire in Africa. The immigrant settler groups
of Southern Africa, largely from Europe, were a part of
the same European immigrant pattern that built the United
States. While Americans were not direct participants in
settling Rhodesia and South Africa, the similarities of
origin, conquest, and development among settler groups
have created a transnational white-dominated cultural system of great importance to American relations with these
African areas, sustaining and legitimizing their conquest,
racial subjection, and exploitation.[4] And corporate investment flows and profits have reflected these ties of
legal similarity and colonial mentality.

THE HISTORICAL PERSPECTIVE

The U.S. relationship with Africa historically should
be seen in terms of its integral ties with European imperialism. Contemporary Western relationships with Africa
emerge from the nearly 200 years of exploration, exploitation, colonization, and national struggle that only in the
present day have reached a new phase of self-determination
within the framework of independent states; this was a
period in which Western ideas as well as economic and
legal systems were imposed upon the African continent.
The central core of this nineteenth-century expan-
sionism was an Anglo-Saxon and Franco racism that believed
in its civilizing mission and that the "primitive" cultures, shiftless patterns of livelihood, and pagan reli-
gions of people less equipped to compete in the Darwinian
evolutionary pattern should be tutored and directed by
those who had developed industrialism, democracy, science,
and Christian forms of life.[5] There were of course less
ethnocentric missionaries and anthropologists whose ideas
and lives did not fit this general pattern, such as
Elizabeth Huxley and David Livingstone; however, in the
main this was the dynamic pattern of life that led to the
pioneering, arduous, and enterprising expansion of the
English- and French-speaking peoples of Europe over two
centuries.
This same racial-cultural imperialism provided much
of the impetus to the colonization and conquest of the

Indian lands of North America. Slavery was a very important economic aspect of this conquest and development,
not only as an economic system but as an expression of
this racial-cultural core. The fact that most slaves
came from Africa is an early relationship that has an important bearing upon the contemporary scene. The Indians--
who could maintain sustained resistance--were eventually
swept aside and eliminated. This is not the historical
emphasis given to children in history books in the United
States or in England, but if the United States and the
underlying forces that have moved her in the world are to
be understood a more realistic interpretation must be made
of the hard core of ethnocentric ideas of mission and
rights that led to the establishment of certain kinds of
economic systems ranging from slavery to industrialism and
capitalism. An analysis that begins with an economic system and the classes of that system seems to miss the crucial explanation of why certain groups such as the Anglo-
Saxons became expansionist and how they subjugated others.
The technology they developed, such as ships, compasses,
gunpowder, and later the assembly line, provided this
group with the means to expand. The essential purpose
leading to the push that produces both power and means to
impose new methods of subjection and exploitation upon
other groups of people in the world is based on the chosen-
people myth of superiority and mission, which is racist.

The American Anglo-Saxon was of course busy subduing
the West and beginning probes into the Pacific at the time
the Europeans were partitioning Africa. However, there
was a general American approval and participation in this
civilizing mission despite certain liberal antiimperialist
statements of men like William James, who served as vice-
president of the Anti-Imperialism League, and William
Graham Sumner, who was outraged by the war against Spain.
But the antiexpansionists were swept aside in the rush to
protectionism and empire, culminating in the presidential
defeat of William Jennings Bryan in 1896. And Teddy
Roosevelt's victories buried the antiimperialist cause
for over half a century. The similarity of values and
means for exploiting so-called weaker peoples between
American imperialists like Teddy Roosevelt and the Europeans had laid down an ethnic-racial affinity between
white Americans and the settlers of Africa. When Woodrow
Wilson refused to meet with W. E. B. DuBois at the Paris
Peace Conference in 1919 and insisted upon the inclusion
of a paternalistic mandate system for the League of Nations, Wilson participated in a repartition of Africa
based on this Anglo-Saxon racial system. To hand over

the Southwest Africans to the racist government of South Africa as a mandate of trust was itself an act of racism.

This Anglo-Saxon racial band linked the United States to Europe's empires and directly to settlers in Southern Africa in the nineteenth-century peak period of expansion. Such ties of sentiment and race were more important relationships than economic ones in this period. Later the profitable exploitation of gold, diamonds, and other metals reinforced the relationship. The attempt of Afro-Americans to return to the motherland through the establishment of Liberia in the early nineteenth century was a weak recognition of the ties black Americans were to strengthen in later years. The relationship, however, was a predominantly white one. A similarity of hardship, the bloody conquest of weaker peoples, and the struggle to reestablish educational and cultural ties with the motherland won respect and sympathy among Anglo-Americans for those whom they saw carrying out the same free enterprise in other parts of the world. The bonds were further forged by the two world wars of this century in which men from all of these areas fought and died together in Europe and in Africa for ideas and political systems they cherished in common.

As Wallerstein notes, during and following the Second World War, the United States established a new relationship with Africa, closely identified with its European allies, which became an important part of the continuing system of the racial and ethnic empire of Europe in Africa. However, this was a short-lived empire.

In the 1970s there have been marked indications of a decline in imperial relations of the United States with all of Africa. This means a conflict within American policy and different possibilities that were not covered in Wallerstein's analysis.

REGENERATION OF COLONIALISM AFTER THE SECOND WORLD WAR

The decade following the Second World War witnessed the return of colonial power to Africa despite the presence of restless new self-determination forces. The United States participated in and underwrote this process in all the major facets of its relationship with Africa despite her higher level of verbal commitment than that of the British or the French to the principles of the Atlantic Charter and the United Nations. Economic participation by the United States was limited to the colonial framework and even the rise of the pro-Nazi Nationalist party to power in South Africa did not deter American corporations from utilizing the white settler and colonial framework as a basis for advancing interests in the exploitation of the minerals and fossil fuels of Africa, from Rhodesia to Libya. The bureaucratic-political-military elite in the United States supported this view of colonial Africa, restored with American Marshall Plan relief and the newly created NATO structure. Africa was seen as a strategic resource and manpower supplier in the developing cold war. Church and academic organizations, including the National Council of Churches, held paternalistic views of colonial gradualism aimed at granting self-government in Africa only after the careful development of certain standards of civilization defined by Western law and institutions.[6] This delayed support for African nationalism and reinforced the racial-economic dominance by the West.

There was very little dissent from this extension of American power as the underwriter of colonial exploitation in Africa and the guarantor of its security against Russian expansion and indigenous revolution. However, in the 1950s the beginnings of countervailing groups and relationships became very important: long-established human rights groups under leaders such as Ralph Bunche in the National Association for the Advancement of Colored People, with a racial empathy for the rights of Africans, participated in the formation of the United Nations and mildly protested this American colonialism.[7] New groups like the American Committee on Africa and the League for the Rights of Man, representing religious as well as civil rights concerns, began to organize support for pacific action at the United Nations on behalf of the independence of Africa and human rights. And in the latter 1950s, small groups of American academics also took up the issue within their organizations but were rebuffed (several scholars within the African Studies Association (ASA), formed in 1958, attempted to persuade that organization to oppose aspects of colonialism; however, all such efforts failed on the grounds that the ASA was "nonpolitical"). Under the threats of McCarthyism and the widespread acceptance of the strategic and economic interests of the West in Africa, the white dominance and colonial lobbies had little difficulty in isolating the African constituency as extremists. American power under the new economic, military, and intelligence agencies gave a

transfusion to the dying colonial system that undoubtedly
sustained it for a decade or longer against the gathering
forces of nationalist liberation that had begun to break
through the structure, weakened in the struggle with the
fascist states.

THE GREAT AFRICAN EMERGENCE

The current period of the great African emergence begins with Ghana in 1957. American policy is said to have
favored colonial withdrawal in Africa and actually to have
facilitated it at key points, such as in the Congo in 1962.
The U.S. policy and relationship in Africa did change but
it followed the lead of the European powers and never supported nationalism or neutralism against those powers.

The acceptance of independence suited the major interests in American relationships with Africa, just as it
did in Europe. Independent African states, as long as
they were led by moderate professionals and middle-class
representatives who maintained the basic economic ties
with the West, were not regarded as a bad investment.
Leaders such as Houphouet Boigny in the Ivory Coast and
Jomo Kenyatta in Kenya, who had put their radical days
behind them and appreciated the benefits of commercial
and tourist relationships, as well as the educational and
religious ties established under colonialism, found great
favor in Washington, as they did in the capitals of Europe.
On the other hand those African leaders like Nkrumah,
Sekou Toure, and Nyerere who "listened to a different
drummer" found much less favor and consequently less aid
than did the Westernized leaders.

The Kennedy administration was generally regarded as
representing the most pro-African presidency and period;
however, this was more image than reality. While foreign
aid figures expanded during that period and the numbers
of diplomatic personnel in Africa increased geometrically,
this was the high point in the growth of American imperial
power, which opportunistically took advantage of the re-
laxation of colonial dominance of African countries to engage in more extended commercial trade and investment, religious activity, and diplomatic cultivation of American
interests in Africa.[8] The major dynamics of this period
were trade expansion and fuel and mineral development.
And the U.S. military and diplomatic services supported
this. The cold war served as a convenient rationale for
the growth of American economic and military assistance,

at least for Congress if not for the former colonial countries themselves. It also made the U.S. relationship easier with former colonial powers--who were ever disengaging politically and permissive of U.S. entry into their previous domains provided the Americans did not disturb continuing neocolonial cultural and commercial relationships--and helped to keep down the growth of Soviet and later Chinese interests in Africa. The U.S. corporate investment in South Africa rose most sensationally in the Kennedy period and afterward by well over 300 percent-- from $286 million in 1960 to $964 million in 1971.[9]

American churches in the main were pleased with this new independence departure and initiated a self-determination program of their own with the creation of younger churches and selection of African bishops that were expected to fit within the wider Western church pattern. Academicians were especially responsive to the new opportunities for research and foundation grants. They flooded into the new African states, writing African histories and constitutions, creating new universities, and utilizing new methodologies. However, Afro-American scholars played a strictly secondary role in these new enterprises at this stage.

This expansion of American corporate, religious, academic, and bureaucratic interests in Africa had some skeptics and opponents among the civil rights and pacific action groups but their dissent was generally discounted by the major influences in American policy on Africa. This dissent was directed at those forms of assistance and growth that were favoring a new African middle-class elite as corrupt and ineffective as the colonial administrations they replaced. Dissenters also objected to the way in which the cold war was being used as a device of favoritism and leverage for U.S. corporate interests and how U.S. aid undermined the development of the nonaligned self-reliance considered so vital to the achievement of real independence.

This period saw the emergence for the first time of a true African constituency[10] in the United States that developed primarily out of opposition to American policies in Southern Africa, where nationalism was stymied by the Portuguese, South Africans, and Rhodesians.

While the new African constituency's organizations, like the American Negro Leadership Conference on Africa, had only weak and periodic black support in this period they were growing in alliance with black political gains. Rebellion was developing among liberal Protestant denomi-

nations whose anger was fueled by conscription and the
heavy tax burdens of military programs necessitated by
maintaining large armies abroad, and by tax subsidies for
American multinational corporations, especially oil companies making gigantic profits and yet paying virtually
no U.S. tax. (An examination of the annual reports of the
leading denominations of the National Council of Churches
reveals this trend beginning in the mid-1960s when church
opposition to the war in Vietnam began to emerge.) Antiimperialist traditions of the "free traders" and "free
silver" populists were stirred against the corporate-
military elite whose links to settler colonialism were
exposed by Gulf Oil in Angola and by Mobil Oil and Newmont Mining in South Africa, and by the indirect subsidies to the growing colonial wars of Portuguese Africa
through U.S. payments, loans, and military aid.

Countering this African constituency was the settler-
colonial constituency that was highly financed by multinational corporations, represented in Washington and at
the United Nations by various European and Southern African embassies, with influential spokesmen within and outside the administrations. The press especially reflected
this view because its norms accorded with the anti-
Communist and Anglo-Saxon political ideas of populace
groups such as the African American Affairs Association
that worked closely with other organizations supporting
the Rhodesians, fostering American oil interests in Portuguese territories, and assisting the South African lobby
in putting together influential programs such as the U.S.
South African Leadership Program. These groups utilized
long-established channels of influence on the Congress and
with the American public to counteract the African constituency. They secured support for the conservative influences around Tshombe in the Congo, maintained business
relationships with Rhodesia, and helped underwrite and
expand business investments in South Africa, Namibia, and
the Portuguese territories. Within the African continent
they undermined the credibility of the more radical regimes and encouraged divisions among African states, especially when it came to assistance for liberation movements, which they termed "terrorist."

During the 1960s the intricate and powerful network
of white dominance in the Western world successfully came
to the support of the settlers and colonialists in Southern Africa. This was directly reflected in American policy in many respects in the Congo, Rhodesia, and South
Africa, and at the United Nations: two dramatic examples

occurred in the Congo and Rhodesia. The American under-
cutting of the Kenyatta Commission of the Organization of
African Unity (OAU), which was attempting to bring a negotiated settlement to the Congo in 1964 and ended in the
Congo paratroop drop intervention, bears out Wallerstein's
analysis of the influence of American economic interests
and strategic considerations. The failure of the United
States to support the African request at the United Nations for the use of force against the Rhodesian rebellion
best illustrated the Anglo-Saxon racial-ethnic links.
Force that could have been used by the British and Americans for questionable ends of intervention in the Congo
was withheld a year later from the Rhodesian crisis when
the legal and practical reasons for a quick, forceful intervention were far more compelling. The political constituencies of both Western powers were placated by these
decisions and the special racial-economic interests in
each case were served, though perhaps not intentionally,
by decision makers whose choices generally lead to consequences they do not perceive.

THE DECLINE OF U.S. INFLUENCE IN AFRICA

American influence in Africa began to decline rapidly
at the end of the 1960s because of a number of long-term
trends; this in turn has led to the emergence of a major
disengagement movement from the overextension of power by
the United States in the postwar world. The struggle
against racial imperialism in Africa is now being fought
within the framework of far more favorable trends within
the American society. This is particularly where this
observer's analysis diverges from Wallerstein's assessment and others that operate on the assumption that the
situation of the 1960s still prevails. My conclusions
are less pessimistic, not because of different moral values but because the options currently are wider and more
open to positive influence by the antiimperialist than
they have been since the defeat of the populists and
Bryan at the end of the nineteenth century.

The United States today is contracting its power
throughout the world as a result of overextension, costly
losses, and changes in American economic circumstances.
This is particularly apparent in regions of the Third
World from policies ranging from the Nixon doctrine in
the Pacific to the reduction of commitments to NATO interests operating in Africa. There are numerous reasons

for this general contraction trend but the most important
are a growing realism concerning the objectives of Communist powers, the diminishing persuasive force of the messianic myth of the Anglo-Saxon culture, and the shifting
of economic priorities within the American economy. Such
basic changes are also reflected in the character of the
American political system, which has important bearings on
what side American decision makers ultimately support in
Africa.

Today American economic interests in Africa are primarily concentrated in independent black Africa, not in
the white settler areas; moreover U.S. economic interests
have begun to focus heavily in black Africa on fuel and
scarce minerals. American heavy investment in manufacturing and mining in South Africa and Southern Africa in
general was in the past several years primarily reinvest-
ment; oil has not been found in the settler areas. And
now that Angola and Mozambique are moving rapidly out
from under Portuguese rule by the advances of nationalist
liberation movements the oil deposits of these nations
move into the black as opposed to the white column.

Thus the economic pressures on U.S. corporations and
the U.S. economy to go with black Africa rather than with
white settler areas may well swing the balance in new
directions. Wallerstein's analysis, which builds on the
dependency of the U.S. economy on a settler-dominated
Southern Africa, is a distortion of reality and misjudges
these current developments.

Figures on the growth of American corporate investment in South Africa and even in Zaire should be broken
down into the different types of industry and their importance to the American economy. The current and growing energy shortage in the United States has the effect
of intensifying American interest in cooperation with
Nigeria, Angola, and North Africa as priority areas.
There has been evidence that some American multinational
corporations such as American Metal Climax, with heavy
stakes in both Namibia and Zambia, are being forced to
choose between settler Africa and black Africa. The
Nixon diplomatic and military strategy in his first term
of office was to expand trade and investment, attempting
to reestablish commercial relations despite the U.N.
sanctions on Rhodesia and entering into a more vigorous
"contacts" policy with South Africa. (The primary economic interests of the United States in Africa are now
petroleum fuels and minerals: 50 percent of all U.S. investment in Africa is in petroleum in seven countries--

Algeria, Angola, Egypt, Gabon, Libya, Nigeria, and Tunisia.) This policy ran into considerable difficulty with black Africa and the U.S. African constituency. There is some evidence that in its second term the Nixon administration began to back off, though the pressures from the settler constituency to stand firm remained fierce. The best illustration of this was the decision in 1971 to allow the importation of chrome from Rhodesia despite U.N. sanctions. The complexities of this issue have been well documented in other studies but the issue serves as an excellent example of how the Nixon administration initially gave in to special economic interests and to the fears of the self-sufficiency advocates of the Pentagon, as well as to the Anglo-Saxon racial sentiments responding to the pressures from the Rhodesian and South African lobbies that had found an able spokesman in the U.S. Congress in Senator Harry Byrd of Virginia. The lower-echelon State Department officials, together with the African constituency, were finally able to persuade the administration to reverse the policy; they prevailed because of the growing recognition that principal U.S. economic interests lay with those African states that might take steps to cut off primary resources to the United States as the Arabs had done over the Middle East issue. American corporations were under fire internally and externally for their racial complicity in South Africa and the administration felt it was far more important to preserve the image of the American corporation in Southern Africa as being cooperative with international standards rather than opposing them. The difficulties of reversing this decision, even with a change in administration policy, is demonstrated by the competing pressures of the settler and African constituencies that have resulted in a slow process toward the repeal of the Byrd Amendment. The U.S. Senate voted for repeal while no action has been taken in the House. The power and influence of the right wing represented by pro-Rhodesian senators such as Peter Dominick (Colorado) and Barry Goldwater (Arizona), who use the corporate interests and play upon anti-U.N. sentiments, reflect the real force of racial imperialism in American society. Their ability to influence these kinds of decisions cannot be quickly reversed though their control is being weakened primarily because they are losing credibility.

Probably the most important reason for the demise of the Anglo-Saxon messianic myth is the detente between the Soviet Union and the United States. The integral rela-

49

tionship between security and the colonial civilizing mission has been a major part of the extension of direct U.S. power into various parts of the world. The defeat of these concepts in Southeast Asia and the adjustments to Arab interests in the Middle East have brought about important long-term changes in American strategy throughout the world as reflected in U.S. military aid programs, economic assistance, and counterinsurgency actions. It is now very difficult for both the right wing and settler interests in the United States to make a case for underwriting either the Portuguese or South African mission in Africa, because their colonial racial systems are now obviously anachronisms. However, the force of Anglo-Saxon solidarity is still very potent in American society and can be counted on to rally sentiment for a beleaguered Rhodesia or whites under attack from revolutionaries and Communists. Moreover these sentiments are closely tied with special business and corporate interests whose sophisticated manipulation of government and shrewd deception of the public is unexcelled.

The sense of strategic U.S. commitment to the Southern African redoubt began dying hard in the Nixon administration; the renewal of the Azores Pact with Portugal and the extension of several million dollars of military aid in 1972 illustrate this point. The United States provided the means for the Portuguese to continue their colonial wars in Africa but the Portuguese army has since decided the struggle could not be won and has opted for disengagement. The United States is clearly not willing itself to take up the struggle directly and favors a gradual transition of power to the African liberation movements it had previously opposed through the indirect supply of weapons and the training of counterinsurgency troops. In the fall of 1973 the State Department bitterly objected to the recognition of Guinea-Bissau at the United Nations. The heavy commitment of U.S. oil companies will nevertheless call for a major turnabout, as in Algeria, of American relations in Guinea-Bissau, Angola, and Mozambique.

South Africa remains the last retreat of the cold war strategists, multinational corporate interests, and the Anglo-Saxon congressional racists. With South Africa they are on stronger ground in the short run but probably not in the long run unless they can create some sort of gotterdammerung to bring the Western countries into a major effort to preserve this "last outpost of civilization."

The major favorable short-term trends for the African settlers are the high profit rates of a booming South African economy in which some 300 American corporations have nearly a billion-dollar stake, and the claim of South Africa to providing the major Western cover for the vital shipping route of oil around the Cape of Good Hope. The limited nature of the U.S. investment in South Africa has already been indicated. In the 1970s this investment has become highly vulnerable to criticism for supporting the racial policies of the South African government that have already had deterrent effects on some businesses. The big multinationals have been defensive of their "enlightened policies" but the pressures at home have already brought one major company to admit that it is not anxious to expand and another to say it would not enter the area. While the State Department has sought to build a reformist image about American companies in South Africa, liberal leaders and blacks in the American Congress are increasingly aware of the importance, in the balance, of the black African states that are the suppliers of an increasing portion of American energy supplies. The African constituency has developed a growing campaign to pressure American companies out of South Africa, which will be very difficult to achieve even with full sanctions by the United Nations; but the influence this pressure has on new U.S. investment and special technological support in South Africa may become very important. The South African economy is overextended and dependent upon skill from abroad that can very rapidly begin to dry up, not only in the case of the United States but also Europe. Thus it is difficult to see how, in anything but the short run the American economy can be regarded as committed to maintaining South African stability or the extension of settler interests into the rest of Africa, as Wallerstein and others have suggested. For instance such a course is not necessarily a foregone conclusion for the United Kingdom although economic and racial interests will oppose and undercut any official British policy of disengagement.

Official U.S. policy will shift gradually to increased economic sanctions and disengagement from South Africa largely as a result of the long-term trends of the international/American political scene. This process is being considerably delayed, not so much by the economic interests in South Africa as by the mistaken sentiments of Anglo-Saxon racism that emerge from the similarities in origin of the American and white-dominated regimes of Southern Africa.

An illustration of this point is the controversy over the building of the new naval base at Diego Garcia in the Indian Ocean, because in the last analysis the racial interests have retreated into strategic argument. The American Navy has sought this base to protect the shipping of oil supplies against the Middle East and the increased activity of the Russian fleet in the Indian Ocean. While the settler interests have long pressed for the recognition of South Africa within a NATO southern tier of the Atlantic, and for the strengthening of the Simonstown Naval Base on the west coast of South Africa, the Diego Garcia base is a step in the right direction as far as they are concerned because it accepts the logic of their concern for protecting shipping around the Cape. The Nixon administration pressed for the base, despite earlier congressional rejection and State Department doubts, because it accepted the strategic logic that Russian submarines are more of a threat to American shipping in the Indian Ocean than off the coast of Guinea or in the North Sea. This is very dangerous because it might lead to a naval arms race in the Indian Ocean that could then actually bring South Africa into the network of direct NATO security. Should the settler interests succeed in linking American security to South Africa, this would give the Anglo-Saxon mythology a new lease on life with incalculable consequences.

The primary hope for offsetting such a step rests in the emergence of the African constituency to a position of influence in the American society and policy that it has not previously enjoyed. This opportunity arises in part from the demise of imperial ambitions, previously discussed, which is in turn linked to the major shift in economic priorities toward black Africa and the withdrawal of Portuguese, British, and French colonial interests with which the United States has been associated.[11]

The major change in the African constituency in the 1970s has been the increased growth of black participation and the emergence of a middle class, largely church-inspired, a loose network of groups with roots in the peace movements and substantial support in the provinces. This is reflected in the growing political sophistication of their activities, now directed more at Congress, as compared to the United Nations, and in an awareness of the techniques of influencing congressional candidates.

The black input into this constituency is the least understood of the African interests though it is potentially the most important. Black radicals tend to exaggerate their importance and frequently fail to support some of their most important leaders, such as Congressmen Ronald Dellums and Charles Diggs, because they discount the role of the black caucus. They also negate their liberal allies and quarrel with them over issues that are frequently secondary, to the despair of their African brothers who realize that only a coalition of blacks and liberals can muster the power to move the white establishment. However, the black power movement of the 1960s has brought many able young Afro-Americans into the struggle and politicized the cultural movement concerning African issues, so that African liberation days are now held in many cities of middle America. The moderate black leaders have tended to underestimate their influence because of the apathy and failures of the past; yet their importance in interpreting Africa academically and publicly has grown rapidly and representatives of their view have begun to penetrate into the highest echelons of American government, religion, business, and finance. From these points of power they are in a position to lead many churches and even businesses into new relationships with Africa. The political-economic base of American blacks in American cities is broadening. The lack of unity is the despair of many black Americans as reflected in their internecine quarrels and the lack of a single leader of preeminence. But unity is not necessarily a measure of effectiveness, which is more often the result of diverse influences than of a single impact. The sum total of this black American input is to support black Africans in their economic efforts, especially in such times as starvation in the Sahel. Their weight is against any economic or military measures that support Rhodesia or South Africa and they favor use of necessary force by the United Nations. They have totally opposed bringing South Africa into the Western security framework and any such step would risk militant black resistance.

The most potent new groups are the respectable middle-class spokesmen who represent a resurgence of the antiimperialism and populism of the nineteenth century though they are falsely accused by the expansionists of being isolationist. The focus of interest for these groups is the hard-pressed consumer and taxpayer who suspects the multinational corporations, yawns over the oddly anti-Communist shibboleths, prefers a less costly army based at home, and hopes the United Nations can fulfill the original ideals of the Charter of Human Rights.

These groups find their expression through the Rotary Clubs, the League of Women Voters, various trade unions, and church social action programs that directly benefit African liberation movements. It is in the awakening sense of outrage that large portions of this class have now developed, from an awareness of the extent to which they have been ravaged and victimized mentally, physically, and spiritually by a corrupt elite, that the hope of democratic society resides. Christopher Lasch saw this when he spoke of "the democratic instinct in middle-class Americans who have no material need to revolt but who are becoming conscious of the degree to which they, too, are corrupted, degraded, and victimized by the very arrangements that have made possible their unprecedented prosperity."[12] The political dimension of this revolt has been charted by Jack Newfield and Jeff Greenfield in A Populist Manifesto: The Making of a New Majority (Praeger, 1972), in which the distinction between the elitist and populist tradition in the Democratic party is outlined from the time of Bryan versus Wilson to Estes Kefauver versus Stevenson in the modern era. The fact that a populist antiimperialist won the Democratic nomination in 1972, though he lost the election, indicates that trend and the strength of the populist wing. One effect of Nixon's 1972 victory was to bring corruption out into the open, thereby giving tremendous impetus to the reformist movements. While the right-wing Wallace groups, in combination with the old elite, might be the beneficiaries of the upheaval, this unrest equally strengthens the populist trend.

In the 1970s the African issues have become more clearly drawn and the protagonists are far more equally divided than previously. Under the Nixon administration no new departure was launched comparable to the Middle East or China policies because the administration was not prepared to risk the wrath of its right-wing supporters over Rhodesia or South Africa. However, in the years ahead, while the dangers of slipping into a defense of white supremacy remain great, the more probable course is the continuation of a gradual disengagement from settler Africa, possibly in concert with several Western European countries working through the United Nations' potential for pacific action. Given the dangers of the short-term, the long-term trends are promising and it will be tragic if, through failure of nerve, insight, or organization, the American people should lose the very real chance we now have to dismantle our own racial empire.

1. James Rosenau, <u>Linkage Politics: Essays on the Convergence of National and International Systems</u> (New York: Free Press, 1969).

2. Joseph Nye, "Comparative Regional Integration, Concept and Measurement," <u>International Organization</u> 22 (Autumn 1968): 855-80.

3. Eric Rosenthal, ed., <u>Encyclopedia of Southern Africa</u>, 1970, p. 178.

4. Racism based on false interpretation of the Bible was widely spread in the Southern United States and South Africa--for example, Noah's curse of Ham, which had no actual racial connotation; see Robert Graves and Raphael Patai, <u>Hebrew Myths</u> (New York: McGraw-Hill, 1964), p. 121.

5. An interpretation of this can be found in Richard Hofstadter, <u>Social Darwinism in American Thought</u> (Boston: Beacon Press, 1970).

6. John Foster Dulles represented this perspective in both his private and public roles: he chaired the International Relations Committee of the National Council of Churches and later as secretary of state under Eisenhower underwrote colonialism in Africa; see John Foster Dulles, <u>War or Peace</u> (New York: Macmillan, 1950).

7. <u>Atlantic Charter and Africa</u> (New York: Phelps-Stokes Fund, 1942).

8. President Kennedy made a great point of receiving African ambassadors and under his administration foreign assistance to Africa reached its highest point; see Waldemar Nielsen, <u>The Great Powers and Africa</u> (New York: Praeger, 1969).

9. <u>Africa Today</u> 19, no. 2 (Spring 1972), and U.S. Department of Commerce, <u>Overseas Business Reports</u>.

10. Ross Baker, "Towards a New Constituency for a More Active Foreign Policy for Africa," <u>Issue</u> 3, no. 1 (Spring 1973).

11. The scope and growth of this black lobby is outlined by Earl W. Yates in "The Need for a Black Lobby on Southern Africa," in <u>Africa Today</u>, Summer 1974.

12. Christopher Lasch, <u>The Agony of the American Left</u> (London: Pelican, 1972), p. 41.

U.S. POLICY:
AN OFFICIAL VIEW
Herbert J. Spiro

Before discussing present trends and goals of U.S.
policy toward Africa it is important to examine the
trends and goals of the past 15 years; this is not to
recriminate or advertise the fact that some observers
have been more right, or at least less wrong, than others
in gauging previous trends but rather simply because the
realities of the present problem regarding Africa cannot
be understood without noting the problems of the past.
And reasonable projections into the future are unlikely
unless some effort is made to figure out why many of the
earlier projections turned out to be wrong.

Africa has exploded into the consciousness of American policy makers and American academics during the cold
war. This fact has shaped their perceptions more than
anything else, regardless of where an individual has
stood on the main issues of the cold war itself. If one
has strongly espoused the policy of containment and has
feared Communist penetration of Africa and the rest of
the world, this obviously has colored his interpretations.
If on the contrary one has considered such fears to be so
many red herrings, one might assign to the newly independent African states the task of helping the parties to
the cold war overcome their conflict. In neither case
have scholars or policy makers been likely to render
"detached" interpretations of African developments or to
look at issues in U.S.-African relations solely on their
merits. As a result Americans interested in Africa have
tended in the past to oscillate between two extreme positions on the spectrum of possible attitudes: excessive
expectation and excessive disappointment. At any one
time, different people were at opposite poles of this

spectrum. For example this observer may have thought in
1962 that the Federation of Rhodesia and Nyasaland would
break up "successfully," that is, without massive incidence of violence, while other observers may have feared
or hoped that either the Federation would be dissolved
violently or the white settlers of Southern Rhodesia
could continue to control the two northern territories
through their "monopoly of the means of legitimate force."

When various expectations were not fulfilled their
holders would veer to the other extreme of disillusion-
ment. If a charismatic African leader failed to usher in
the millenium for his country or the continent, his erstwhile admirers turned to denouncing him as a latent
"totalitarian dictator" in cahoots with Moscow and/or
Peking. On the other hand when extreme pessimism about
Africa's "lack of social structures" and lack of political
experience was disappointed by some incipient proto-
Communist leader being overthrown, the erstwhile pessi-
mists would execute a total about-face and urge the United
States to grant massive assistance to the newly liberated
country in order to integrate it into the free world.

CONTEMPORARY U.S. AND AFRICAN ATTITUDES

Today the indicator on the dial registering American
attitudes toward Africa hovers closer to the midpoint of
the spectrum; that is the basic present reality. But the
indicator is still hovering because it is subject to opposing attractions from both the positive pole of excessive hopes and the negative pole of excessive disillusion-
ment. It is necessary that this situation be kept in
dialectical tension, that it be kept hovering, so that
the dynamism of U.S. policies will not be lost, but
neither will it be allowed once again to overoscillate
between two unrealistic extremes.

By now we have come to realize that among all the
so-called developing areas. Africa was neither the
closest geographically to the United States nor the most
important economically nor the most threatened strate-
cally. Beyond that U.S. resources for worldwide development assistance turned out to be more limited than some
anticipated in the heyday of independence movements.

Americans in like manner have come to understand that
the African governments will want to set their own goals
and priorities, move toward them at their own pace and in
their own ways, and in the process preserve both the

appearance and reality of sovereign equality. Moreover
as a result of the general movement away from the cold
war and toward detente the United States has been able
to view with greater equanimity than ever before the conduct at the United Nations and elsewhere in the international system that is genuinely nonaligned. The United
States has in other words abandoned the liberal paternal-
ism of the grand donor and the illiberal insecurity of
the grand protector; it now approaches African governments, as it approaches all governments, as equals and on
the merits of specific issues arising in mutual relations.
The present state of U.S.-African relations will be examined below, as seen in the Department of State, under
regional headings.

WEST AFRICA

In West Africa, the region hardest hit by drought,
thousands of inhabitants are dependent on foreign donors
for food. Widespread livestock losses and the resettle-
ment of many nomadic tribesmen near food distribution
centers are providing profound social and economic changes
in the area. Despite increased prices the United States
has pledged to provide to the area the same volume of
commodities supplied in 1973, and is hopeful that other
donors will do likewise. In 1973 the United States was
the area's single largest donor, contributing over $48
million worth of emergency assistance out of a total of
$154 million. For the medium and long term, the United
States is cooperating with the special Sahel Committee
made up of representatives of the six most affected countries in West Africa to develop a recovery and rehabili-
tation program for the area. Congress has already authorized $25 million and appropriated (but not yet authorized)
an additional $50 million for this purpose. Furthermore
the Massachusetts Institute of Technology has been commissioned by the Agency for International Development
(AID) to determine long-term development options for the
problems arising from the continuing drought in the Sahel.
With the notable exception of oil-producing Nigeria
the nations of West Africa are suffering the adverse impact of spiraling petroleum prices. For most countries
of the region the increased cost of petroleum imports
will drive trade balances deeply into deficit. The area's
leaders also worry that economic recession in the industrialized countries will reduce demand for the raw

materials and agricultural exports of Africa. Congress' attitude toward replenishing international development associations is interpreted as signaling a sharp reduction in levels of assistance previously provided by the developed countries. All of these factors underlie a general desire in various regions to maximize domestic returns from exports and from foreign investments. Nationalization of overseas firms has become more common, and talk of producer alliances more frequent. New regional economic organizations evidence in part a move away from traditional rivalries to an awareness that growth can be accelerated by economic cooperation and integration.

Nigeria has become the fourth largest producer of crude oil in the world and the third largest supplier of U.S. oil. With 70 million inhabitants and quadrupled oil revenues, Nigeria appears destined for rapid development and an increasingly prominent role in world affairs. Ghana's more modest potential may be more fully realized once rescheduling has lightened the burden of debt repayment. Wider overseas interests and revision of existing concession agreements are not expected to alter the unique intimacy of relations between Liberia and the United States. There is however a quickening of interest in the markets of Francophile Africa on the part of the American business and banking communities.

In the political sphere U.S. relations with the nations of West Africa are very sensitive to American attitudes toward the liberation movements in colonial and Southern Africa. America's preference for peaceful solutions in West Africa conflicts with the increasingly militant advocacy by some West African states of insurrectionary violence. Key issues for the immediate future are the outcome of administration-backed efforts to repeal the Byrd Amendment and the renewal of our Azores base agreement with the Portuguese.

CENTRAL AFRICA

Many of the same factors apply to U.S. relations with the countries of Central Africa. As world resources become more scarce and inflationary trends intensify, there is the same tendency among the Central African governments toward increased control of primary products.

Zaire for example is moving to decrease Belgian management of its copper mines; moreover all other mining

ventures will require 50 percent ownership by Zaire. In
cooperation with other copper producers Zaire is seeking
to form a cartel that will be aimed at effectively controlling export prices. The government of Gabon is taking steps to unilaterally control the price of uranium.
Cameroun is a member of the "Geneva Group" that has agreed
to cooperate in the control of coffee prices, designed to
avoid the wild fluctuations of the past.

In addition to control over resources Central African
governments are seeking greater control over enterprises
that are key elements in their economies; these are sometimes called "strategic enterprises." These countries
insist on joint ventures for all foreign investments including the diamond industry in the Central African Republic, various manufacturing in Cameroun, phosphates in
Brazzaville, minerals in Madagascar, and the export-import
enterprises in virtually all of the countries of the area.
Foreign investors are also being placed under great pressure to advance the training and placement in managerial
positions of indigenous workers.

The countries of Central Africa see themselves increasingly as part of what they regard as the "Third
World" that must unite to end "exploitation" by the developed industrialized world. Decisions made in the context of this "Third World solidarity" are becoming increasingly locked in, and the U.S. government is having
decreasing success in countering this trend with its consequent effect on bilateral relations. The nonaligned
support of Prince Sihanouk is an excellent example of this
trend.

With Zaire as one of the major pioneers, the United
States is seeing increasing references to "African authenticity"--the changing of names to eliminate European
names in favor of traditional African names and greater
use of traditional African clothing, songs, art, and so
on. This search for an African identity, especially at
the earliest stage, can mean greater chauvinism and xeno-
phobia. These negative aspects of "authenticity" are
present in Zaire but the entire process nevertheless appears to be making a contribution to nation building.

SOUTHERN AFRICA

The area in Africa that has drawn the most attention
and the most criticism is Southern Africa. This interest
is focused on South Africa because of its unique policies

of racial discrimination and the lack of any political role, at least in the central government, for the nonwhite majority. Faced with these problems the U.S. government has evolved a policy of restraint in its relations with South Africa.

Thus for example the United States continues a strict embargo on military and security equipment that began in 1962; neither encourages nor discourages investment; and places various limitations on commercial trade promotion and on normal activities of the Export-Import Bank. On the positive side the U.S. government has actively encouraged American business firms in South Africa to improve the wages, working conditions, and fringe benefits of their black employees while working within the framework of the law.

Moreover the United States expects to continue its efforts of recent years to maintain and expand contacts with all the various elements within South Africa. Another aspect of that policy is the expanded U.S. international visitor program that has made it possible to bring larger numbers of leaders from various segments of South African society to the United States. The aim of this program is to encourage peaceful change in the extraordinarily complex South African society.

Future trends are difficult to predict: there are many forces working for change just as there are reasons to believe that meaningful change will be an exceedingly difficult process. Among the forces that will bring change are the expanding South African economy with its need for more and more trained black members of the working force, outside pressures, and the steady development of Bantustans, or homelands. The latter, although creations of the white government, are producing a new generation of black leaders who have begun to articulate demands that have not been heard within South Africa for some years. Although the South African government is taking stern measures to suppress black leadership in the urban areas of the kind it considers potentially dangerous, it will doubtless be extremely difficult to contain growing black pressures for meaningful change, however difficult it may be to foresee the nature of these developments.

On the question of Namibia the U.S. government takes the view that the Republic of South Africa is illegally occupying Namibia and we fully support the authority of the United Nations regarding the area. Both in bilateral and multilateral forums the United States has sought to

persuade the Republic of South Africa not only to with-
draw its administration from Namibia and respect the
rights of the people of the territory, but to achieve an
orderly withdrawal from Namibia by peaceful rather than
violent means.

Since May 1970, the United States has officially
discouraged American investments in Namibia. The United
States also announced at that time that the Export-Import
Bank's facilities would no longer be available for trade
with Namibia and that any further investment there made
on the basis of rights acquired from the South African
government after the termination of the mandate would not
receive U.S. government protection against claims of a
future legitimate government in Namibia.

The United States continued to support peaceful and
practical efforts within the United Nations to enable the
people of Namibia to exercise their right to self-
determination and independence.

The Portuguese African territories presented the
United States with a very difficult policy problem: seemingly a conflict of interest. On the one hand there were
U.S.-Portugal ties that revolved around the U.S.-NATO
relationship and the use of the Azores base. On the
other hand the United States and Portugal had divergent
views on the political future of the Portuguese African
territories of Angola, Mozambique, and Portuguese Guinea.
The Portuguese saw these territories as integral parts of
Portugal, while the United States believed these territories should be allowed ultimate self-determination and
supported peaceful advances to this goal. In this connection the United States has since 1961 enforced an embargo on the shipment of U.S. arms for use in the insurgencies that were taking place in the Portuguese African
territories. The United States required and received as-
surances from the Portuguese in each instance that any
military equipment supplied to them for NATO use would
not be used outside the NATO area of operations.

This stance has not won the United States any
friends; African nations have been greatly disappointed
with U.S. failure to countenance or support liberation
movements in the Portuguese territories. The events of
the past few years in Portugal and in Guinea-Bissau,
Mozambique, and Angola have focused African attention on
U.S. attitudes toward the new situation in Southern
Africa. African nations have held unrealistic expectations of U.S. ability to influence the Portuguese. Conversely the Caetano government did not consider the

United States a solid ally; it saw the insurgencies as a part of a great Communist conspiracy against Southern Africa and was baffled that the United States did not support Portugal in her fight.

This left the United States caught in the middle. The U.S. government did not necessarily view the liberation movements as viable alternatives to Portuguese control and had grave reservations about the movements' claims of territorial control and of loyalty from the local populations. At the same time The United States believed in and foresaw the coming of self-determination for the peoples of the Portuguese territories. America desires to see self-determination come peacefully and to include all elements of the societies of these areas; and it seems that this is now possible given the changed attitude of Portugal toward African independence and the African response to it.

The situation of the three landlocked, black majority-ruled independent states of Southern Africa--Botswana, Lesotho, and Swaziland--remains a key factor in determining a coherent Southern African policy for the present and in attempting to anticipate future changes in the subcontinent. These three nations, independent since the late 1960s, continue to evolve an increasingly independent political posture in relation to South Africa and Rhodesia as they attempt to decrease their considerable economic dependence on their white-ruling neighbors. (This economic dependence is founded on (1) these countries' need to export labor, (2) lines of transportation and communication that run inevitably through white-ruled areas, (3) membership in the Southern African Customs Union and the Rand currency area, and (4) the fact that these nations are integrated into the Southern African economic region, which is dominated by industrialized South Africa.)

U.S. policy toward Botswana, Lesotho, and Swaziland is to encourage and assist them in their efforts toward economic development. Progress in that area will enable them to play a more independent political role in the face of their white minority-ruled neighbors. The United States fully supports the nonracial policies of these countries and in part sees them as models in Southern Africa of how multiracial nations might progress in peace.

RHODESIA

The principal reality of Rhodesia is that a white-minority regime is increasingly hard pressed to remain in political control of an African majority that outnumbers it by a ratio of 21 to 1. The question becomes whether the dominant means toward change will be peaceful or violent in nature.

The main effort toward a peaceful resolution of Rhodesia's problems is occurring in the new approaches between Prime Minister Smith of the illegal white regime and leaders of the African nationalist movements, recently released from detention to permit the initiation of these contacts. Any agreement between Smith and the African leaders would have to be ultimately acceptable to the British and would have to contain in it measures designed to bring about eventual majority, or black, rule in Rhodesia.

Before the new effort toward peaceful settlement fighting continued and incidents increased, many of them initiated by the guerrilla forces. In return the white-controlled government took harsh measures in dealing with the African population to try to meet the guerrilla threat. These measures have included the creation of "no go" areas in some regions, the gathering of rural Africans into "protected villages," and the granting of extraordinary powers to local administrative officals, including that of impressing labor. With respect to whites the regime has broadened the military draft and stepped up its efforts to attract white immigrants to the country.

U.S. policy remains in full support of economic sanctions against the Smith regime as an instrument to encourage a peaceful settlement. Within that context the Senate voted in December 1973 to repeal the Byrd Amendment and the administration is currently supporting and encouraging efforts by congressmen to pass a similar bill in the lower house.

EAST AFRICA

The diversity of political outlooks in East Africa makes it impossible for U.S. policy there to have a regional focus; U.S. relations with Zambia and Tanzania for example are reasonably good but would undoubtedly be much better if the U.S. government were prepared to take the more aggressive position on Southern African questions that both countries favor. As for Uganda, since the military takeover in 1971 it has become increasingly difficult for the United States to maintain any sort of rational political or economic relationship with Uganda

given the foibles of General Amin. It was in recognition
of the fact that the United States could not conduct diplomatic relations effectively in Kampala, Uganda, that
the American Embassy there was closed in 1973.

The economies of the East African region are equally
disparate: Zambia relies on copper, Kenya on tourism and
coffee, and Uganda on coffee; Tanzania and Malawi, having
relatively few natural resources, are much less favored
economically than the other three countries and have
therefore concentrated on agriculture. The promising
economic union, the East African Community encompassing
Kenya, Tanzania, and Uganda, which ultimately could have
embraced Zambia and Malawi as well, has faltered because
of the differences in the economies (and political attitudes) of the community's three partners.

For the foreseeable future there is little likelihood
that the United States will reopen its embassy in Kampala,
although it looks forward to the resumption of normal relations with Uganda when circumstances permit. The preoccupation of both Zambia and Tanzania with Southern
African issues and their growing belief that peaceful
change is a chimera will probably prevent any close relations with the United States so long as the United States
remains wedded to a nonviolent approach to Southern African questions. However, the U.S. government anticipates
that it will be able to work constructively with these
countries in a number of bilateral areas. Barring changes
in the policies established by the leaders of both Kenya
and Malawi, it is likely that the pattern of close and
cooperative relations between the United States and these
two countries will continue.

The most important international problem facing each
of the two independent nations in the Horn--Ethiopia and
Somalia--is the antagonism of the other. Somalia's long-
standing irredentist claim to that part of Ethiopia's
Ogaden region inhabited mainly by ethnic Somali nomads
poses a continuing threat to the integrity of Ethiopia.
This claim and fears of a preemptive Ethiopian military
strike overshadow all other Somali foreign policy considerations.

Both countries are among the 25 poorest nations in
the world and face the similar problem of internal dis-
sension. The urban populations of both countries are
being squeezed by the ever-increasing cost of living. In
Somalia this has so far resulted in sullen grumbling among
the people; in Ethiopia it has led to a military revolt
that toppled the cabinet and casts a cloud over the

future political stability and economic development of
the country.

The United States, conscious of the Horn's strategic
location in relation to the Red Sea-Indian Ocean-Persian
Gulf region, has maintained close and fruitful relations
with Ethiopia and has operated a military communications
facility there (now being phased down) since World War II.
Because of this close bilateral relationship Ethiopia has
received a large amount of U.S. economic aid and over
60 percent of all American military assistance to Africa.

At the same time the United States has tried to maintain good relations with Somalia. After the October 1969
military coup in Somalia, however, U.S. law forced the
termination of the U.S. economic assistance program there
because Somali flag vessels continued to trade with North
Vietnam and Cuba. The new regime viewed this act as an
attempt to destroy it and bilateral relations with the
United States became very strained. These relations have
subsequently improved somewhat as the Somali government
seeks international economic assistance sources to help
Somalia's development. The USSR is currently Somalia's
largest military and bilateral economic aid donor.

The United States will use whatever influence it has
to help maintain the fragile peace existing between
Ethiopia and Somalia and will continue to encourage other
African nations to try to resolve the territorial dispute
between these two countries.

NORTH AFRICA

A number of factors distinguish North African countries from others in Africa. Perhaps the most important
is the fact that the North African countries are Arab
countries; their language is Arabic and they are drawn by
their history and their social heritage to the Arab countries of the Middle East. For the peoples of the Maghreb
the Arab-Israeli dispute and the problem of the Palestin-
ians are not abstract political questions but issues of
great importance in which they feel personally involved.

Because of what they consider unreasonable U.S. government support for Israel, the two major oil exporters
of this region--Algeria and Libya--joined with the other
members of the Organization of Arab Petroleum Exporting
Countries to embargo petroleum exports to the United
States. The U.S. relationship with Libya has been severely strained because of Libya's attitude toward U.S.

policy on the Arab-Israeli question. Progress toward
permanent peace in the Middle East would do more to improve U.S. relations with the countries of North Africa
than any other single factor.

Economic, political, and strategic factors also affect U.S. policy in this region. Access to the Mediter-
ranean is important to the United States, and Morocco
lies on one side of the Strait of Gibraltar. The United
States seeks new sources of energy, and both Libya and
Algeria have such resources. The United States seeks
friends in the Arab world; Morocco and Tunisia have been
such friends for many years, and the United States is
developing closer ties with Sudan and Mauritania.

Algeria's reserves of oil and natural gas and its
desire to develop them for the benefit of its economy are
a natural point of cooperation: the United States wants
and needs new energy sources while Algeria wants and needs
the American market, access to American technology, and
the capital equipment necessary to exploit these resources. This process has already begun with the El Paso-
Sonatrach project that will provide 10 billion cubic
meters per year of Algerian liquefied natural gas for the
U.S. market beginning in 1976 when the facilities, now
being constructed by U.S. companies with the financial
assistance of the U.S. Export-Import Bank, are completed.
Despite political differences, the United States looks
forward to growing cooperation with Algeria in the energy
field.

Morocco, Tunisia, Sudan, and Mauritania are not
blessed with petroleum but they have other raw materials
such as phosphates and iron ore that will become increasingly important in the years ahead. These countries also
have the potential to develop their agriculture and become
self-sufficient in food production; the United States
hopes to be able to cooperate with them in their economic
development for the benefit of all.

ECONOMIC POLICY

One aspect of our relations with Africa should be
discussed separately: U.S. economic policy. There is no
such thing as U.S. economic policy toward Africa. This
statement holds true for all the regions within the State
Department's area of responsibility. The United States
has only global economic and aid policies.

With respect to bilateral assistance the Congress has legislated the U.S. global aid philosophy. The problem is that this philosophy is difficult to apply: each country has its own development problems and its own priorities, and quite frequently these are in conflict with what is permissible or desirable under U.S. assistance legislation. The classic U.S. problem concerns infrastructure. In the case of multilateral assistance the United States is even farther removed from regional policy. In recent years both the International Bank for Reconstruction and Development and the International Development Association have provided increasing amounts of aid to African countries. This is a simple question of fact; it reflects increasing attention on the part of the World Bank group to the needs of the least developed countries.

In the negotiating forum of the General Agreement on Tariffs and Trade the United States will pay increasing attention to the developing countries because the U.S. government would want the discussions to move toward an examination of the problem of access to raw materials. This problem has been discussed to some extent in the U.N. Conference on Trade and Development in connection with the Charter of Economic Rights and Duties of States and the special session of the U.N. General Assembly in April 1974.

The United States still disagrees with the Europeans over trade preferences, but this disagreement involves only the Europeans, not the Africans. The United States hopes that African countries will stand firm in their opposition to reverse trade preferences for the Common Market, but it is their decision to make. However, the countries granting reverse preferences will not be eligible for the U.S. generalized preferences. In any event these are of only marginal interest to African states. The age of special relationships may be coming to an end together with preferential trading relations.

Regarding American commercial interests the focus is in contrast to the above policy; there is a more aggressive posture in promoting exports to Africa and the United States is attempting to develop country resource management programs for Zaire, Nigeria, and Algeria, the major markets in African developing countries. The United States will need a substantial increase in exports to offset its growing deficit with Africa resulting from its imports of petroleum and higher-priced raw materials.

There has been a steady growth in American investments in tropical Africa, while investments have declined
in North Africa because of the nationalization in whole
or in part of American oil companies in Libya. Most of
the American investments in tropical Africa have been in
the extractive industries, with very little in manufacturing and service industries. The extractive area is
becoming a more difficult field for private investment;
insurance against expropriation risks is unavailable in
this area, and there is greater opposition to foreign
ownership of natural resources. The darkest cloud on the
horizon as far as economic relationships are concerned is
the growing debt repayment burden: debt service is growing at a faster rate in Africa than in any other part of
the developing world. The future apparently holds in
store a number of debt rescheduling negotiations. An
important element in this picture is a large amount of
debt held by branches of American banks in Europe.

In summarizing the present realities of African-U.S.
relations one finds little cause for complacency. One
particular reality that will have grave implications for
the U.S. role in Africa is the diminishing AID program.
Foreign assistance appropriations for Africa for the
fiscal year 1974 totaled $147.5 million compared with a
total of $163.1 million for 1973. This meant an effective
cut in the regular program of 25 percent, and the outlook
for fiscal 1975 is bleak. Added to this gloomy picture
is the decline in the PL 480 surplus commodity program.

Relative public indifference to African issues is
another reality. One yardstick for measuring public interest on an issue is the flow of mail received by the
government. A random check of the weekly report of public mail for February 18-22 indicated that combined mail
received by the White House, the secretary of state, and
the State Department amounted to approximately 2,000 letters. One-third of this mail was on the Middle East. As
for Africa the report stated, "Again a very quiet week,
with a few letters supporting the importation of chrome
from Rhodesia." American congressional candidates have
not had to defend their voting records on African issues
as they have in the case of the Arab-Israeli question.
This lack of a widespread American popular constituency
for Africa is reflected in such congressional actions as
the defeat of the International Development Association
replenishment resolution (1974), the passage of the Byrd
Amendment (1971), and Senator Fulbright's resolution to
end AID (1974).

The energy crisis and the impact of rising oil prices on developing countries could have serious consequences for U.S. policy toward Africa. By a conservative estimate African countries will pay $800 million to $1 billion more in calendar year 1974 than they did in 1973 for oil imports alone. At the present cost of oil only three African countries have the necessary foreign reserves on hand to pay for their oil imports for the next two years. Kenya for example, with $230 million in reserves, is facing an oil bill of $180 million that leaves very little for development or even for basic needs such as food. The Arabs have offered the Africans $200 million in guarantees for commercial borrowing and have proposed funding a Bank for African Development with $500 million. The Iranians have also indicated that they would provide direct assistance to the developing countries and would participate in a special fund for these countries. The United States welcomes these overtures. What the oil-producing nations do with their surplus funds will have an obvious impact on America's own AID Program for Africa as well as on the programs of other donor countries.

Related to the energy crisis is a fourth reality: although most African countries are not petroleum producers many of them do have valuable resources such as copper, bauxite, cobalt, and phosphates. The Arab success in manipulating oil both to achieve higher prices and to gain political objectives has not gone unnoticed by the Africans. In the general rush for primary commodities the developed nations are confronted with a growing determination on the part of Africans to control their own resources. While this development in itself is not a threat to the United States, nationalization of resources can pose serious problems not only for American investors but also for a host of interrelated industries dependent on the raw materials. On the subject of economic interdependence the State Department holds the view that interdependence is made more critical by the scarcities around us, the rate at which resources are being depleted, and the degree to which commodities essential to modern life are concentrated in a few countries.

Another reality is the cohesion among Third-World countries on political issues in the General Assembly. The Third World, in the past so critical of blocs, has now created its own bloc. It has been a long time since the United States could count on an automatic majority at the United Nations. The African countries alone constitute one-third of the U.N. membership. Allied with the

Arab world on such issues as Israel, apartheid, and the liberation movements, the African countries are a force to be reckoned with and the way in which they use their voting strength can do much to affect American attitudes toward the United Nations itself.

The Sahelian drought is perhaps the harshest reality with which the United States must deal. Still it presents the kind of clearcut challenge that Americans with their "can-do" philosophy prefer. There are no conflicting goals in this problem, only people to feed, animals to save, and land to reclaim. The problem is enormous, but compared with other realities this one is more easily definable and therefore more susceptible to solution.

The foregoing should demonstrate the most important reality: there are definite limits to U.S. power. The United States has very little control over the development of situations of interest to the Africans, and sees little value in rhetorical resolutions that can only exacerbate already difficult problems. What then can the United States do? Be patient and realistic, recognizing the limits of its power to influence others to do things they do not want to do. The United States can keep its priorities straight, recognizing that they will not always accord with those of the Africans but that it is worth searching for areas of agreement. The United States can also adopt the long view of history, recognizing that time is often the key to what is sought and that nations, no more than men, live only for today.

Spiro's study in this volume together with his article in Issue[1] include most of the State Department's position with regard to Africa: the former cold war orientation of U.S. policy in Africa was a mistake, as was the belief that instant democracy would result upon decolonization in Africa on the basis of one man, one vote; the U.S. government is now willing to deal realistically with individual African states on the basis of mutual respect and equality regardless of the kind of African government that exists; the United States believes in self-determination and majority rule, but will support only peaceful evolution; the United States will urge South Africa to evolve racially, but will not isolate South Africa and will maintain "communication";[2] and the United States cannot right the racial wrongs in Africa, for its global responsibilities have tied its hands and sapped its energies.[3]

Spiro's addition to the standard line has to do with those whom he identifies as the academics, blacks, and professionals of the "Democratic era," 1960-68. Most of his criticism of old policy and claims to the establishment of new policy is based upon a rewriting of history and the consideration of policy out of historical context. In the first place Spiro indicates that Africa emerged on the American policy scene in 1960; however, aid to Africa as preparation against the day of independence actually began in 1948 under President Truman and was dispensed through the colonial powers. Several American foundations and organizations were busy aiding development in Africa in the 1950s--the Institute of International Education (IIE), the African-American Institute (AAI), the American Committee on Africa, the American Society on African Culture, the Ford Foundation, the Carnegie Corporation of New York, the African Liaison Committee of the American Council on Education, the American Federation of Labor-Congress of Industrial Organizations (AFL-CIO), etc. The Bureau of African Affairs of the Department of State was established on August 20, 1958. Libya began the independence process in 1951. Spiro is too much impressed by formal governmental definition of what policy should be.

THE REVOLUTION OF COLOR

Scoffing at the cold war effect on the liberation
process in Africa is easy at this point of detente, but
the cold war was very hot until the Eisenhower administration began to cool it. Much more was at stake in the
1950s and 1960s than the cold war competition between
Russia and the United States; there was in fact the whole
revolution of color set off by the polarization of power,
with one pole asserting color exploitation as a function
of capitalism. The nonwhite people of the world had been
held in thrall by Europe, the British Empire, and the
United States until the West rejected Hitler's racism and
World War II secured the emergence of Russia and China as
powers. Colored people now demanded and achieved independence everywhere; and the price of delay or of attempts
at assimilation in European political systems was wars of
national liberation, often with Communist support and
sometimes capture by a Communist power--Algeria, Vietnam,
Kenya, Cameroun, and the Congo. These political conditions were the cause of the U.S. drive for decolonization,
not the U.S. heartland's devotion to 1776. The latter
only provided support for the policy.
    This color revolution, as the 1960s showed, was
about to flood the United States, for the black population of America understood that it needed to no longer
tolerate discrimination and indignity in every aspect of
life--legal apartheid, physical violence, and lynchings.
Had the reforms beginning with Brown v. Topeka in 1954
not been under way one would suspect that the violence of
the 1960s in America would have had much wider support
among black people. Spiro seems to think that the emergence of independent black African states and the presence
of their representatives in the United States was the
stimulus for the emergence of the civil rights movement
among black Americans.[4] Without the civil rights movement the international position of the United States today
would not be much different from that of the Republic of
South Africa. In the context of the world and domestic
color revolution that the United States moved to accommodate by urging decolonization abroad and effecting an
end to legal segregation and discrimination at home,
Spiro's summary judgment of the pre-Nixon era--"by now
we have come to realize that among all the so-called developing areas, Africa was neither the closest geographically to the United States nor the most important economically nor the most threatened strategically"--seems

73

particularly blind to reality.[5] The historical revision-
ism of Spiro makes one wonder what country he lived in
from 1950 to 1970.

The deriding of academicians and professionals who
were working in the African field during the 1950s and
1960s overlooks three factors: the inadequacies of
political science in those years to deal with government
in developing areas; the pervasiveness of the old ex-
cuses for colonialism in terms of future independence
with the capacity for self-government; and the pervasiveness of inappropriate socialist slogans for colonial
liberation.

Not everyone working in the African field, and especially black Americans, has been so naive as to think that
instant government of, by, and for the people would appear upon the exit of the colonialist. The record of sustained free governmental institutions is a slim one even
among the nations of Europe. In 1958 in a volume edited
by this writer, St. Clair Drake had an article evaluating
African societies from the social-anthropological point
of view and urged the development of societies and governments in Africa in terms of pragmatic pluralism. In
the same volume Martin L. Kilson examined the social
class origins of black nationalist organizations and
parties in British West Africa, and Hugh H. Smythe analyzed the emergence of the black elite in Nigeria.[6]
While numerous white political scientists (Henry Bretton
was a marked exception) were rationalizing the emergence
of one-party states in Africa through social relativism,[7]
Kilson demonstrated that this particular path had no
turning. Kilson later was able to forecast the military
coup in Ghana, which occurred within two months of his
prediction.[8] W. Arthur Lewis condemned the lack of
imagination and adaptation in the transfer of democratic
institutions, especially party systems, from Europe to
Africa and predicted the rise of coalition government
under military dominance.[9] In Pan Africanism Reconsidered there is recorded this writer's opening address to
the second major international conference of the American
Society of African Culture in 1960 in which the dangers
and pitfalls of the emergent African national state system were noted as well as the circumstances that offered
hope.[10]

Finally, it can be said about the 1950s and 1960s
that the United States in those years achieved its real
policy aims in Africa: decolonization without the loss
of any major African country to the Russians or the

Chinese; there was no hot war in Africa that involved U.S. troops or Russian or Chinese troops, and there were only two outbreaks where it could be said that the fighting was carried on by surrogates.

Having set the framework of U.S. relations with Africa as characterized by detente, noninterference, equal treatment and respect, sympathy for African "mammoth problems," and the relative unimportance of Africa as compared to other continents, Spiro proceeds to describe and defend U.S. policy toward each region of Africa and most of the states in each region. What therefore emerges is a statement of bilateral relations within State Department and National Security Council (NSC) determinations. Such a formulation supports the thesis of "helplessness" on the part of the United States and "unreasonableness" and "ingratitude" on the part of African states.[11] Given Africa's least importance in the rank order of continents and America's international responsibilities, Spiro outlines a reasonable and generous policy.

Nothing could be further from reality, present or past, than this picture of the determinative quality of bilateral relations based on expert, fair policy. There are two reasons for this. First, the United States serves in Africa as the main actor of the "Western" state system (including some not so western states) within the interdependent international political system;[12] the other members of the Western state system have something to say about what the United States does in Africa.[13] Speaking before the Royal Commonwealth Society in London on March 14, 1973, David Newsom, the then Assistant Secretary of State for African Affairs, said,

> The United States does not desire--even if it had the capabilities and resources to do so--to replace the former colonial powers in trade and economic relations with African nations. . . . We continue to believe, however, that the traditional ties of language, education and business that link these [African] nations with the metropole nations in Europe are important to both partners.[14]

And second, many forces in America besides the policy makers have some effect on U.S.-African policy.

With regard to the first point, it has been precisely because France, Britain, Belgium, and Portugal have been

part of the Western state system (or subsystem) of which
the United States is the main actor that our policy in
Africa has been subject to attack from African nationalists, especially of late with regard to Belgium, Portugal,
and South Africa, but not excluding France and Britain in
the past. It was French insistence upon assimilation in
Algeria that placed us upon the horns of a dilemma: either
political chaos in France or Russia in Algeria. It was
both the reluctance of Belgium and the reluctance and in-
capacity of Portugal to serve as midwives of decolonization that brought a near confrontation with Russia in the
Congo, open interference by the United States in the
Congo, and the refusal of the United States to assume the
burdens of decolonization in Portuguese Africa. In black
Africa both France and Britain were willing to serve as
midwives of decolonization. Without a postwar presence
of any importance in Africa the United States gave help
and cooperation;[15] this did not make fast friends for
America among the nationalists of Africa.

THE AMERICAN DILEMMA IN SOUTHERN AFRICA

The dilemma in which the United States presently
finds itself in Southern Africa results from our commitments to the Western state system and to its role in the
international political system. Tied to Portugal and
South Africa, the United States espouses the principles
of national self-determination and majority rule in the
desperate hope that the color revolution backed by the
socialist state system will not make Southern Africa a
battleground where the United States, with its large
black population, fights on the side of the whites. Portugal had sought assimilation of its African colonies but
has now decided on independence for the territories.
Portugal and the Azores are now revealed as not only important to NATO, but to U.S. Middle East policy and U.S.
ability to secure military aid to Israel.[16] South Africa
not only guards the Cape and Indian Ocean route but its
minerals are important to Western technology and its
productivity is important to British investment. South
Africa in effect is a minority, white-ruled, racist state
in a black and brown continent. South Africa supports
"illegal" Rhodesia and illegally administers Namibia contrary to both the decisions of the General Assembly of
the United Nations and the advisory opinions of the International Court of Justice. The United States is careful

to be only legally and symbolically opposed to the acts of the Republic of South Africa.[17]

These factors do not constitute the limitations of U.S. global responsibilities or U.S. bilateral policies with African nations. The racist members of the Western state system are in direct conflict with the policies of the black sub-Saharan state system that is antiracist, anticolonial, and antiimperial, all of which positions the United States also espouses. The United States after all is part of the international political system that takes these three positions, and has been at great pains not to lose the black African regional subsystem to the Western state system.

The second point noted above was that many forces in the United States besides the State Department and the NSC affect policy in Africa. For example one can note such forces as government organizations that implement policy; business organizations, especially those in the extractive industries; the Africanist academicians and professionals; the Council of Churches and specific Protestant denominations, as in the case of the Sudan recently and in Angola now; the Catholic Church, as in the decolonization of both French West and French Equatorial Africa; the Congress; "unreconstructed" southern and conservative congressmen, as in the Byrd Amendment; and black political power, as focused on Africa by Congressman Diggs.[18]

FUTURE REALITIES

As far as future realities are concerned this writer will elaborate only on black political power, for it should be clear that black urban political power, especially as practiced within the Democratic party, is considerable. In the 1976 presidential election that power will in all probability be determinative in most statewide elections in the pivotal large urban states--the elections for presidential electors, governors, and senators. Black political power in municipal elections is already clearly demonstrated. Through Diggs' urban political leadership, the Black Political Convention and its assembly, of which Diggs is president, and the black man in the street have all been made mindful of U.S. policy toward Africa. Under Diggs' leadership the Subcommittee on Africa of the House Committee on Foreign Affairs has made thorough investigations of U.S. policy in Africa and of political conditions in Africa, and has produced admirable reports.[19]

The future president may well have to deal with
black political power dedicated to the solution of Southern African racism and colonialism--black political power
well represented in the House and influential in the election of most important senators.[20] This representation
will be supported by substantial pressure-group activity
from a host of black organizations as well as church-
related organizations that are capable of intense activity in crisis situations involving Southern Africa. Most
Americans for example are aware of both the Congress of
African People and the African Liberation Day Committee.
Besides these a large number of black organizations have
continuing or sporadic Africa-related activity.[21]

A future reality in terms of Rosenau's concepts will
be political linkage between the drive for black economic
equality in the United States and black freedom in Southern Africa.[22] Both questions will be raised by blacks
politically in the United States, and politicians will
react by responding first to one and then the other.
Nationalists in Southern Africa will be emboldened by this
support and will in all probability experience increasing
American support for their own position. Black Americans
will support black freedom in Southern Africa and will
use their political power as Jews have previously done
for their kith and kin in Europe and now in Israel, and
as the Irish did for theirs in Ireland. But it is more
than this; it has been but a few years since black people
in America were subjected to color-caste discrimination
and legalized segregation when at the same time blacks
everywhere in the world also faced these horrors and colonialism. Black Americans see U.S. support of Portugal
and South Africa and shilly-shallying on Rhodesia as a
threat to their status in America.[23]

The single remaining major problem for blacks in
America is the fate of the lowest class of urban poor,
especially the teenage members of this group. Political
action to solve this economic deprivation, unless there
is still deeper unemployment in the American society, will
in all probability be black nationalist and anticapitalist
and will in all probability be linked to nationalist,
anticapitalist movements in Southern Africa. Accommodation to demands for full employment that includes the
poorest is not to be expected in the United States; this
has never existed since World War II and economists now
generally identify--foolishly, in terms of political de-
cision--such "welfare" demands as the cause of world inflation.

LACK OF REALISM IN U.S. POLICY

Spiro's regional analysis of U.S. bilateral relations
with African nations is often unrealistic in terms of the
dragons he fears and the sources of U.S. difficulties.
His complaints against joint ventures, producer alliances,
and nationalization in West, Central, and East Africa
overlook not only the availability of other profitable
relationships but, more important, the causes of such
economic steps. Terms of trade in the past have run consistently against the developing nations, and mineral-
and oil-producing countries have seen their liquid holdings
eroded by inflation. The Western state system's market
has obviously not been a free market; the European Economic Community (EEC) is not based on the idea of free
and equal access to all. Why then complain about the
awkward economic steps of the developing nations?--elim-
inate the causes of these steps.

It is of course in Southern Africa that Spiro most
fails to face reality. In South Africa the Department of
State places hope in peaceful change, world pressures,
"communication," and leader exchanges as means of ending
racism in a state that was always racist and has become
steadily more racist and repressive since 1948.[24]

The U.S. steps to put pressure on South Africa have
always been hedged by steps backward and by loopholes in
U.S. restrictive actions. For example the U.S. financial
community came to the rescue of South Africa after
Sharpeville in 1960 when there was a flight of capital
from South Africa. The United States sent a black economic officer to South Africa, but the U.S. ambassador
there, contrary to past practice, gave an all-white reception on Republic Day and went hunting on notorious
Robben Island with black political prisoners as beaters.[25]
The United States embargoed military sales and equipment
to South Africa, but brought no pressure on or spoke no
evil of France and our other allies who broke the U.N.-
sponsored embargo. Between 1963 and 1971 the United
States sold South Africa 1,967 light, transport, and
helicopter aircraft, according to Bruce Oudes in the
January-February 1973 issue of _Africa Report_. We encouraged, somewhat ineffectively, American business firms to
improve black wages,[26] but the administration did not
support the Diggs fair employment bill covering U.S. firms
in South Africa. The United States may neither encourage
nor discourage investment, but U.S. firms still receive
U.S. tax credits for taxes paid to South Africa. The

U.S. Export-Import Bank guarantees and insures American exporters to South Africa, which has an unfavorable balance of trade and imports capital for investment. South Africa still enjoys a sugar quota in the United States. The United States takes the position that South Africa illegally occupies Namibia, but refuses to join the U.N. General Assembly's Council for Namibia that first China and then Russia did join.

Not only does the United States follow this waltzing policy but, contrary to what Spiro notes, the United States can bring real and effective pressure to bear on South Africa to modify the racist policies without condoning or using force. It is important in this regard to note South Africa's current problems, for she is far more vulnerable than she appears:

1. Except for Britain's resumption of obligations under the Simonstown Naval Base agreement, South Africa is still not formally included in the Western defense system.

2. South Africa needs access to African markets; she is the most highly industrialized country in Africa and could be in a stronger competitive position vis-a-vis other manufacturing countries.

3. She needs to improve relations with African states where she faces near isolation. South Africa's outward-looking policy is an admission of this need as well as an attempt to split African nations on her isolation.

4. South Africa has a half-billion dollar deficit in her balance of payments yearly as the result of investments in sympathetic neighboring countries like Mozambique (Cabora Bassa and Cunene).

5. Oil is not available to South Africa except from non-Arab, pro-Western sources. The country is both water and energy shy, factors which will further affect her balance of payments.

6. South Africa is isolated from U.N. organizations and from most nations of Africa.

7. South Africa depends on the West for new capital investment, new technology, and new sophisticated weapons.

It is clear that the United States could compete with South African goods in the African hinterland, if necessary through dumping activities; make it difficult for American capital to flow to South Africa; invest in the African states surrounding South Africa as soon as they become independent on a majority rule basis; refuse to sponsor South Africa's outward-looking policy by indicating U.S. disagreement with it to France and African states until South Africa accepts the Lusaka Manifesto; make it clear that the defense of South Africa is not a commitment of the United States; step up efforts to take gold out of the world monetary system; retaliate against France, in capital and technology flows, for her arms and technology support of South Africa; put the situation in South Africa and all of Southern Africa on American telecasts and in the American press; make it clear that South Africa's rejection of the Lusaka Manifesto means that at some point the United States will be forced to abandon its principle of evolution in Southern Africa by peaceful means only; invest in personnel and education in the Bantustans; and join the Council for Namibia and scrupulously follow all the legal requirements involved in recognizing the legality of U.N. presence in Namibia and the illegality of South Africa's.[27]

The collapse of Portuguese colonialism in Africa has made the State Department's defense of its policy toward the Portuguese territories patently laughable. Spiro notes that "African nations have held unrealistic expectations of U.S. ability to influence the Portuguese." What has been so unrealistic about it? The Portuguese were clearly not in a position to stand the strain on their resources and their youth from continued fighting with guerrillas in Africa. So weak a nation would certainly have responded to U.S. pressure if it had been applied. What the United States did was to provide Portugal with a total aid package of $436 million. And the Portuguese have changed their attitude and are willing to turn the territories over to independent African governments.

Spiro notes that "conversely the former Portuguese goverment did not consider the United States a solid ally; it saw the insurgencies as a part of a great Communist conspiracy against Southern Africa. . . ." Yet the Communist party is now most active in Portugal and has a role in the politics of the country. And Spiro adds that "the U.S. government did not necessarily view the liberation movements as viable alternatives to Portuguese control and had grave reservations about the movements' claims of territorial control and of loyalty from the local population." Evidently the Portuguese themselves differ with us on these positions. The present Portuguese government is going to be very different from the previous one and the U.S. government will have to deal with it on that basis. One hopes that the desire to maintain Portugal as a hinge of NATO and the Azores as an access route to Israel will not lead to any attempts at restoring the status quo in Portugal to secure our international state system.[28]

RHODESIA

In Rhodesia, U.S. policy waits on Britain as always in former British Africa--but not to the extent that the Byrd Amendment at the behest of Union Carbide and Foote Mineral cannot break the embargo on chrome. The administration and the Democratic party that controls the Congress are both in favor of an embargo on chrome; it all has an Alice-in-Wonderland quality. Although Spiro does not mention it, presumably any settlement of the Rhodesian question will require the approval of the U.N. Security Council, from which the policy of economic sanctions emanated and which at Britain's behest has jurisdiction over the matter. Meanwhile South Africa, by making the rand available to Rhodesia at a fixed rate and through trade, supports Rhodesian defenses as France ignores sanctions. And British delay further erodes the power of moderate black Rhodesian leaders while the charisma of the young socialist trained leaders in the field grows.

Brief comments suffice for the rest of Africa, since at the present time Southern Africa is, as Waldemar Nielsen pointed out long ago, the "African Battleline."[29] Conflict between the state systems harasses U.S. bilateral relations in most of East and North Africa. As Spiro notes, U.S. relations with Zambia and Tanzania will not improve much until the United States can take a more positive role in Southern Africa, a function of U.S. relations with Britain, Portugal, and South Africa. The Ethiopian-Somali conflict is threatened by the East-West conflict; and U.S. relations with North Africa, as Sprio notes, await a settlement in the Middle East, where the United States supports Israel, a member of the Western state system.

Another offshoot of the U.S. systems attachment should be noted; Southern Africa's systems-and-principles conflict results in a low-profile U.S. posture of non-interference and nondiplomatic hostility no matter how justified. The price the United States has paid for this in terms of decency and honor in Uganda and the Sudan is not mentioned by Spiro.

There have been certain general changes in U.S. economic relations with Africa that seem to be or may be bringing changes in policy. As the United States is faced with a rising cost of minerals and petroleum, partly in response to the action of producer countries, and is buffeted by world inflation and unfavorable balance of payments, there seems to be a tendency to move toward hard credit. The United States has not yet fulfilled its obligation to the International Development Association. The nonpetroleum- and nonmineral-producing countries in Africa are hard hit by the rise in petroleum prices, with the cereals-importing countries being the hardest hit. Discriminating economic policies will be needed; otherwise the poor countries will be in deep crisis as population rises faster than food production.

Spiro notes the increased U.S. investment in petroleum and minerals in Africa. The U.S. balance of trade with Zaire, Nigeria, and Algeria in each case indicates the need to export goods to each. Nigeria and Algeria account for 50 percent of all African exports to the United States. The U.S. investment in South Africa is roughly $1 billion and it will be $2.5 billion in Nigeria by 1976 as the liquefied natural gas project gets under way. In 1972 trade with South Africa grew 2 percent to $972 million and with Nigeria it grew 28 percent to $384 million.[30] Nigeria, Zaire, Algeria, Libya, Zambia, and perhaps soon-to-be-independent Rhodesia and Angola are going to be far more important to the United States economically than South Africa. To say, as has been said ad nauseam, that Africa is unimportant to the United States economically because its total investment in Africa is only 5 percent of its overall investment abroad, and because African-U.S. trade is relatively small for both parties, is to miss the point altogether. The United States must have Africa's nonferrous minerals and oil. How much oil or rare and costly nonferrous minerals need to be denied the world market without serious repercussions for the United States or the Western state system?

NOTES

1. Herbert J. Spiro, "The American Response to Africa's Participation in the International System," Issue 3, no. 1 (Spring 1973): 2-23.
2. See discussion of NSSM 39 and "communication" in John Seiler, "The Failure of U.S. Southern African Policy," Issue 2, no. 1 (Spring 1972): 21.

3. Cf. U.S. Department of State, Africa: Excerpts
from . . . United States Foreign Policy, 1972, A Report
of the Secretary of State (Washington: U.S. Government
Printing Office, 1937), pp. 108, 448-50. See also speech
by David Newsom, assistant secretary of state for African
affairs, before Mid-America Committee, Chicago, June 28,
1972, in Current Foreign Policy, U.S. Department of State,
Publication #8671 (Washington: U.S. Government Printing
Office, August 1972), pp. 1-2.
4. Spiro, "The American Response to Africa's Participation in the International System," op. cit., p. 21.
5. Cf. John A. Davis, "Black Americans and United
States Policy Toward Africa," Journal of International
Affairs 23, no. 2 (Summer 1969): 236-49; A. R. Preiswerk,
"Race and Colour in International Relations," The Yearbook
of World Affairs 24 (1970): 54-87; George W. Shepherd,
Jr., Racial Influences on American Foreign Policy (New
York: Basic Books, Inc., 1970); George W. Shepherd, Jr.
and Tilden LeMelle, eds., Race Among Nations (Lexington,
Mass.: D. C. Heath and Co., 1970); Nathan I. Huggins,
Martin L. Kilson, and Daniel M. Fox, Key Issues in the
Afro-American Experience (New York: Harcourt Brace
Jovanovich, Inc., 1971), vol. 2, pp. 167-302.
6. John A. Davis, ed., Africa Seen by American
Negroes (Paris: Presence Africaine, 1958), pp. 2, 11-83.
7. See Gwendolen M. Carter, ed., African One-Party
States (Ithaca: Cornell University Press, 1962), pp. 1-11,
55-61, 177-230; for opposite point of view see pp. 357-70.
8. Martin L. Kilson, "Authoritarian and Single-Party
Tendencies in African Politics," World Politics (January
1963), pp. 262-94; Martin L. Kilson, "Politics of African
Socialism," African Forum 1, no. 3 (Winter 1966): 17-40.
9. W. Arthur Lewis, "Beyond African Dictatorship:
The Crisis of the One-Party State," Encounter (London:
August 1965), pp. 3-16.
10. John A. Davis, "Pan-Africanism: Nascent and
Mature," in Pan-Africanism Reconsidered, ed. John A. Davis
(Berkeley: University of California Press, 1966), pp.
32-33.
11. U.S. sensitivity to African criticism is used to
justify a low-profile U.S. policy and charges of ingratitude; John H. Collins, "Foreign Conflict Behavior and
Domestic Disorder in Africa," in Conflict Behavior and
Linkage Politics, ed. Jonathan Wilkenfeld (New York:
David McKay Co., 1973), pp. 251-93, studying seven domestic disorder variables and eight foreign conflict behavior variables by use of zero-order correlations, multiple

regression, and time lag analysis, found that negative
"diplomatic" communication messages, antiforeign unofficial behavior, negative behavior, and diplomatic hostility
are all strongly predicted by domestic disorder. In the
face of such data the United States should at least not
abandon holding all African states responsible for humane
behavior.

12. See Morton Kaplan, System and Process in International Politics, rev. ed. (New York: John Wiley and
Sons, Inc., 1964). Kaplan viewed the states of the world
as an interdependent political system; this concept has
been enlarged upon to include a bipolar, tripolar, or
multipolar system or two competing systems with principal
and maverick actors and subsystems. See also Herschelle S.
Challenor, "Dialogue and Dissent: The Discontinuities of
Global and Regional Interaction over the Situation in
Southern Africa," paper delivered at the 1972 Annual Meeting of the American Political Science Association, Washington, D.C., mimeographed; Oran Young, "Political Discontinuities in the International System," World Politics
20 (1968): 369-98 (cited and relied upon by Challenor to
evolve her basic concept); J. David Singer, "The Level of
Analysis Problems in International Relations," in International Politics and Foreign Policy, rev. ed., ed. James
N. Rosenau (New York: The Free Press, 1969), pp. 20-29.

13. Cf. Waldemar A. Nielsen, The Great Powers and
Africa (New York: Praeger, 1969), chaps. 1-4 and 10.

14. David Newsom, "U.S.-African Interests: A Frank
Appraisal," Current Foreign Policy, U.S. Department of
State, Publication 8701 (Washington: U.S. Government
Printing Office, May 1973), p. 3.

15. Nielsen, The Great Powers and Africa, op. cit.,
chaps. 1-4.

16. Bruce Oudes, "In the Wake of the Middle East
War," Africa Report 19, no. 1 (January-February 1974):
11-13, 35, 50.

17. On Southern Africa see John A. Davis and James K.
Baker, eds., Southern Africa in Transition (New York:
Praeger, 1966); Waldemar A. Nielsen, The Great Powers and
Africa, op. cit., chaps. 10 and 11; Waldemar A. Nielsen,
African Battleline (New York: Harper and Row, 1965).

18. Ross K. Baker, "Towards a New Constituency for
a More Active Foreign Policy for Africa," Issue 3, no. 1
(Spring 1973): 12-18. James N. Rosenau, Domestic Sources
of Foreign Policy (New York: Free Press, 1967).

19. See Congressman Diggs' numerous articles in
Issue, op. cit. and the four volumes of published hearings

of his committee in this country and Africa in 1971 and 1972.

20. See Joint Center for Political Studies, Black Politics '72, parts 1 and 2, Washington, 1972; Focus 2 no. 7 (May 1974): 7, Focus 2, no. 5, p. 6. There are now 17 black members of Congress, 239 black legislators in 29 states, and 111 black mayors, including those in the cities of Los Angeles, Atlanta, and Newark, and approximately 800 black aldermen and councilmen.

21. Selected Directory of African Programs of U.S. Organizations (Washington: Africa Catalog, 1973); International Directory for Educational Liaison (Washington: American Council on Education, 1973), pp. 97-178.

22. See James N. Rosenau, ed., Linkage Politics (New York: Free Press, 1969), p. 44; Rosenau defines linkage as "any recurrent sequence of behavior that originates in one system and is reacted to in another." It would follow from this that national states, their foreign policy, and the international state system or systems are inevitably affected by crossnational linkages. Cf. James N. Rosenau, "Theorizing Across Systems: Linkage Politics Revisited," in Conflict Behavior and Linkage Politics, ed. Wilkenfeld, op. cit., pp. 25-29. See also Hans J. Morgenthau, "United States Policy Towards Africa," in Africa in the Modern World, ed. Calvin W. Stillman (Chicago: University of Chicago Press, 1955); Hans J. Morgenthau, Politics Among Nations (New York: Knopf, 1967). Since Morgenthau believes that politics among nations are determined by the interests of given state-units forming the system, differences between national state systems (especially as to domestic values) are not crucial to the true understanding of international behavior or how a nation should act. In terms of U.S. policy achievements in Africa until Southern Africa was reached in the decolonization process, the Morgenthau thesis explains much.

23. Davis, "Black Americans and United States Policy Toward Africa," loc. cit.

24. Thomas Karis and Gwendolen M. Carter, eds., From Protest to Challenge 1882-1964, vols. 1-3 (Stanford: Hoover Institution Press, 1972-74); John A. Davis and James K. Baker, eds., Southern Africa in Transition, op. cit.

25. Joel Carlson, "Comment on Bruce Oudes' Observation on America's Policy Problems in Southern Africa," Issue 3, no. 4 (Winter 1973): 33-34.

26. Ruth First, "The South African Connection: From Polaroid to Oppenheimer," Issue 3, no. 2 (Summer 1973): 2-7.

27. For a discussion of ideas with regard to South Africa's value to the United States and its vulnerability see Colin Legum and Margaret Legum, "South Africa in the Contemporary World," Issue 3, no. 3 (Fall 1973): 17-28; Bruce Oudes, "Observations on America's Policy in Southern Africa," Issue 3, no. 4 (Winter 1973): 26-43; Elizabeth S. Landis, "American Obligations Toward Namibia," Issue 1, no. 1 (Fall 1971): 15-19; Charles C. Diggs, Jr., "Action Manifesto," Issue 2, no. 1 (Spring, 1972): 52-60; John A. Davis, "Economic Development and Political Independence of the Bantustans as a Strategy of Erosion of Minority Rule in the Republic of South Africa" (Barranquitas: Conference of Black Africanists, January, 1972, mimeographed).

28. Cf. John Marcum, "The Politics of Indifference: Portugal and Africa, A Case Study in American Foreign Policy," Issue 2, no. 3 (Fall 1972): 9-18; John Marcum, The Angolan Revolution, The Anatomy of an Explosion, 1950-1962, vol. 1 (Cambridge, Mass.: MIT Press, 1969).

29. Nielsen, African Battleline, op. cit.

30. Bruce Oudes, "In Washington: Nigeria, Humphrey and the Chrome Caper," Africa Report 18, no. 2 (March-April 1973): 15.

4

U.S. POLICY
AND SOUTHERN AFRICA
George M. Houser

The policy of the United States is much more dynamically keyed to the forces attempting to maintain the
status quo in Southern Africa than to the forces of change.
Waldemar Nielsen put this very politely in terms of South
Africa when he noted:

> There is a considerable degree of truth in
> the designation of the United States as
> one of South Africa's chief allies. For
> the fact is that although the United States
> has repeatedly expressed criticism of
> apartheid in recent years, it has simul-
> taneously appeared to contradict its
> statements by other actions. . . .[1]

In a preelection interview in 1972 former President
Nixon said:

> I wouldn't want to leave the impression
> that . . . Africa will not get atten-
> tion . . . [it] will, because none of
> our present policies are sacred cows.
> I'm going to look at the African policy
> to see how our programs can be improved
> in those areas.[2]

The "improvements" made under the Nixon administration are indicative of the direction of U.S. policy toward Southern Africa. Under the appropriate headline
"U.S. Widens Ties to African Whites," Terence Smith sum-
marized some of these policies in an article in the New
York Times of April 2, 1972. He pointed to the direct

U.S. sale of Boeing 707 airliners to the Portuguese government; the sale of small civilian jet aircraft to South Africa; the permission given Union Carbide to import a shipment of chrome from Rhodesia in 1970 that was said to have been purchased before U.N. sanctions came into effect (in spite of this request having been denied both in 1968 and 1969); the agreement with Portugal to renew the lease for the American air base in the Azores and the quid pro quo of export-import loans to Portugal; and the greatly increased negative U.S. voting record at the United Nations on issues related to colonialism in Southern Africa. To this list one could add the weak U.S. administration position on the sanctions-breaking Byrd Amendment in 1971, the continued provision of military training for members of the Portuguese army and air force, and the unsympathetic treatment accorded South African political refugees seeking entrance into the United States.

In appraising U.S.-South African relations during 1973 Ken Owens, Washington correspondent for the Johannesburg _Star_, commented that "the democratic administration's draft towards a policy of isolating South Africa has been checked and, in marginal areas where it was politically feasible, reversed."[3]

Owen wrote a follow-up article (in the _Star_ of February 9, 1974) dealing with the shift in the emphasis of David Newsom during his term as the assistant secretary of state for Africa; the article was cast in the framework of what Owen called "a casual remark of approval" from Cornelius Mulder, the South African information minister for Newsom at the time he left South Africa for a new assignment in Indonesia. According to Owen, Newsom had shared the orthodox critical view on South Africa of most of the State Department's African bureau at the beginning of his term of office; but at the end of his stint with the bureau Newsom is quoted by Owen as saying that "South Africa has within itself the dynamics for change . . . [and that he] indulges the cautious hope that this process will render not only violence but even outside pressure unnecessary." Owen noted further that Newsom was now reporting that African leaders in independent states were giving no better than secondary consideration to the liberation of Southern Africa.

Newsom set the theoretical context of U.S. policy toward Southern Africa in a speech before the Mid-America Committee in Chicago on June 28, 1972. He outlined three constant elements in that policy that certainly antedated the Nixon administration: support for the principle of self-determination; abhorrence of the institution of apartheid; and support for peaceful change in Southern Africa through constructive alternatives to the use of force. The contradiction between stated policy and practice is what deeply concerns those who are sympathetic with the liberation struggle in Southern Africa.

It is important to note that the policy of the Nixon administration was different only in degree, not in kind, from American policy in the early 1950s when the emergence of African independent states first made it imperative to develop a policy toward Africa. This writer, in testimony given at the hearings conducted by the House Subcommittee on Africa on U.S.-South African relations in March 1966, commented that American policy toward South Africa could at best be characterized as one of "reluctant concern":

> The United States has reluctantly been
> pushed by the African countries to state
> an increasing concern about the injus-
> tices in South Africa. But the United
> States has dragged its heels at almost
> every point.

Wallerstein elaborated on this view in an article in 1969:

> U.S. foreign policy on Africa has been con-
> sistent throughout American history. Wash-
> ington has pursued the goal of a minimum
> amount of trouble purchased with a minimum
> expenditure of time, money and energy. . . .
> Beginning with the Eisenhower Administra-
> tion and continuing under John F. Kennedy
> and Lyndon B. Johnson, the policy of
> neglecting Africa changed somewhat but
> more in style than in substance. Washing-
> ton continued to want little trouble with
> less effort, but didn't want the Africans
> to know about it.[4]

Clearly U.S. policy has been noninitiating, and it has always lagged well behind the changed circumstances in Africa. In 1952 when the racial situation in South Africa first became an item on the U.N. agenda, the United States opposed the formation of the U.N. Commission on the Racial Situation in South Africa. The U.S. position exactly paralleled that of South Africa: that the world organization was not competent to deal with the internal affairs of a member state. It was not until 1958 that the United States revised its position enough to vote with a majority resolution expressing "regret and concern" over South Africa's continual flouting of the U.N. Charter. But even at this time the United States refused to permit the word "condemn" to be included in the resolution. This is typical of the development of American policy over the years; by the time the United States finds it possible to vote for a somewhat condenmatory resolution, the majority of world opinion has taken another long stride ahead leaving the United States again in the minority with the colonialist nations.

Only during a portion of the Kennedy administration was there an exception to the general stance of American policy. By the end of 1960 there were 26 independent African states. Thus the Kennedy administration coincided with a period of great optimism in Africa. It was assumed even in the State Department that soon all of Southern Africa would be under majority rule. In the cold war atmosphere of the early 1960s the United States and the Soviet Union tried to compete for influence, particularly among Southern Africans. The U.S. government was so concerned about reports of the number of Southern African students going to Soviet bloc countries to study that a U.S. team was sent to East Africa in 1973 to make a survey of the actual student situation. The survey team found that there were nine students going to Communist countries to study for every one who came to the United States. Subsequently an expanded student program was set up by the United States, and a growing number of students from Southern Africa came to American colleges. They too shared the optimism in the United States that their countries would soon be independent and that their advanced education would put them in a preferred position for leadership roles in their countries.

During this period Francis Plimpton, Deputy Permanent Representative of the United States to the United Nations (1961-65) often reiterated the U.S. position on apartheid: "The United States abhors apartheid. We rejoice in the bravery of the men and women of South Africa who fight on day by day for racial justice." After the Angolan uprising of March 15, 1961, the United States voted to condemn Portuguese policy in the U.N. Security Council. And in August 1962 the United States voted for a Security Council resolution calling for a ban on the sale of arms to South Africa.

But on the whole U.S. policy has been the familiar
one of not unduly disturbing the status quo in Southern
Africa. Up to the time of the Nixon administration U.S.
votes on colonial issues had frequently been abstentions
(such as the astounding abstention in December 1960, at
the end of the Eisenhower administration, on the key U.N.
resolution on Granting Independence to Colonial Countries
and Peoples). But under the Nixon administration, especially as the demands of the African states became more
urgent, the United States tipped the balance of its voting record to the negative. In the 1972 General Assembly
for example, of the eight major resolutions on Southern
Africa and colonial issues the United States voted nega-
tively on seven and abstained on one. For the most part
the United States was joined in these votes by both South
Africa and Portugal.
     The fact is that U.S. pronouncements in support of
the idea of self-determination (not necessarily independence) have not been reflected in performance. Government spokesmen explain this in a variety of ways. They
say that other international issues take precedence; that
U.S. government resources must be directed toward the difficult domestic racial problems; and that no powerful
pressure groups have arisen to force the United States to
give top priority to the struggle for freedom in Southern
Africa. But the fact most obvious to onlookers including
those actively engaged in the liberation struggle is that
American interests reflect not only concrete considerations of economic involvement in Southern Africa but
global military strategies.

THE NECESSITY FOR A UNITARY APPROACH
TO SOUTHERN AFRICAN PROBLEMS

     Foreign policy cannot exist in a vacuum: it may be
judged realistic to the extent that it relates effectively
to an objective situation. What is the objective situation in Southern Africa to which foreign policy must relate if it is to be realistic? Southern Africa can be
considered as a unit because the vast majority of the
people in the area share common problems. First, they
have been the victims of conquest by a European power.
While this was the experience of the whole African continent as well as other parts of the world, the difference is that for the Southern African countries (and in
this discussion Guinea-Bissau is included as part of this
complex) the conquest is still a fact of life.

Second, the people of Southern Africa also share a
history of racial domination by a white minority. Racial
laws were put into effect with the aim of keeping the
people permanently in a position of subjugation. Apartheid was codified into a system of laws in South Africa.
Essentially the same tactics were used in all areas of
Southern Africa to limit the movement of the African people in their own countries. African labor could then be
exploited and competition on the basis of equality avoided.
In spite of some differences in the areas under Portuguese
domination, a basically similar racist system prevailed
from one area to another. As Eduardo Mondlane pointed
out, "The most that the assimilado system even sets out
to do is to create a few 'honorary whites,' and this certainly does not constitute non-racialism. . . ."[5]

Third, the majority of the people in Southern Africa
share a common economic domination by the white minority.
The greater portion of the land--the richest and most pro-
ductive--as well as the industries, the managerial positions, and the better-paying jobs are all in the hands of
the white minority.

Fourth, the African people in these dominated areas
of Southern Africa all have in common a political subjugation. Prior to the April 1974 coup d'etat in Portugal
no African political organizations were permitted in the
Portuguese-controlled areas. In the other areas the most
dynamic African political groups have been banned, and
nonwhites either cannot serve in the legislatures of the
countries or, as in the case of Rhodesia, are for all
practical purposes permanently in a position where majority political control is an impossibility.

Finally, the majority of these people in the areas
of Southern Africa share a determination to protest and
struggle against this domination. In effect Southern
Africa is the area where the struggle for freedom on the
African continent continues. A policy that does not relate to the reality of this struggle is either terribly
mistaken or irrelevant.

The problems of Southern Africa will not disappear.
One consideration is that the African states will not let
the rest of the world forget that a liberation struggle
is continuing to take place. This has been clearly indicated at the United Nations. In 1973 the U.N. General
Assembly voted to reject South African credentials by a
vote of 72 to 37 with 13 abstentions; and when South African Minister for Foreign Affairs Hilgard Muller rose to
address the General Assembly at least 100 of the delega-
tions walked out leaving him with an almost empty hall.

The oil-producing Arab states, in response to pressure from the Organization of African Unity, announced at their conference in Algeria on November 28, 1973, that they would embargo oil exports to Portugal, Rhodesia, and South Africa. Attention to Southern African problems is urgently called through many such international conferences, perhaps the most significant of which was held in Oslo in April 1973 to outline ways of supporting the liberation movements and their struggle against colonial and white-minority governments.

Another consideration is that the guerrilla warfare that has continued to break out in vast areas of Southern Africa makes it appear now that the struggle will be a protracted one. Although there may be differences of opinion regarding the amount of territory in the Portuguese areas that is under the control of the liberation movements, there is no contesting the substantial advances of these forces in the last decade nor the fact that the wars have been very costly to Portugal. Likewise South Africa and Rhodesia are spending increasing amounts of money to try to protect themselves from an actual or potential military challenge.

Finally, the possibility is generally recognized that a wider race conflict may be in the offing. As Colin Legum and Margaret Legum pointed out in their paper prepared for the 1973 session of the African Studies Association:

> The present drift of events is towards,
> rather than away from, race war--the only
> logical outcome of a confrontation between
> white societies embattled in defense of
> their supremacy and black societies un-
> willing to accept the permanence of such
> a relationship.[6]

This view is reinforced by the current degree of military cooperation among the colonialist and white-minority regimes.

Although the countries making up Southern Africa have many things in common, they also have differences. In detailing the nature of the Southern African situation it is perhaps useful to evaluate these differences in terms of the vulnerability of the various territories to change toward majority rule.

RHODESIA'S VULNERABILITY TO CHANGE

The Rhodesian minority regime seems particularly vulnerable to change. Of the Rhodesian population of some five million only 5 percent is white. Although this white minority is in power and has unilaterally declared its independence from Great Britain, no countries have formally recognized this independence. On the other hand both Portugal and South Africa assist Rhodesia particularly in bypassing U.N. sanctions. Although South Africa has military units in Rhodesia, it is most unlikely that South Africa would agree to incorporate Rhodesia into the Republic of South Africa since this would increase the European population of the Republic by only 250,000 while adding more than five million to the African population.

African opposition to the white-minority regime is growing. The myth that Africans would meekly accept the permanence of white-minority control was dramatically dispelled when the Pearce Commission, in conducting its "test of acceptability" for a new proposed settlement between the Rhodesian and British governments, met with staunch African opposition. The African National Council was organized almost spontaneously around the issue of opposing the British-Rhodesian settlement. Although more than 1,700 Africans were arrested during the two-month Pearce Commission investigation, the commission was deluged by thousands of protest letters, and Lord Pearce reported that 80 percent of the Africans rejected the proposed settlement.

Guerrilla action has steadily intensified in Rhodesia since 1973. An announcement in early February 1974 that the Rhodesian government was doubling its military draft was an indication of the seriousness with which the white minority looks upon black nationalist action. Zambia provides friendly borders from which the Zimbabwe guerrillas can act. Furthermore there has been substantial military cooperation between Zimbabwe guerrillas and the Mozambique Liberation Front along the northeastern border of Rhodesia. The evacuation of thousands of Africans and the creation of a "no-go" free firing zone on the Rhodesian side of this border is a clear indication of the Rhodesian regime's concern over this development.

Except for its links with South Africa and the former Portuguese government, Rhodesia is an isolated

country. Britain has no intention of interfering militarily at this point. But despite their limited effectiveness international sanctions can be expected to continue and in many ways to make life hard for the European
minority.

NAMIBIA

Partly because of its international status, Namibia
also seems vulnerable to pressure for change. Although
the apartheid laws of South Africa extend to Namibia,
they are applied there a little less rigorously--African
political organizations have not been banned for example.
The South West African Peoples' Organization (SWAPO) that
is carrying on at least limited guerrilla action, especially in Caprivi, still exists as an aboveground organization and has been very active in Namibia since 1973.
However, the repressive measures taken against SWAPO members in the early months of 1974 led to an exodus of
thousands of them in mid-1974. The South West African
Convention, a relatively new coalition of organizations
committed to oppose apartheid and to gain independence,
also exists legally in Namibia. These events in Namibia
draw particular international attention because the United Nations, both in the General Assembly and in the
Security Council, has terminated South Africa's mandate
over the territory of Namibia and the International Court
of Justice has termed South Africa's continued presence
in Namibia illegal.

The Namibian ties with South Africa are of course
very close. A majority of the European population in
Namibia (about 13 percent of the whole) are Afrikaners
from South Africa. The economy of Namibia, based heavily
on mineral wealth, is geared to South Africa's. Yet it
is doubtful that South Africa would make an all-out effort to defend her actual presence in Namibia.

Neither Namibians nor South Africans take seriously
the advisory council established by Prime Minister Vorster.
The "homelands" policy that the South African government
is attempting to implement in Namibia is rejected by the
African political organizations and has become a focus of
political opposition.

Opposition to South Africa's continued presence in
Namibia is almost universal. But more significant, active opposition inside the country is growing. Particularly important was the strike of some 15,000 contract

workers from Ovamboland in December 1971. This type of action can be expected to continue.

The United Nations has rejected a continued dialogue between the U.N. secretary general and the government of South Africa over Namibia. Although there may be occasional efforts to reopen discussions, nothing important can happen until South Africa agrees to the two basic principles advanced by both the African nationalists and the United Nations: the establishment of a unitary state, and independence. This requirement was confirmed by the unanimous vote of the Security Council in December 1974; the resolution adopted gave the government of South Africa until May 1975 to begin withdrawing from Namibia.

IMMINENCE OF INDEPENDENCE IN REMAINING PORTUGUESE TERRITORIES

Until the coup d'etat in Portugal of April 25, 1974, the Portuguese had given no indication that they were prepared to leave any of their colonial territories in Africa. They maintained the fiction that Guinea-Bissau, Angola, and Mozambique together with their offshore islands were overseas provinces of Portugal. White immigration to Africa had been encouraged in an effort to implement a policy of assimilation. In a 40-year period from 1930 to 1970 the white population in Angola grew from 30,000 to about 350,000, and in Mozambique from 18,000 to 150,000.[7] In spite of various reforms introduced by Portugal virtually no observers were deluded into thinking that the relation between Portugal and the overseas territories was anything other than that of a colonial power to a colonial people.

With the struggle for independence expanding over the past decade, Portugal has been forced to employ over 150,000 troops and to commit at least 50 percent of its annual budget for the wars in its three colonies. Prior to the coup d'etat liberation movements already controlled significant areas of the land and received military support from the Organization of African Unity (OAU), from many African countries bilaterally, and from the Communist countries. In addition support for nation-building activities came from some Western European countries, from a multitude of private Western organizations, and from U.N. specialized agencies. The African Party for the Independence of Guinea and the Cape Verde Islands (PAIGC) proclaimed the existence of their state in September 1973, and the Republic of Guinea-Bissau was recognized by at least 100 countries by the time Portugal acceded to the fait accompli of total independence in September 1974.

Undoubtedly one of the factors that made it difficult for the Portuguese to negotiate for complete independence in Africa is that they do not have the neocolonialist option that has been open to the French, the British, and the Belgians in Africa. Portugal itself is an underdeveloped country. Its major economic enterprises both in Angola and Mozambique are already in the hands of U.S., South African, and British interests that dominate the oil and diamond industries, the sugar estates, and the hydroelectric and irrigation projects in the Portuguese African territories.

Portugal's African wars have been extremely unpopular among the Portuguese people. Portugal has had a shrinking population as its people have migrated to France or to West Germany in an effort to better their economic lot. Deserters and draft-dodgers in Portugal amounted to about 15,000 a year in 1967 and by 1974 numbered more than 100,000.[8] The political opposition in Portugal, finally able to express itself after 40 years of repression, has come out against the wars in Africa.

While pressures had steadily mounted on the Portuguese regime both in its African colonies and at home in the metropole, the coup compressed great changes into a few days. The new regime in Portugal has now recognized the independence of Guinea-Bissau; and a transitional government with a Mozambique Liberation Front (FRELIMO) majority has been established to direct Mozambique to total independence by June 25, 1975. At the time of this writing negotiations for Angola's independence in 1975 are proceeding.

Whatever the events of the future, they will not eradicate the record of the past, nor invalidate the thesis presented in this study: that U.S. policy in Southern Africa up to the time of this writing has been one of support for the dominant white-minority and colonial regimes. Southern African policies may well continue to change in the future; but so far there is no indication of any change in the basic components of U.S. policy. And so long as that is true America will continue to play a role that impedes the movement of the people of all of Southern Africa toward freedom.

SOUTH AFRICA: KEY TO SETTLEMENT
IN SOUTHERN AFRICA

Of all the countries of Southern Africa the Republic
of South Africa seems the least vulnerable to change.
With a European population comprising almost 20 percent
of the total population, the white minority in South Africa is in firm control and is committed to maintaining
that control. This means that the struggle for fundamental change will be long and hard. Prime Minister Vorster
probably spoke for the majority of the white population
of South Africa when he said during the 1970 election:

> We are building a nation for whites only.
> We have a right to our own identity just
> as blacks and other non-whites have a
> right to theirs. Black people are en-
> titled to political rights, but only over
> their own people--not my people.[9]

Many of the South African whites come from genera-
tions of whites who were born and raised in South Africa--
this is their home. They control a wealthy and strong
country. South Africa prides itself on having 40 percent
of all the automobiles in Africa, 57 percent of the electric power, 50 percent of the telephones, 80 percent of
the coal, and of course 64 percent of all of the Western
world's gold.

For a nation of its size South Africa has a very
powerful military force, more powerful than the combined
forces of the rest of the continent excluding Egypt.
South Africa now produces 80 percent of its weapons. According to the Financial Mail of December 8, 1972, South
Africa was at that time "producing more than 100 kinds of
ammunition, rifles, sub-machine guns, explosives, cannon,
vehicles such as armored cars, electronic equipment like
radar detection systems and walky-talkies, and aircraft."

Expenditures for defense in South Africa rose from
$64.4 million in 1960-61 to $422.4 million in 1972-73 and
will double in 1975. The purpose of this strength is to
protect white South Africa from any threats against its
external or internal security.

Just as South Africa is building a "whites only"
society it is attempting to impose a black society on
its African population. However, it is impossible to

look upon the Bantustans (homelands) policy of the apartheid government as a serious permanent development; these
Bantustans represent a divide-and-rule tactic. They are
a schematic necessity to make rational the claim that
South Africa is not one nation but many. For Africans
who live in them the Bantustans represent a way of surviving on the fringes of the system. Only 6.9 million
of the African population of over 15 million in South
Africa live in any of the reserves now, and over a third
of these are migratory laborers. The Bantustans do not
represent a national base for the millions of men and
women who were born and have worked in the urban areas
for many years. Furthermore the Bantustans are on the
whole uneconomic; their arable land is greatly limited,
and their natural resources and industry are almost non-
existent. Whites and blacks alike realize that the economy of white South Africa is dependent upon black labor.
Therefore the theory of the Bantustans simply perpetuates
the idea of a permanent migratory labor scheme.

Is apartheid slowly being eroded? Can change come
about peacefully from within South Africa? While change
may not necessarily be accompanied by an Armageddon of
violence, it nevertheless seems clear that change cannot
come without persistent struggle and strife. One simply
cannot take seriously the superficial signs of change
that are popularly pointed to at the present time. For
example the so-called outward look and certain emphasis
on "dialogue" does not, as Colin Legum and Margaret Legum
point out, represent "a change in policy, but of tactics,
designed primarily to strengthen South Africa's capacity
to resist change at home and to reduce the impact of international pressures."[10]

South Africa needs friends: It needs friends in
Africa in order to minimize the risk of military action
from other African states and to obtain markets for South
African products that blacks in South Africa, existing on
subsistence wages, cannot afford to buy; and it needs
friends elsewhere in the world, particularly in the West,
not only to encourage economic relations, commerce, and
investments but also for some protection against the Communist states that are committed to support the liberation forces. This reality has been responsible for the
creation in South Africa of the "enlightened" policy of
encouraging diplomatic relations with some black African
states, although Malawi is the only state that has openly
accepted the invitation thus far. This reality has also
been responsible for South Africa's accelerated public

relations campaign, particularly in the press of the United States and that of Britain. To prove that apartheid is actually being eroded apologists point out that an increasing number of black American athletes, the most notable being Arthur Ashe, can now compete in South Africa. They further point to "evidence" such as the recent decision of the Johannesburg City Council to eliminate petty apartheid (except in toilets) in Johannesburg.

Although for a time a few African states campaigned to open up dialogue with South Africa, the Organization of African Unity voted overwhelmingly to reject the concept of dialogue at its meeting in June 1971: 28 countries voted against and 5 in favor with 6 abstaining. The overthrow of Dr. Busia in Ghana (1972) and of President Tsirinana of the Malagasy Republic (1972) has further weakened the voice of those in Africa who have called for dialogue.

None of the superficial changes in South Africa have had any effect whatsoever on the basic aim of apartheid—the control of the black majority by the white minority. The pass laws still stand intact with over 600,000 being arrested under them every year. The possibility of black participation in the political process of South Africa is as remote as it was when the Nationalist party came to power in 1948. Organizations committed to the dismantling of the apartheid system are still banned. Leaders of both radical and liberal opposition movements are banned, have their passports withdrawn, and have their homes raided. This has happened to leaders of the South African Student Organization, the Black Peoples Convention, the National Union of South African Students, the Christian Institute, and even the South African Institute of Race Relations. Even the leader of the nonracial South African Amateur Swimming Federation has been placed under ban because he was considered too outspoken. The government's recently enacted "affected organizations" law will among other things have the effect of cutting off all international financial assistance to blacklisted organizations.

No doubt the effectiveness of the police state apparatus in South Africa will be able for some time to forestall any fundamental challenge to the institution of white supremacy. The most effective opposition to the system will probably come in the industrial structure as the great mass of workers—the Africans—demand better positions, increased pay, and the right of trade-unionism. Evidence of an accelerated campaign along these lines could be seen among the thousands of workers in the Durban

area who went out on strike in 1973. One must expect
growing police violence such as took place September 12,
1973, at the Western Deep Level Mine in Carletonville,
where 12 Africans were killed and 27 injured as workers
demonstrated for increased pay. Action by workers may be
the most effective way of challenging the system because
such action will not seem to the white-minority regime to
be a direct attack on the political structure of apartheid. But mass action on the part of Africans will inevitably lead to political action.

The basic reality of the South African situation is
that a confrontation exists between a white minority determined to maintain power and a black majority rejecting
injustice and domination. How peacefully the change to
majority rule will be made depends largely on the white
minority.

In April 1969 a conference of East and Central African states in Lusaka adopted a manifesto on Southern Africa. This was looked upon as a moderate document. Its
principal message is found in the twelfth paragraph,
which reads in part:

> On the objective of liberation . . . we
> can neither surrender nor compromise. We
> have always preferred . . . to achieve it
> without physical violence. We would pre-
> fer to negotiate rather than destroy, to
> talk rather than to kill. We do not advo-
> cate violence. . . . If peaceful progress
> to emancipation were possible . . . we
> would urge our brothers in the resistance
> movements to use peaceful methods of
> struggle even at the cost of some compro-
> mise on the timing of change. But while
> peaceful progress is blocked by actions of
> those at present in power in the states of
> Southern Africa, we have no choice but to
> give to the peoples of those territories
> all the support of which we are capable in
> their struggle against their oppressors.

To summarize, there exists in Southern Africa a confrontation between a white minority and black majority
that has taken the form of a liberation struggle. This
struggle will continue until the forces of white supremacy and colonial domination have given way. Ultimately
the will of the majority will prevail. It is assumed

that unitary states will be established, and it is hoped
that multiracial societies will emerge but this possibility will become increasingly remote as the struggle in-
tensifies. It is to this reality that future U.S. policy
must relate if it is to be relevant.

U.S. POLICY IN PRACTICE

An examination of actual U.S. practices in Southern
Africa can be divided into five components--trade and investment practices, military considerations, cooperative
schemes, liberation movements, and the nature of diplomatic relations.

Trade and Investment

South Africa. In the last several years a great deal of
attention has been given to U.S. trade with and investments in South Africa. This is rightly so because U.S.
economic ties with South Africa dominate the relations
between the two countries. The official policy of the
U.S. government is, as frequently stated, that "the U.S.
government neither encourages nor discourages investment
in South Africa." Because investment in South Africa has
always been profitable for American businessmen encouragement has never been necessary. John Blashill noted in
this connection:

> The Republic of South Africa has always
> been regarded by foreign investors as a
> gold mine, one of those rare and refresh-
> ing places where profits are great and
> problems small. Capital is not threatened
> by political instability or nationaliza-
> tion. Labor is cheap, the market booming,
> the currency hard and convertible.[11]

U.S. investment in South Africa has grown dramatically from an estimated $50 million in 1943 to $284 million in 1960, to $800 million in 1970.[12] The U.S. De-
partment of Commerce figures for 1971 show a total book
value for U.S. investment in South Africa of $964 million,
about 11.1 percent higher than the figure for 1970; U.S.
investment is about 17 percent of total direct private
foreign investment in South Africa; and repatriated

earnings from this investment contributed about $58 million to U.S. balance of payments in 1971.[13]

Over 300 American firms are involved in South African investments and the general rate of return has been about 19 percent. By comparison the average return on U.S. investment throughout the world in 1969 was 12.2 percent. It is interesting to note that the return on U.S. investments in South Africa reached a high of 46 percent in mining in 1970. Overall, manufacturing dominates U.S. investments in South Africa, especially automobile manufacturing. In this sector the U.S. investment in 1970 represented 25 percent of all U.S. investments. Mobil and Caltex refine over half of the oil imported into South Africa; 60 percent of South Africa's automobiles are produced by American corporations; and a large share of the capital investment in South Africa for mining machinery and the construction industries is from American companies.

Loans by two banking consortiums have been made directly to government and its agencies rather than to private industry in South Africa. One consortium loan of $40 million was ended in 1969 after considerable pressure from American groups that had protested the loan. A second loan organized under the European-American Banking Corporation and totaling over $210 million began in 1970 and it too was to the South African government and its agencies. The U.S. portion of this loan is $18.5 million.

The United States has a favorable trade balance with South Africa. For example in 1972 South Africa's exports to the United States amounted to $324.7 million and imports from the United States amounted to $597.1 million. Major South African exports to the United States have consisted of diamonds, other precious stones, metals and sugar, while the imports from the United States are mainly machinery and electrical equipment, chemicals, textiles, base metals, precision instruments, and paper. Despite increasing competition from Japan, France, and West Germany, the United States is still--after Britain-- South Africa's second largest trading partner. The U.S. Department of Commerce projected that U.S. exports to South Africa in 1973 would amount to $728 million, a 22 percent increase from 1972. This maintains approximately the 17 percent U.S. share of total South African imports.

Namibia. The United States officially discourages investment in Namibia and a formal announcement of this policy

104

was made on May 20, 1970, in response to the judgment of the International Court. This policy applies to all investments made in the Namibian territory prior to October 27, 1966, when the U.N. General Assembly terminated South Africa's mandate over Namibia. Furthermore the policy of the U.S. government is not to protect present investments in Namibia against the claims of any future lawful government, and credit guaranties or other facilities from the U.S. Export-Import Bank are no longer extended for trade in the territory.

Most American investment in Namibia has been in the petroleum and mining industries. In 1971 three American oil companies (Exxon, Caltex, and Gulf) relinquished their offshore oil concessions in Namibia, to be replaced by Aracca Exploration Limited, Continental, Getty, and Phillips. The terms of the concessions are for nine years with an initial investment of $1.2 million and drilling to begin after three years.

However, the most significant American investment in Namibia is the joint control by Newmont Mining and American Metal Climax of the Tsumeb Corporation through approximately 58 percent of its stock. Tsumeb accounts for approximately 80 percent of the base mineral production in Namibia. Other U.S. corporations in Namibia include U.S. Steel, Bethlehem Steel, Nord Mining, Navarro/Zapata, Phelps, Dodge, and Tidal Diamonds; the total U.S. investment is in the neighborhood of $50 million.

There are no separate U.S. trade statistics released for Namibia since these are integrated into the figures for trade between the United States and South Africa. A considerable portion of Namibian exports to the United States consist of karakul pelts and fish products, but other major exports are diamonds and copper.

Rhodesia. Investment and trade with Rhodesia have been reduced since the adoption of the U.N. sanctions that the United States supported in the Security Council in 1966 and 1968. Prior to UDI and U.N. sanctions there were some 53 U.S.-owned and -related corporations in Rhodesia; in 1969 there were only 31. These were primarily distributors, such as export brokers of tobacco, and mining concerns such as Union Carbide and American Metal Climax.

U.N. sanctions in Rhodesia included a complete trade embargo as one of the mandatory provisions. In October 1971 the Congress passed Section 503 of the Military Procurement Act, the so-called Byrd Amendment, which stipulated that the president could not prohibit the importation

into the United States of any strategic material so long
as such material was not prohibited from a Communist-
dominated country. Thus by legislative action the position of the executive branch of the U.S. government taken
at the United Nations was undermined. In March 1972 the
first shipments of chrome from Rhodesia came into the
United States under the Byrd Amendment. It was noted in
a study published by the Carnegie Endowment for International Peace: "The most persistent lobbyist against the
Byrd Amendment was the State Department--and its efforts
were vitiated by the refusal of the White House to weigh
in with phone calls to wavering Senators."[14]

The executive branch of government was severely em-
barrassed by the passage of the Byrd Amendment and key
representatives of the administration appeared at congressional hearings urging the repeal of the amendment in
late 1973. Among these were John Scali, permanent U.S.
representative at the United Nations, who said before the
Senate Foreign Relations Committee's Subcommittee on African Affairs: "The United States importation of Rhodesian goods under section 503 has become an extremely
serious issue in our relations with African countries."
During the second time around, before the Senate voted
to repeal the Byrd Amendment in December 1973, Secretary
of State Kissinger indicated that the administration
wanted the Byrd Amendment repealed.

There have been other leaks in the enforcement of
total U.S. sanctions, as indicated by export-import figures for 1971, when for example $807,000 worth of Rho-
desian goods were imported into the United States and
$652,000 in U.S. goods were exported to Rhodesia. An in-
cident that attracted some attention involved the sale
of three Boeing 720 jetliners. They were bought by a
dummy company in Switzerland and put into service in
Rhodesia in September 1973. According to an article in
the Washington Post these airliners now are the mainstay
of the Salisbury-Johannesburg run.[15]

A pamphlet issued by the special Rhodesia project of
the Carnegie Endowment for International Peace reported
other American transactions with Rhodesia that violated
sanctions.[16] It detailed violations of sanctions through
the use of credit cards; advertisements for Rhodesian industries, banks, hotels, touring companies, and commercial enterprises appearing in such publications as the
Journal of Commerce in New York; and arrangements for
renting cars in Rhodesia through Hertz and Avis offices
in the United States. It is notable too that one can
stay in a Holiday Inn in the Rhodesian city of Bulawayo.

<u>Portuguese Territories</u>. The single largest U.S. investor
in the Portuguese territories is Gulf Oil through its
Gulf Cabinda subsidiary. Gulf began prospecting for oil
in Cabinda in 1954 and made its first oil discovery there
in 1966. By the end of 1972 Gulf's Angola investments
had reached $209 million. Payments by Gulf to Portugal
for its Angolan concession amounted to about $61 million
in 1972, representing about 13 percent of the total Angolan provincial budget for that year. Payments to Portugal were even greater in 1973, reaching a figure of
$91 million.

By mid-1973 the U.S. State Department reported that
four U.S. corporations were investing in oil in Angola--
Tenneco, Texaco, Gulf, and Mobil; eight others had received offshore concessions. Other U.S. capital investments in Angola total about $50 million.

In Mozambique U.S. investment is over $30 million.
In 1970 there were some 15 U.S. firms in Mozambique of
which five or more were primarily involved in the distribution of finished products. Oil exploration was
undertaken by Texaco, Sun Oil, Gulf, and Hunt International; Bethlehem Steel prospected for minerals in the
Tete Province.

Trade with Mozambique has been very modest. In 1972
for example Mozambique's exports to the United States
were only $23.2 million and imports from the United States
were $17.8 million. Cashews are the primary cash export.

Trade with Angola has been relatively more extensive.
In 1970 Angola's exports to the United States were worth
$76 million or 16.7 percent of its total exports, and im-
ports from the United States were $48 million or 13.6
percent of Angola's total imports. The major Angolan export is coffee although this has dropped from 58 percent
of the total in 1971 to 46.5 percent in 1972; other exports include crude oil, sisal, and beryllium and fish
products. The U.S. exports to Angola consist mainly of
steel and iron products and heavy equipment.

Defense Considerations

<u>South Africa</u>. Official U.S. policy, originally announced
at the United Nations in 1961 by the then Ambassador Adlai
Stevenson, is to embargo military equipment and supplies
to South Africa. This action was taken unilaterally by
the United States even before the resolution calling for
a military embargo against South Africa was introduced
in the Security Council. The question, however, is how

well this embargo has been observed. Certainly the United States is not in the position of France, currently the chief supplier of military hardware to South Africa. Nevertheless the U.S. commitment to embargo has been compromised by a number of transactions and events.

According to the Johannesburg Star of April 17, 1971, Mrs. Olive Beech, head of the American Beechcraft Corporation, announced in Johannesburg that South Africa's defense force could now buy light American aircraft for reconnaissance and training purposes. Although according to the Star this was denied by Undersecretary Newsom he went on to say that "normal trade with South Africa in civilian type goods for non-military purposes continues and we are prepared to consider licensing for VIP transport purposes limited numbers of small unarmed executive civilian type aircraft which will not strengthen South Africa's military or internal security capacity." The critical question is whether the United States can police South Africa's use of small aircraft to prevent their being converted to military use. It would be particularly difficult for the U.S. government to do this inasmuch as flying is such a popular activity among whites in South Africa. The small aircraft that the United States is now authorized to sell to South Africa could easily be used by the Air Commandos, a volunteer group made up of private pilots commissioned for military activity in times of emergency.

Furthermore the U.S. government has authorized the sale of helicopters to South Africa, such as the amphibious Sikorsky 62 that is capable of flying 400 miles without refueling and was used extensively by the U.S. Army in Vietnam. Here again the question of U.S. ability to police the use of these helicopters is critical.

Testifying before the House Foreign Affairs Committee on June 16, 1971, Jennifer Davis, speaking for the American Committee on Africa, said:

> Beech has sold 25 planes [to South Africa] in the last six months. By 1969 Cessna had already sold more than 1,000 planes in the southern Africa area . . . which extended over South Africa, Namibia, Angola and Mozambique, and had sent a special six-man selling team to South Africa to launch three new models in October 1970. Several executive jets had been sold by late 1969, and it is interesting to note

that the technical report which appeared
in the South Africa _Financial Gazette_
stressed that the Lear-jet 24D can land
and take off from nearly all landstrips in
Southern Africa.

Several U.S. corporations have helped to supply
South Africa with equipment that can be used for military
purposes. For example IBM has supplied at least four com-
puters to the South African Department of Defense, while
ITT's equipment and expert knowledge has been applied to
the South African regime's communications systems. General Electric, through its South African subsidiary, supplies about 95 percent of the diesel locomotives for
South African railways. Again equipment essential for
communications and transport falls into a nebulous area
that can be interpreted as having either war or peacetime
value depending on whether a society seems to be in a
state of war or not.

In early February 1973 the South African minister
for information, Cornelius Mulder, spent several days in
the United States, and a considerable amount of that time
in Washington. He met in quiet conversation with a number of prominent political and governmental leaders including minority leader Gerald Ford. But of particular
concern in the present context was Mulder's visit to the
Pentagon to meet with Vice Admiral Ray Peet, deputy assistant secretary in the office of the assistant secretary
of defense for international security affairs. Although
there was no public announcement of the topic discussed
by Mulder and Peet, an interpretive memorandum from the
Southern Africa Committee quite logically suggested that
the discussion had implications for South African and
American strategies in the Indian Ocean. The memorandum
noted that the United States had opened a communication
center on the British island of Diego Garcia and that the
Pentagon had announced plans to construct a $29 million
air and naval support facility on this island in the Indian Ocean. Furthermore the memorandum referred to the
recommendation by a U.S. research team on naval warfare
from a 1970 U.S. school of naval warfare proposing a
"multi-national naval presence in the area." The research
team report had stated that since South Africa possessed
the only strong maritime force in the area "the navy of
the Republic of South Africa should be invited to participate even though political differences are to be anticipated." Fears that the United States is approaching a

military detente with South Africa were further strength-
ened by the "unofficial" visit of the head of the South
African armed forces, Admiral Hugo Biermann, to Washington, including the Pentagon, in May 1974.

Portugal. Since the 1961 uprising in Angola the United
States has had an announced policy of prohibiting Portugal's use of NATO military equipment outside the North
Atlantic zone. In terms of actual policy the United
States has attempted to remain neutral in Portugal's African wars while simultaneously maintaining a military alliance with Portugal as a European country. A State Department officer put it this way:

> U.S. policies towards the Portuguese terri-
> tories in Africa are influenced by two
> principal factors. On the one hand we de-
> sire to maintain friendly, cooperative re-
> lations with Portugal that are consistent
> with our international undertakings, and
> to continue U.S./Portuguese cooperation in
> the North Atlantic area as envisaged by
> the NATO treaty and by our defense facili-
> ties agreements with Portugal. On the
> other hand, we believe that the long range
> interests of Portugal and of the peoples
> of the overseas territories would be best
> served by full Portuguese acceptance of
> the principle of self-determination.[17]

The contradiction between these two aims has laid U.S.
actions open to constant questioning on a number of important issues.
    Most troubling has been the presence of the American
airbase in the Azores, used by the U.S. Air Force since
the Second World War. Until 1962 formal agreements between the U.S. government and the Portuguese determined
the use of the base. However, following the insurgency
in Angola, which led to U.S. votes at the United Nations
that were critical of Portuguese policy in Africa, Salazar's government decided not to enter into formal agreement although the United States continued to use the base.
Meanwhile in the summer of 1961 the Joint Chiefs of Staff
had decided that the Azores base was essential to American security. It was noted by Arthur Schlesinger:

> The problem led to continual wrangling in
> Washington--the Bureau of European Affairs

versus the Bureau of African Affairs; the
Mission to the U.N. versus the Pentagon.
. . . This dilemma left us no choice but
of moderating policy on Portuguese questions in the U.N.--never enough for the
Nationalists in Africa and always too much
for the Pentagon and Dr. Salazar.[18]

For a time in the late 1960s it looked as if the
Azores would be officially regarded as of little strategic value to the United States. Having previously been
looked upon as an important refueling point, the Azores
represented less apparent value with the development of
planes capable of flying long ranges. Writing in a New
York Times column on March 5, 1969, James Reston noted
that the need for the Azores no longer existed "but the
old arrangements go on."

In the December 1971 formalized agreement with Portugal for the use of the Lajes airbase in the Azores, the
United States agreed to a $436 million economic aid pack-
age to Portugal to be spread over a two-year period. The
bulk of this amount was in Export-Import Bank loans total-
ing $400 million to buy American goods for development
projects in Portugal. Other aspects of the package included the loan of an oceanographic ship, a grant of $1
million for educational projects in Portugal financed by
the Defense Department; a minimum of $5 million for road-
building machinery, cranes, hospitals, and port and har-
bor equipment; and access to a $15 million loan for sur-
plus agricultural commodities from the United States.

A number of the Export-Import Bank's press releases
issued in 1973 indicated how some of the loan funds have
been used. For example on June 21 the bank announced the
sale of 22 General Electric locomotives to Mozambique at
a cost of $9.5 million; on July 19, $4 million was announced to finance the sale of tire production facilities
in Mozambique; on August 10, $30.2 million for the sale
of one Boeing 747 to Portugal; on September 11, $7.8 mil-
lion for the sale of goods and services required for a
pulp and paper manufacturing facility in Portugal; and
on October 5, $6 million to help finance the sale of one
Boeing 737-200 jet aircraft, spare parts, and related
ground equipment purchased by Mozambique's Harbors, Railways and Transport Administration.

According to former Premier Caetano the treaty was
"a political act in which the solidarity of interests between the two countries is recognized and it is in the
name of that solidarity that we put an instrument of

action at the disposal of our American friends, who are also now our allies."[19]

The Middle East war of October 1973 added another dimension to the U.S.-Azores question. With the countries of Western Europe refusing landing rights to American planes flying military supplies to Israel, the Azores served an urgent purpose. The Financial Times of London commented on November 28, 1973: "There is a change in Washington's sulky attitude of the past few months, which implied that the Azores base was no longer useful." Up to 800 tons of war equipment each day went by American planes, particularly the new supercargo plane, the C-5, through the Azores. On December 17, 1973, Secretary of State Kissinger, visiting Lisbon, commented:

> On this trip through the Middle East, I was reminded of the fact that Portugal stood by its allies during the recent difficulties and the United States is extremely grateful for this. . . . I would like to say that as far as the United States is concerned, our journey together is not finished.[20]

Portugal was able to allow the use of the Azores and to ignore threats of an oil embargo by Arab countries, which had been supplying almost 90 percent of her crude oil, because Gulf Cabinda produces enough to supply all of Portugal's requirements. From this vantage point Portugal was able to use her newfound strategic position as an ally of the United States to exert additional pressure. Appeals by the Portuguese embassy in Washington to members of the U.S. Senate were no doubt partly responsible for the watering down of the Tunney-Young Amendment to the Foreign Aid Bill. The original purpose of this amendment was to make into law the prohibition of the use in Africa of American arms supplied to Portugal. The final version that was passed by the Senate struck out any reference to Portugal and substituted "any non-African country." The bill in its final form required the president only to report "as soon as practicable" on the use of economic, military, or agricultural assistance from the United States for military activities in African territories.[21]

One of the complications in U.S. military policy toward Portugal was that the Portuguese did not make the distinction the United States tries to make between Africa and the North Atlantic area. Any military assistance to

Portugal, whether directly from the United States or through NATO, could from the Portuguese point of view be used either in Europe or Africa.

Under its Military Assistance Program the United States maintained a 21-man military advisory group in Lisbon to "permit the training of key Portuguese military personnel." In addition provision was made for some training of military officers in the United States. For example in 1968, 107 military personnel were trained in the United States at a cost of $120,000 and in 1970 the training of 33 officers cost $88,000. In the late 1960s and early 1970s under the Military Assistance Program about $1 million a year has been given by the United States to Portugal. In the 20-year period prior to 1967 approximately $326 million was spent overall under the program.

In the last few years the United States has sold to the Portuguese commercial airline--TAP--seven 707s, three 727s, and two 727-Cs, all from Boeing. Sales have also been made from Boeing to DETA, the commercial airline in Mozambique. It is common knowledge in Mozambique that commercial aircraft have been used for military purposes. In fact DETA had a formal contract with the military authorities in Mozambique under which it guaranteed to "give the Military Region of Mozambique regular air transport on a charter basis." At the formal signing of the contract various military personnel, including the commander-in-chief of the armed forces of Mozambique, were present.

In 1972 North American Rockwell had sold four aircraft to a private airline company in northern Mozambique; in 1973 and again in 1974 helicopters were sold by Bell Aircraft to several government departments in Mozambique.

Reports from some of the liberation movements, particularly the Peoples Movement for the Liberation of Angola (MPLA), of Portuguese use of herbicides to destroy crops in liberated areas raised serious questions about increasing U.S. exports of herbicides to Portugal and directly to Mozambique in 1972. It was precisely during this period that complaints persisted about Portugal's chemical warfare in Mozambique.

Cooperative Programs

The U.S. government has had some limited cooperative programs with Southern African countries, primarily with South Africa. A description of these programs follows.

National Aeronautics and Space Administration (NASA) stations. In 1961 NASA established three space tracking stations in South Africa, the most important of which were the deep space instrumentation facility and the station for satellite tracking and data acquisition, with an operating budget of $2.5 million per year; with equipment, technical supplies, and finances supplied by NASA; and with staff (most of whom were trained by the United States) provided by South Africa's Council on Scientific and Industrial Research. In the later 1960s the question of racial segregation at these facilities was raised. In response to this the State Department affirmed that no discrimination at the facilities would be countenanced; however, the issue was actually avoided by using South Africans in almost all of the approximately 250 positions at the facilities, with the major exception of one person from the California Institute of Technology's jet propulsion laboratory. According to an article that appeared in the July 10, 1970, issue of Science Magazine, employment was "in accord with the Apartheid regulations," and the program was of considerable help to South Africa because among other things it helped train South African personnel in advanced technology. In a four-year training program partially financed by NASA in which South African secondary graduates may receive a diploma for work done at the NASA installations, 30 or 40 students had completed the course in 1970. The 15-year agreement between NASA and South Africa expires in 1975 and the U.S. government has announced that the agreement will not be renewed.

Atomic Energy. Since 1962 the U.S. Atomic Energy Commission has worked with South Africa's Atomic Energy Board and cooperated closely with South Africa. The development of South Africa's first nuclear reactor was inaugurated at Pelindaba near Pretoria in 1965. For this project many South African staff members were trained at Oak Ridge; the United States supplied both a consultant for the Pelindaba reactor and the enriched uranium to start the reactor. Furthermore the main contractors for the project were Allis-Chalmers and eight other American organizations. All 900 employees at Pelindaba are white.

Cooperative Scientific Arrangements. In the field of astronomy the Smithsonian Institute plans to set up an observatory in South Africa, and there is a plan for U.S. cooperation in lunar research inasmuch as South Africa has some of the oldest rocks on earth. This is to be a cooperative scheme with the geology department of Witwatersrand University. There has also been a cooperative arrangement between the United States and South Africa on an Antarctic research program; and there have been exchange programs between a number of South African and American universities including Massachusetts Institute of Technology, the University of California, and the Colorado School of Mines.

In 1972 an agreement was made between NASA and the South African Council for Scientific and Industrial Research that involved the provision for study of satellite pictures of South Africa to the South African Department of Agriculture, Planning and Mines.

Visitor and Exchange Programs. The U.S. government has for many years sponsored a visitors' program for South Africans coming to the United States. On September 27, 1973, John W. Foley, Jr., director of the State Department's Office of Southern African Affairs, in testimony before the House Subcommittee on International Organizations and Movements, said that in the fiscal years 1968 to 1973 the State Department had awarded a total of 91 leader grants to South Africans, of whom the vast majority were black.

In addition to the government-sponsored program private agencies such as the American Field Service, the United States South African Leadership Exchange Program, and the Rotary Club have sponsored exchange programs between the two nations.

American Attitude Toward Liberation Movements

The official U.S. attitude toward liberation movements was probably best stated by Newsom in his June 1972 address, mentioned previously, to the Mid-American Committee in Chicago:

> The question of U.S. official relations
> with leaders of opposition movements in
> colonial territories has always posed a
> dilemma for American policy makers. . . .
> These movements are a political fact. On
> the one hand, the absence of contact or
> support from us leaves the leaders sub-
> ject to certain other outside influences.

On the other hand, the United States has
traditionally been unwilling to recognize
the opposition elements in colonial territories until an internationally recognized
transfer of power has taken place.

This policy was reflected in 1972 votes in the U.N.
General Assembly when the United States opposed two reso-
lutions--one conferring observer status on representatives of liberation movements from Namibia, Zimbabwe, and
the Portuguese colonies at U.N. committee discussions on
colonialism and the other affirming the legitimacy of the
struggle against apartheid and colonialism "by all available means."

Furthermore the United States made it clear that it
will not respond to the appeal of the PAIGC to give recognition to the newly proclaimed Republic of Guinea-Bissau.
Prior to the formal cessation of control over Guinea-
Bissau by Portugal the U.S. government maintained that
Guinea-Bissau did not meet the standards of an independent state: its geographical area could not be clearly
defined; it did not have control over a given area; and
it was not in a position to conduct foreign relations.
In a letter to Congressman Donald Fraser, national chairman of the Americans for Democratic Action, Claude G.
Ross, acting assistant secretary for African Affairs, reported on November 9, 1973:

> The best information we have indicates
> that the PAIGC . . . does not control as
> much as one-third of the territory in
> question. . . . there is clearly no
> settled capital where governmental affairs
> are conducted or where foreign representa-
> tives could be received or live. . . .
> Portugal completely controls about two-
> thirds to three-fourths of the territory.
> . . . The PAIGC probably controls be-
> tween 25,000 to 50,000 people out of a
> total Portuguese Guinea population of
> 490,000.

A similar letter to the African Studies Association
dated December 3, 1973, and signed by Carol C. Laise,
assistant secretary for public affairs, ended with almost the same wording: "Because the U.S. Government must
take into account both the facts it possesses and the

possible far reaching implications of extending recognition to any new claimants of independence, we do not recognize the PAIGC claim of an independent Guinea-Bissau."

The State Department was particularly careful not to disturb Portugal by exhibiting any relationship with the liberation movements in the Portuguese colonies. There was the occasion for example when a FRELIMO delegation of three came to New York City in 1967 and asked this writer, in his capacity as executive director of the American Committee on Africa, to arrange a meeting for them with the State Department. I then called the Mozambique desk officer at the State Department who indicated after consultation with the department that the best that could be done would be to arrange for a representative to meet the FRELIMO delegation in some out-of-the-way restaurant either in Washington or New York City. The delegation refused this invitation.

Similarly, American diplomats in Africa were discouraged from maintaining relationships with representatives of liberation movements even though in some cases such relationships had been established between the parties in the United States.

In a conversation that I had with the American ambassador in Conakry in 1970 it transpired that he had no contact with the PAIGC. Although he had met one of its leaders at a diplomatic reception the ambassador did not even remember the name of this leader who I subsequently learned was Aristides Pereira, now the secretary general of the PAIGC.

The most sensitive capitals for contacts with liberation movements in Africa have been Lusaka and Dar es Salaam; and at the U.S. embassies in these cities there has been one political officer whose major responsibility is to try to maintain contact with the liberation movements, with the main objective of gathering information. This function is of no use to the liberation movements, which have increasingly downgraded the importance of these contacts.

The most substantial U.S. government program related to the liberation movements was the assistance to students from Southern Africa that was initiated in 1962. Two programs were funded by the government and administered by the African-American Institute (AAI). One of these provided secondary education for students from Southern Africa, essentially political refugees, who were not ready to enter university. Two schools were established under this program, one at Kurasini in Tanzania and the other at Nkumbi in Zambia. The students who went to these two schools were in effect nominated by the liberation movements. Between 1962 and 1972, according to U.S. government figures, this program cost $7,135, 000. In December 1969 the Kurasini facility was turned over to the government of Tanzania and a year later the property at Nkumbi was turned over to Zambia.

This Southern African student program brought to American universities about 500 students from Southern Africa during the period from 1963 to 1973. According to U.S. government figures the program cost $8,585,000 and the AAI estimated the administrative cost of the program to be $1,500,000.

The Nature of Diplomatic Relations

The U.S. government maintains diplomatic relations with Portugal and South Africa, and the post of ambassador to Lisbon has been regarded as an important one. Within the Portuguese structure the embassy in Portugal has presumably had direct relationships with the U.S. consulates in the Portuguese territories. U.S. consulates are maintained in Lourenco Marques and in Luanda but not in Bissau.

The U.S. embassy in South Africa is located at the administrative capital in Pretoria; in addition there are consulates in Cape Town and in Durban.

The apartheid pattern in South Africa has caused some strains in American diplomatic practices especially because of pressure from civil rights forces in the United States. On the whole the United States has followed a fairly timid policy aimed primarily at avoiding the exacerbation of official diplomatic relations. The current policy and practice was outlined by Foley in a statement before the House Subcommittee on International Organizations and Movements on September 27, 1973:

> We consider it important to maintain contact with all segments of the South African population and promote interracial communication in South Africa. Our embassy and consulates in general in South Africa have wide ranging contacts among all racial groups. Multiracial social events at the homes of American officials serving in South Africa bring together

various South Africans who might otherwise
not meet. We were pleased to note that
the American ambassador's last Fourth of
July reception, traditionally multiracial,
was attended by South African government
officials who for the first time accepted
invitations.

It is notable that while previously such multiracial
gatherings were held only annually on the Fourth of July,
now they are held more frequently.

The U.S. government has begun to break down racial
barriers very cautiously in the assignment of American
personnel to South Africa. In his abovementioned speech
before the Mid-America Committee in Chicago, Newsom
pointed out that black diplomatic couriers have been
placed on runs to South Africa and that in 1971 three
black foreign service officers were given temporary as-
signments in South Africa. In 1973 the first permanent
assignment of a black American to a diplomatic post in
South Africa was issued, and black Americans have also
been sent to South Africa under the official cultural exchange program. Pressure from civil rights organizations
protesting the visit of U.S. naval vessels to South Africa has caused such visits to be suspended since 1967.

Namibia has of course never been looked upon as separate from South Africa until recently and even though
the United States supported the U.N. resolution terminating the mandate of South Africa over Namibia there is no
U.S. consular office in Windhoek.

Prior to UDI some 20 countries including the United
States maintained consular establishments in Rhodesia.
Since the adoption of sanctions against Rhodesia all of
these offices have been closed.

THEMES OF U.S. POLICY

A number of constant themes have run through U.S.
policy toward Southern Africa for the past 20 years.
Some of these themes are clearly stated, others merely
implied. In general U.S. policy has been weak and non-
initiating--reactive rather than active. A major objective has been to avoid confrontation with the colonial
and white-minority governments in power. The toughest
policies have in fact been emasculated: sanctions
against Rhodesia have been compromised by the import of

chrome and other strategic materials under the Byrd Amendment; support for the termination of South Africa's mandate over Namibia and the discouragement of investment in that country has been weakened by the unwillingness of the United States to engage in implementing action through the United Nations and particularly by its refusal to serve on the U.N. council for Namibia; the embargo on arms to South Africa, as noted previously, has been weakened by permitting some planes and other materials convertible to military use to go to South Africa; and the arms limitation on Portugal stipulating that NATO arms cannot be used in Africa has been vitiated by the fact that Portugal does not recognize the distinction between its activities in the North Atlantic area and the wars in Africa.

In view of these facts U.S. policy can be characterized as follows:

1. U.S. policy toward Southern Africa is low on the scale of American foreign policy priorities. Secretary of State Kissinger, in his maiden speech at the United Nations, did not mention Africa in spite of the fact that the General Assembly agenda was, as usual, loaded with African issues. Justifications for this low priority position are either that more pressing issues exist elsewhere in the world or that African independent nations are not pressing as hard in private contacts with the U.S. government as in their public declarations. It has also been pointed out that the cold war between the Soviet Union and the United States is tempered, and certainly it is not actively pursued in Africa at this point. Colin Legum and Margaret Legum commented that Southern Africa has low priority for the Russians and Chinese as well, "which is one major reason why Western policymakers can afford to relegate it to 'tomorrow's problems' rather than today's"; but they noted further that Chinese and Russian "diplomacy and long term strategy can proceed in low key, but with purposeful support for the challengers of apartheid, while the West is still principally engaged in tactical diplomacy of avoiding active involvement with either side."[22]

2. U.S. policy is one of dialogue and communication. When Nixon became president he ordered a review of U.S. policy toward Southern Africa, and in April 1969 the report on this review was submitted to the National Security Council for discussion of various U.S. options. It was decided that the former Kennedy and Johnson policies of verbal attacks on apartheid should now be played down

and a program of increased communication substituted on the theory that friendly persuasion rather than constant condemnation would be more likely to make the Southern African white-minority governments modify their racial policies. In furtherance of this policy the United States helped pave the way for American black athletes such as golfer Lee Elder and tennis player Arthur Ashe to go to South Africa. In line with the Verligtes policy of the Vorster regime South Africa cooperated by granting visas. The policy was working well enough so that in January 1973 when Mulder came to the United States he had no difficulty in seeing such highly placed individuals as Senate Minority Leader Hugh Scott, Thomas Morgan, chairman of the House Foreign Affairs Committee, Senator John Tower of Texas, former Governor Ronald Reagan of California, and reportedly a number of black leaders including Mayor Thomas Bradley of Los Angeles.

The United States enthusiastically endorsed the proposal of Kurt Waldheim, secretary general of the United Nations, for entering into dialogue with the Republic of South Africa on Namibia on the grounds that the United States was reluctant to eliminate the possibility of future talks with South Africa in the belief that such discussions were the most realistic way of gaining self-determination of the people of Namibia.

The African states that had temporarily endorsed the dialogue approach to South Africa on the Namibian question reversed their position by a formal vote at the OAU in 1973, and in the Security Council they voted for the secretary general to discontinue his efforts. From an African perspective these discussions with South Africa had not led to any constructive developments, and South Africa had continued with its policy of formalizing the Bantustans in Namibia.

At an early stage the Nixon administration extended this policy of dialogue and communication to Portugal. Seymour Finger, speaking for the United States, told the Fourth Committee at the United Nations on November 14, 1969:

> It is not at all certain that a conciliatory approach to Portugal would lead toward the goal of self-determination. . . But we are convinced it is worth trying . . . condemnation of the colonial war which is allegedly being waged by Portugal against the people in its African

territories . . . is hardly likely to
achieve a constructive dialogue with the
government of Portugal.

3. U.S. policy is opposed to isolating South Africa.
It was noted in the 1969-70 Foreign Policy Report, "We do
not believe that isolating them [South Africa] from the
influence of the rest of the world is an effective way of
encouraging them to follow a course of moderation and to
accommodate change." But in fact this policy, contrary to
the claims of those who say that isolation would not yield
results, has worked most effectively in the area of sports.
The exclusion of South Africa from the last two Olympic
Games and from participation in many international sporting events seems to have had an effect on policy at home.
Although apartheid has by no means disappeared from
sports, and probably will not as long as the present
South African regime is in power, it has been eroded by
making a distinction between domestic and international
sporting events.
4. U.S. policy strongly advocates peaceful as
against violent change in Southern Africa. In a speech
that Newsom made on September 17, 1969, he put this very
clearly: "We do not believe that the use of force is the
answer. We do not believe it is a feasible answer given
the strength of the white regime. We do not believe it
is a just answer because violence hardly brings justice
to all."
At a meeting in Atlanta in October 1971 Newsom expanded on this theme: "We believe change will come in
Southern Africa. Economic and demographic pressures make
this inevitable. In South Africa itself there is a lessen-
ing of rigidity. Change is a central theme of discussion.
. . . We cannot expect change to come quickly or easily,
our hope is that it will come peacefully."
The indication by Newsom implied that somehow "economic and demographic pressures" will bring this change
about is in effect an argument for U.S. noninvolvement in
the struggle for change in South Africa. As Jennifer
Davis pointed out in a study presented to the African
Studies Association on November 19, 1971: "There is violence in South Africa every moment of the day; there is
violence when 33 out of 100 babies die before they are
one year old; there is violence in the daily arrest of
2500 men and women for infringements of the pass laws;
there is violence in a system of forced labor. . . ."
The majority in Southern Africa find it understandably

difficult to take seriously an argument against violence
that comes from a government that indiscriminately bombed
Southeast Asia to the horror of the world. And yet part
of the American rationale for voting against the U.N.
resolutions giving legitimate status to the liberation
movements is based on this argument for "peaceful change."

5. U.S. policy is both white and European oriented.
Support for Portugal in votes on U.N. resolutions reflects
this U.S. policy. It is interesting to note that the
first veto that the United States cast in the Security
Council on March 17, 1970, came on an issue condemning
Britain for not using force in Rhodesia. Newsom, in his
aforementioned Chicago speech in June 1972, tried to rebut
this position when he said: "We have had to deny both in
Africa and in this country that we have chosen sides in
this southern conflict and that the United States would
intervene on the side of the white regimes in the event
of trouble."

While the question of U.S. intervention to uphold
the white status quo and protect its economic interests
in Southern Africa is a matter of conjecture, it is a
concrete fact that U.S. policies are focused almost exclusively on the white regimes; it is assumed that the
white regimes will initiate the policies that will help
to bring about change. The aim of U.S. policy has therefore been to remain on good terms with the white minority
in South Africa and with the colonialists in the Portuguese territories. As for policy on relations with the
liberation movements, such policy has been virtually non-
existent.

It was this European- and white-oriented policy that
finally led to the resignation of Congressman Diggs from
the U.S. delegation at the United Nations in 1971. The
immediate cause of the resignation was the renewed agreement with Portugal for the use of the Azores. In a statement issued at the time of his resignation Diggs said:

> I object most strenuously to the U.S. com-
> mitment to bail Portugal out of the eco-
> nomic and political consequences of its
> nefarious policies in Africa without any
> commitment and definitive action towards
> Portugal towards ending the wars and to-
> wards granting independence to the people
> of these areas.

Diggs noted further that in the Azores agreement "this
administration has announced both an open alliance with

Portugal and a decision which I can interpret only to mean 'partnership' in the subjugation of the African people."

6. U.S. policy toward Southern Africa is pretty much "business as usual." A partial exception to this may be seen in policy toward Rhodesia, but American economic involvement there has never been great and, in any event, imports from Rhodesia under the Byrd Amendment have virtually equaled what they were in 1965 or before. It is impossible to judge the net effect of the U.S. policy of discouraging new investment in Namibia. In the case of both the Portuguese territories and South Africa trade and investment have continued and in fact grown; in this case the rationale of the U.S. government is that improvements in labor practices can be a catalyst for change in the South Africa situation. This idea is enlarged upon by noting that U.S. firms can improve labor practices and thus become a force for overall change in South Africa.

The late Amilcar Cabral, former leader of the liberation movement in Guinea-Bissau, speaking to a gathering of a few friends one evening in New York, related a conversation with a secretary in the American embassy in Conakry regarding the offshore presence of Continental and Exxon in Guinea-Bissau.

> I told him that we considered this an un-
> friendly attitude of the United States to-
> ward our people. And he said, "Oh, no, we
> can do nothing at all through our govern-
> ment, because these are private companies
> and you see, Mr. Cabral, they would very
> much like to be the first, because when
> you'll be independent, they will be the
> first there." I told him, "You are a
> Christian. You must remember that Christ
> said that maybe the first will be last."
> He was not too happy with that.

7. Legality and international law are central in U.S. policy toward Southern Africa. This has been particularly clear in the case of Namibia. The United States looks upon the decision of the International Court of Justice on June 21, 1971--declaring South Africa's presence in Namibia illegal--as of vital importance. In the Rhodesian case U.S. policy prior to UDI was based essentially on the legal arrangement between the white-minority government of the self-governing colony and

Britain. When Britain declared that the Smith regime had violated this legal relationship the United States supported Britain. Within this context the United States could support Britain in its call for sanctions against the illegal regime.

This same approach apparently carried over in the relationship between Portugal and her territories in Africa. George Bush told the Security Council on November 22, 1973:

> Under international law, sovereignty over the Portuguese territories is invested in the state of Portugal. Now we recognize Portugal's sovereignty, even while we continually urge Portugal, as we do, to permit the exercise of self-determination in these territories.

TWO DIFFERENT PERSPECTIVES

African nations and the United States see the world from two different perspectives. Most of Africa wants secure nationhood, political stability, improved education, expanded health facilities, and genuine economic progress. But the going is difficult. And the unfinished struggle for freedom in Southern Africa is part of this perspective. In Southern Africa the mass of the people--the Africans--are not free to build their own institutions or to find their own national identity; minority white regimes are trying to keep them in subservience, and this has resulted in racial confrontation.

In contrast the United States, including the government and most of its people, feels generally satisfied with the world as it is since Americans have, relatively speaking, good educational and health facilities, national identity, and economic security--and they want to keep what they have. They do not want their own world to be disturbed by reminders of gross injustice and inequality elsewhere. The dynamics of the Third World of which Africa, and certainly Southern Africa, are a part are disturbing; Americans are generally uncomfortable in the presence of the dynamics of the Third World. There is relatively much more comfort and ease in the seeming stability of the white South African world. Nevertheless there is always the annoying feeling that even in that relatively comfortable environment everything is

not quite all right. But there is also the seemingly
naive hope that somehow it will be possible for things to
change in Southern Africa with little or no inconvenience.
And this simply is not so.

To avoid facing the uncomfortable reality of the
dynamics of change in Southern Africa, the United States
has taken a number of protective actions. For example it
has resigned from the U.N. Committee on Decolonization.
It had been embarrassing for the United States to be con-
stantly the butt of criticism not only of African countries but of some Asian countries and the Communist countries while it was trying to participate half-heartedly
in a committee whose function was to implement the anticolonial resolution on which the United States had abstained in 1960. Similarly the United States did not accept an invitation to attend the Oslo Conference held in
April 1973. The argument might have been given privately
that the conference could not be effective or that it
would be unrealistic. But the fact is that it would have
been an embarrassment to the United States to be confronted with the dynamic demands of the Third World countries in Africa. And the United States did not take a
seat on the U.N. Council for Namibia because to have done
so would have meant an acceptance of the logic that the
United Nations and the Republic of South Africa are in
direct confrontation over the issue of the independence
of Namibia.

Perhaps one of the clearest examples of the problem
of U.S. policy in a dynamic Third World context is on the
issue of the recognition of the Republic of Guinea-Bissau.
It may be possible to argue about the actual percentage
of the territory of Guinea-Bissau controlled by the PAIGC
as against that controlled by the Portuguese. However,
the point is that the U.S. government believed, or seemingly wanted to believe, that the Portuguese, not the
PAIGC, controlled three-fourths of Guinea-Bissau. But
most of the members of the United Nations believed the
contrary--that the PAIGC had sway over most of Guinea-
Bissau and the allegiance of most of its people. It was
comforting to the United States to accept a legalistic
approach to the issue of recognition that involved secondary questions such as the location of the Guinea-
Bissau capital. Pointing to a large tree in one of the
liberated areas of Guinea-Bissau, Cabral said to a visitor, "You see, once we have independence this wouldn't
be bad as a capital for our country: a tree where you
could rest after a trip to the villages."[23] If the

United States had really wanted to recognize the Republic of Guinea-Bissau a way could have been found to have done so.

The sad fact is that U.S. policy is not related to the dynamics of change in Africa nor to the reality of the Third World. On the contrary it relates most effectively to the static reality of the status quo that, as events have demonstrated, is likely to be temporary. Thus U.S. policy is one of accommodating the white and European regimes, of hypocritically emphasizing peaceful change, of avoiding confrontation, and of carrying on "business as usual." The official attitude toward liberation movements is at best paternalistic. On the whole the Nixon administration merely pursued a policy that had been in existence for the previous 20 years. However, there was less pretense; consequently there were more negative votes than either abstentions or affirmative votes on the key resolutions in the United Nations. The attitude seemingly expressed by the Nixon administration was, "We are a big power and we are no longer going to be pushed around by these mini-Republics."

Can the United States continue to get away with pursuing this type of policy on Southern Africa? Of course America is a big and powerful country and therefore can withstand a great deal of international animosity. But if the present policy continues it will be at considerable cost. First, there will be periods of great tension with many countries in the world. The kind of criticism the United States has been subjected to over the last two years since being saddled with the Byrd Amendment is a small sample of what may follow. Second, as the crisis in Southern Africa deepens, as I believe it will, the United States may well be subjected to joint and concerted action by many of the countries of the Third World. There has been some indication of the possibilities of such joint action in the recent crisis in the Middle East and in the embargo on oil to countries aiding Israel. It is by no means inconceivable for the African countries, joined by some of their friends elsewhere in the world, to undertake similar action.

Third, if present U.S. policy continues the United States can hardly expect good relations to be established when independent states emerge in all of Southern Africa. Although the United States could survive without having the best of relations with countries controlled by African majorities in all of Southern Africa, it would not be a simple burden to bear.

Finally, if the present policy continues in the face of an increased crisis in Southern Africa it can add to tensions on the home front. In his book The Great Powers and Africa, Nielsen said that once the "Vietnam agony" was over, Southern African issues would be "the next foreign policy focus. . . ."[24] This prediction has not as yet been borne out. The "next" focus has in fact been the Middle East, not Southern Africa. Yet I believe that there will be a major focus on Southern Africa in the near future. A growing number of segments in American society are not only conscious of the struggle in Southern Africa but are keenly dissatisfied with American policy toward it. As yet the coalitions of concerned citizens are not very large although there has been increasingly effective action by churches, by some student groups, and by some community organizations.

The most effective action has been and probably will be taken by the various elements in the black community. The congressional black caucus has provided a legislative focus for this concern. The first national black convention held in Gary, Indiana, in March 1972 gave primary attention to the question of U.S. policy toward Africa. On May 27, 1972, the number of people (mainly black) celebrating African Liberation Day was estimated as high as 30,000. They gathered from all over the country to press for support of the liberation struggles of Africa and for a change in U.S. policy. A permanent organization, the African Liberation Support Committee, has grown out of this effort. When the first shipment of chrome from Rhodesia came into a Louisiana port in March 1972, it was a combination of black longshoremen and students from Southern University in Baton Rouge that mounted a protest demonstration against the violation of sanctions. And in the fall of 1973 and spring of 1974 a coalition of organizations in port cities such as Baltimore, Philadelphia, New York, and Boston, led primarily by black longshoremen, delayed by their protest and boycott, and in some cases actually prevented, the unloading of some Rhodesian metals. In early 1974 the annual convention of the international longshoremen voted officially to refuse to unload any further shipments from Rhodesia.

This may be only a beginning. Such efforts will increase as the internal struggle in the Southern African countries deepens--many Americans understand the connection between the struggle for equality at home and the struggle for liberation abroad.

THE POSSIBILITY OF CHANGE IN U.S. POLICY

Can the United States basically change its policy toward the liberation struggle of Southern Africa?--it would be difficult without some rather fundamental changes within the country itself. Nevertheless one lives in hope. But rather than trying to blueprint the elements of a different policy, it should be noted that a new policy, adequate to meet the demands for change in Southern Africa, would be a positive one. And it would be geared to support for the liberation struggles rather than to support for the minority regimes. With this change of orientation a whole set of specifics would become possible, such as massive support for the liberation movements; large contributions to the U.N. Trust Fund for Southern Africa; acceptance of a position on the U.N. Council for Namibia; the grant of political asylum to refugees from Southern Africa; a ban on oil prospecting in South Africa by American firms; and a move toward the withdrawal of American capital from countries controlled by white-minority regimes.

NOTES

1. Waldemar Nielsen, _African Battleline_ (New York: Harper and Row, 1965).
2. Bruce Oudes, "Sacred Cows and Silver Linings," _Africa Report_, November-December 1972, p. 9.
3. Johannesburg _Star_, January 5, 1974.
4. Immanuel Wallerstein, "From Nixon to Nixon," _Africa Report_, November 1969.
5. Eduardo Mondlane, _The Struggle for Mozambique_ (Baltimore: Penguin Books, 1969), p. 50.
6. Colin Legum and Margaret Legum, "South Africa in the Contemporary World," _Issue_, Fall 1973.
7. _Africa-Asia_, September 20, 1971.
8. William Minter, _Portuguese Africa and the West_ (Baltimore: Penguin Books, 1972), p. 35.
9. United Nations Association--U.S. National Policy Panel, _South Africa: Proposals for Americans_, 1971.
10. Legum and Legum, op. cit.
11. John Blashill, "The Proper Role of U.S. Corporations in South Africa," _Fortune_, July 1972, p. 49.
12. Corporate Information Center, National Council of Churches, _Church Investments, Corporations and South Africa_ (New York: Friendship Press, 1973).

13. U.S. Department of State, Employment Practices of U.S. Firms in South Africa, February 1973.

14. Diane Polan, Irony in Chrome: The Byrd Amendment Two Years Later, Carnegie Endowment for International Peace, 1973.

15. Washington Post, December 16, 1973.

16. Stephan Park, Business as Usual: Transactions Violating Rhodesian Sanctions, Carnegie Endowment for International Peace, 1973.

17. Letter from Edward Holmes, of the U.S. State Department, to Richard Parker (United Church of Christ), November 21, 1968.

18. Arthur M. Schlesinger, Jr., 1,000 Days: John Kennedy in the White House (Boston: Houghton Mifflin Co., 1965), p. 562.

19. John Marcum, "The Politics of Indifference: Portugal and Africa, A Case Study in American Foreign Policy," Issue 2, no. 3 (Fall 1972): 12.

20. Statement of Henry Kissinger, reported in State Department Bulletin, January 14, 1974, p. 25.

21. Christian Science Monitor, November 21, 1973.

22. Legum and Legum, op. cit.

23. Gerard Chaliand, "The Legacy of Amilcar Cabral," Ramparts, April 1973, p. 19.

24. Waldemar Nielsen, The Great Powers and Africa (New York: Praeger, 1969), p. 363.

In commenting on Houser's comprehensive, informative, and well-documented treatment of U.S. policy toward Southern Africa I will focus primarily upon what he calls the reality of the subcontinent. First it should be noted however that there exists the grim possibility of a race war in Southern Africa in the not-inconceivable near future. The change-over of government in Portugal and its effect on the resolving of the wars of liberation in the Portuguese territories must lead to a change in strategy by the white-minority racist regimes of South Africa and Rhodesia. It is quite possible that their reaction to the assumption of political power in the Portuguese territories might advance the probability of racial conflict in Southern Africa.

There are three points that I consider important to an appreciation of Houser's study: the need for the United States to change its policy toward Southern Africa; the possible impact of a tough U.S. policy toward Southern Africa; and the fallacy underlying the argument for continued American cooperation with the racist regimes of South Africa and Portugal and the colonialist wars of Portugal.

Houser identifies U.S. policy toward Southern Africa as marked by a contradiction between stated policy and practice. This contradiction arises from the fact that America's perceived military and economic interests in Southern Africa outweigh its moral judgment and its sense of justice and humanity; this has bedeviled American policy, Houser notes, causing it to lag "well behind the changed circumstances in Africa."

SOUTHERN AFRICA AS A UNIT

An important contribution of Houser's study is that it treats the Southern African subcontinent as a unit on the basis of a similar configuration of political and economic problems in the constituent countries. And this is the reality to which American policy must address itself. For the same reason any international action to remedy the situation in the various countries must be concerted and directed to all the territories simultaneously,

if only because the minority white regimes of the area
have constituted themselves into a bloc--the white re-
doubt--to frustrate the emergence of majority rule.

Houser suggests that the white regimes in Southern
Africa are going to be under increasing pressure from the
freedom fighters, the domestic insurgents, the African
states, and certain quarters of the international community. All the Portuguese territories will have become
independent by the end of 1975 and it is now clear that
events in Rhodesia are leading to some form of majority
rule. The situation in Namibia will then come to a head
and can be resolved in only one way--the enforcement of
international decisions on the future of the territory.

South Africa will be the toughest nut to crack. The
verligtes are fortified by a fundamentalist ideology of
race that amounts to a divine revelation. In addition
the regime disposes of a formidable security system designed to cope with both internal and external threats.
However, despite all this the signs are that the economic
disaffection in South Africa exemplified by the recent
strikes will be transformed into political unrest.

U.S. ENTANGLEMENT IN SOUTHERN AFRICA

The sections of Houser's study that deal with U.S.
entanglements with the racist regimes and with Portugal
are particularly instructive: the fact that the network
of relationships consists of trade, investment, military
cooperation, supply of equipment, other cooperative
schemes, and diplomatic relations. There are no direct
relations with Namibia or Rhodesia but South Africa is
always a convenient conduit. Relations with Portugal and
the attitude toward the Portuguese territories in Africa
are undoubtedly undergoing feverish reappraisal following
the change of government in Lisbon. American assistance
to Portugal has ostensibly been given under NATO aus-
pices; but Portugal has never hesitated in turning this
to its military advantage in its colonial wars in Africa.
It is to be hoped that the new Portuguese government will
truly break with the past and come to terms with the nationalist movements on the basis of independence. This
will take American policy off the hook as far as the Portuguese territories are concerned.

Most official explanations of American prevarication
over Southern Africa have never been convincing and the
nature of the collapse of the fascist regime in Portugal

gives little credence to most of the diplomatic rationalization that had been coming from the State Department. U.S. officials are correct however in pointing out that there is a lack of strong public opinion in support of a tough U.S. policy in Southern Africa. Annual surveys carried out by the University of Michigan's research center indicate an alarming decline, particularly from 1964, in the confidence of the American people in their government. Political analysts are not unduly alarmed by the overall government crisis to which the Watergate affair is only a contributory factor, as they regard this state of affairs as signifying a mature stage of a political system. Yet it is this development--giving political representatives a sense of lack of mandate from the public--together with the naturally high degree of sensitivity of democratic politicians to public opinion as well as to the inexplicable, or perhaps conspiratory, neglect of Southern Africa by the national mass media that inhibit American policy from taking a radical and tough stance against the minority regimes in Southern Africa.

THE RESPONSIBILITY OF THE AFRICAN GOVERNMENTS

Clearly Africans, their governments, and their friends in the United States have a great responsibility in bringing before the American public the reality of the situation in Southern Africa. So far the African governments have hardly made any effort to mobilize American public opinion in support of African problems. It seems high time for African governments to take concerted action to put their case to the American public. South Africa, which has no case at all, manages to influence American centers of power in its favor through a consistent propaganda campaign. Admittedly South Africa has powerful allies in the U.S. corporate community and certain racist circles. However, the rest of Africa is not without friends in the United States; but to mobilize them, to maintain and channel their interest, and to augment their ranks with as yet uncommitted or uninterested groups requires an African effort that has as yet not been forthcoming. The situation in Southern Africa is primarily an African problem that cannot be delegated. To change the policies of other governments relative to this problem will require a tremendous effort in those capitals in which Africans wish to influence policy.

A reality of the Southern African situation is the internal politics of the liberation movements. This has received scant attention both from scholars and press correspondents. It is becoming increasingly apparent that the squabbles and splits that have been a feature of the liberation movements are not entirely tribalistic in nature or simply prompted by the protracted and frustrating struggle; they are, above anything else, manifestations of fierce internal ideological clashes. When the nationalist movements were driven underground in Southern Africa in the early 1960s part of their leadership that escaped mass arrests, detentions, and imprisonment fled to neighboring black Africa where they regrouped to organize insurgency against racist regimes. This old leadership is still largely in power; but a new and younger leadership cadre is emerging within the movements. This younger group has been trained and groomed in socialist countries or in Africa by socialist experts. This has sometimes resulted in grave outbursts of differences between the Western-educated older nationalists and the socialist revolutionaries who are mostly those actually bearing arms. The conflicts usually arise on the issue of what types of societies should emerge from the ruins of the existing systems. Contrary to what cynical observers may be led to think, such a question has crucial strategic relevance in the actual liberation efforts; for in their competition for mass support with the racist regimes the guerrillas must outdo their enemy by promising a better future to the ordinary man. A socialist has no problem in conjuring up a rosy future for the black majority in white-dominated Africa where the national resources are unequally distributed among the different racial groups. Thus it is in the course of answering this vital and strategic question of the nature of a future society that grave clashes flare up, with the older nationalists preferring a modified Western system and the younger socialists advocating a radical reorientation of their societies. The more protracted the struggle for liberation becomes, the more likely that the older "moderate" leadership will be replaced. It would seem to be in the long-term interest of the United States that independence in Southern Africa emerge under this leadership. There is no doubt that majority rule will eventually come to Southern Africa, and it would seem to be eminently sensible for Americans to cultivate the groups that will ultimately rule the countries of the region.

RESPONSE TO A TOUGH U.S. POLICY

How is the Southern African situation likely to respond to a tough and African-oriented American policy? This question must be viewed in the context of how a speedy revolution can be brought about. A coalition of the three forces already operating against racist regimes can lead to majority rule in the foreseeable future. The first force is the liberation movements. The second is comprised of the black peasants, wage-earners, and political movements and organizations such as the African National Council in Rhodesia and the Bantustans in South Africa; this group is trying to hammer out and wring out political settlements and economic concessions from the whites. These two forces have no problems in coalescing. In fact indications are that in Rhodesia they are merging in a significant way. During the military thrusts of guerrillas the fighters have had no problem in passing their messages to the people through traditional religious leaders; these have become the main transmitters of the war messages from the liberation movements to the peasants. The Rhodesian regime is now confessing that it is dealing with a vast army of guerrillas that has merged with the peasants.

The third force consists of dissidents within the white elements themselves. The chief representative of these in Rhodesia is the Rhodesia Party, a recent breakaway faction of Smith's ruling Rhodesia Front. The fact that must always be borne in mind is that the so-called white redoubt is not a monolithic white society entirely lacking in self-destructive factionalism. Herbert Adam has argued very forcefully that, if anything, white oligarchies will destroy themselves.[1] In support of his argument he points to the failures of nationalist movements in the late 1950s and early 1960s; the ability of the apartheid system to offer limited satisfaction to its black majority; the military weaknesses of black African states precluding them from mounting a military confrontation with powerful white Africa; the relatively recent (but what I consider to be already extinct) efforts by very few black states to come to terms with racist white Africa through dialogue; and what he thinks is a grave lack of unity in the guerrilla movements. In short he concludes that external challenges to white regimes are too weak and therefore the hopes for their

destruction must be pinned on their own endogenous negative forces. As an important rider to his thesis he sees
racial or ethnic conflicts in plural societies as a function of competition for limited resources. As the material
resources of such societies increase so too do the conflicts tend to disappear.

While there is nothing natural preventing the emergence of multiracial societies in Southern Africa, and
while the white regimes are likely to crumble from within,
I disagree very strongly with much of this analysis, which
seems to underestimate the growing African political and
economic aspirations and consequently arrives at the wrong
conclusion that Africans can be satisfied within the framework of the apartheid system.

The implications of this argument go a long way toward supporting continued American economic relations with
Southern Africa. There can be little doubt that American
officials draw upon such so-called scholarly works when
they claim to see in white Africa internal dynamics for
change that will render not only violence but even outside
pressure unnecessary. In its total perspective the argument runs as follows: the United States and its allies
must continue to invest in and trade with white Africa to
stimulate economic growth, which in turn will encourage
the whites to share the resultant wealth equitably among
the members of the different racial groups. How on earth
the crumbs falling from the sumptuously provided table of
the rich and prosperous white baas will transform into
political self-determination for the blacks is never explained. One may very well ask whether there is any evidence that the whites, particularly in South Africa, are
sharing the fruits of their current healthy economy with
their black fellow citizens.

White officials in Southern Africa and some scholars
who are sympathetic to these regimes go to painful lengths
in trying to show that the real wages of the blacks have
been increasing in proportion to the region's economic
expansion. Beyond manipulating the figures so that they
can say what officials want them to say, there is the per-
verted exercise of comparing black wages in white South
Africa with those of their counterparts in black Africa.
Some do not even have any scruples about comparing the
standard of living of Africans suffering similar forced
poverty at the hands of the Portuguese with that of Rhodesian and South African blacks, and then telling the
world that the latter are a lot better off. At worst
nothing can be more of an underestimation of the black

man's intelligence. And at best this is a political game
designed to obscure the naked truth. First, even if statistical data can be twisted to demonstrate that the
blacks of Rhodesia and South Africa earn more now than
they did ten years ago, the bare fact of their slavery
remains that the gap between white wages and black wages
in the same country has been widening at an alarming rate
during the same period. Even worse is the fact that the
cost of living has been rising at a much faster rate than
the rate of increase in black wages. It may turn out,
when the increased basic necessities of an average black
family are taken into consideration, that the black worker
has actually grown poorer than he was ten years ago. It
must also be pointed out that blacks in white-dominated
Africa do not sit down to compare their economic lot with
that of their brothers and sisters in black Africa.
Naturally they compare their standard of living with that
of their white neighbors and white coworkers. Furthermore the whites are using the wealth of the Southern African countries to build huge defense systems against the
forces of majority rule. Obviously a prosperous Southern
Africa works against the interests of the Africans.

In view of these fallacies of the arguments for continued economic relations with white Africa, how can a
tough policy against the racist regimes help to bring
about a coalition of the forces noted above? American
support for guerrilla movements would not only boost their
already high morale but would also increase their prestige
in the eyes of the white dissidents, and thereby bring
these two groups together. The termination of U.S. diplomatic, economic, and military support for the white regimes will effectively isolate them and force them to seek
compromises with the blacks. It has been shown by Colin
Legum and Margaret Legum that Western pressures on Southern Africa are dynamically related to internal forces of
change, since any threats in the past to isolate South
Africa have frequently led to internal explosive situations that have been accompanied by a softening of apartheid policies.[2] The analysis by Legum and Legum is supported by current developments in Rhodesia, laboring
under international economic embargo and threatened with
isolation by the emergence of a black revolutionary government in Mozambique.

The difficulties being experienced by the whites in
Rhodesia are compelling them to consider a settlement
with the guerrilla movements, as evidenced by the contacts
between Rhodesian blacks and whites in Lusaka in December
1973.

On the other hand Savory was much more radical in his suggestion, which was to settle the war once and for all by negotiating the country's political future with the liberation movements. The subsequent uproar from other white leaders against what they regarded as an irresponsible suggestion by Savory forced him to change his statement slightly to say that he had meant nationalist leaders now in prison and detention. However that may have been, the bielections showed that almost 28 percent of the white electorate are now in favor of sitting down with black nationalists, though the whites are somewhat still opposed to a settlement with the people who are actually fighting. In short, international pressures have the wholesome effect of instilling sense in the whites to come to terms with the aspirations of the black majority. This casts serious doubts on the current thinking of American officialdom that outside interferences force the racists to fortify their apartheid laagers.

There is an additional, and somewhat intriguing, argument advanced in favor of continued American economic participation in Southern Africa. It is an argument that carries very little weight with those familiar with the workings of imperialism. It is based on the fact that imperialists, when engaged in their enterprise, will always use philanthropic and humanitarian sentiments as a cloak for their economic motives. Thus it is noted that if the United States as well as its Western allies cut off their trade with and investment in Southern Africa it will be the black man who will suffer first. Nothing could be more removed from the facts; domestic colonial systems such as in Rhodesia and South Africa do not respond to international economic siege by forcing their black subjects into further economic deprivation. In actual fact the whites get hit harder by international economic action long before the black masses feel its impact. The imported goods, which are always destined for the whites, become scarce and prices go up, increasing the cost of living for the whites to almost unbearable proportions. To see this one need only look at the prices of automobiles in Rhodesia. At the same time domestic agricultural products--now no longer exported--become so abundant that they glut the market, thereby forcing their prices down to well within reach of the poorly paid African. In actual practice the racist regimes try to control prices, but nevertheless the forces of the market still produce this reverse type of situation so that on the whole it can be argued that international sanctions against white Southern Africa do not generally hurt the blacks.

Moreover such an economic siege scares away white immigrants. For instance Rhodesia has been registering more losses than gains in its white immigration balance sheets. Only diehard racists have continued to trickle to Rhodesia from overseas. And it is a combination of these racists and the South Africans who for example are running the only institution of higher learning in Rhodesia. The effect of this, as might have been expected, has been the intensification of racism and the exposure of black students to mass arrests and imprisonment by the Rhodesian government. In any case these flighty racists are not useful for the defense of the minority regime, as they come under expatriate terms. But the wholesome thing about the imbalance between white emigration and immigration is that jobs previously reserved for whites open up to blacks. If on the other hand the siege is accompanied by guerrilla attacks most of the male population is drafted into the army. And as the military is a preserve of the whites additional jobs in the economy fall to the blacks. So for the first time in the long history of a domestic colonial system the black subjects begin to enjoy some measure of economic mobility in their own country.

This is not all. It is erroneously believed overseas that an international siege compels the white rulers to use the available economic resources to look after the whites and forget the blacks. Nothing of course could more greatly accelerate a black revolution than such an obvious policy--and the whites know it. The fact is that the white ruling group soon finds itself involved in the competition with the guerrillas for the hearts of the black peasants and wage-earners. In an effort to outbid the liberation movements massive capital is diverted to the African rural areas frequently neglected in peacetime. For the first time the idea of the African paying for his own development is shelved and the white taxpayer's money flies with amazing ease to the black areas. Currently Rhodesia, apart from constructing concentration camps for short-term purposes, is with the help of South Africa improving the agricultural situation of the so-called tribal areas on the northeast border, where the war has been raging. It is most likely that when the war front reaches the major urban areas there will be massive increases in black wages--or will that be too late?

In attempting to refute the argument that American economic action against Southern Africa would hurt the

African, I have tried to sharpen the edge of Houser's message appealing to American leaders to support economic action against the white minority regimes in Southern Africa.

NOTES

1. Herbert Adam, _Modernizing Racial Domination_ (Berkeley: University of California Press, 1971).
2. Colin Legum and Margaret Legum, "South Africa in the Contemporary World," _Issue_, Fall 1973.

Houser's study is a broad general review of current U.S. policy toward the white regimes in Southern Africa, whereas any complete review of American policy in this region would have to include some consideration of our relations with Botswana, Lesotho, Swaziland, Malawi, Zambia, and perhaps even Tanzania and Zaire. The absence of this information detracts from the comprehensiveness, though not from the validity, of Houser's work.

In general this writer agrees with Houser's analysis and his orientation to Southern African issues--particularly his argument about the continuity of U.S. policy across Democratic and Republican administrations, and his assumptions that rightly point out that any relevant policy must accept the protracted struggle for liberation as a central factor of Southern African life. Houser and I seem in agreement on ends but we look at Southern Africa from quite different perspectives. He is primarily a lobbyist and activist; my orientation is essentially that of an academic.

This comment will focus on the international structure within which Southern African policy is being made, the regional context in which it is being implemented, and the strategic appraisals which currently appear to guide policy choices.

The evolution and development of U.S. foreign policy toward Southern Africa does not take place in a vacuum. Events in other parts of the world, shifts in relations between the major powers, and alterations in the posture taken toward Southern Africa, the continent of Africa, and the Third World by other Western and Communist powers--all of these affect policy.

THE CHANGING STRUCTURE OF INTERNATIONAL RELATIONS

Recent years have seen substantive changes in Western strategic planning and in the defense structure associated with that planning. From the vantage point of the United States these changes have been most markedly noticed in the rapprochement with the Soviet Union, the opening of relations with China, the gradual cutting back of American armed forces, and the reduction of America's

forward commitments around the world. To a lesser degree
the United Kingdom's all but complete withdrawal from
East of Suez, and decolonization generally, reflect concerns not dissimilar to those motivating American policy
makers.

In the current era the Western foreign policy of containment and the associated military strategy of deter-
rence--practiced since World War II--have lost their validity. In America the Vietnam experience has resulted
in the collapse of domestic support for a U.S. role as
world policeman or, as Kissinger has more delicately put
it, there is "a reluctance to sustain global involvements
on the basis of preponderant American responsibility."[1]

The Soviet Union has achieved military parity with
the United States--the SALT agreement recognizes this with
regard to nuclear weapons--and with the expansion of its
navy the Soviet Union has achieved global superpower
status that only the United States possessed for most of
the post-World War II era. The multiple efforts to re-
align relations with the Soviet Union and China have been
followed in America by a call for reassessment of relations within the Atlantic alliance, with Europe generally,
and with Japan. Some suggest that we are moving into an
era of "five major units--the United States, the Soviet
Union, China, Japan, Western Europe."[2]

The changes in the international system have many
profound implications for the future shape of international relations, for strategic planning, and for diplomatic and military interactions in the years ahead. There
is considerable informed speculation on these matters.[3]
Current strategic thinking generally argues that by accepting and legitimizing their nuclear parity, the Soviet
Union and the United States have substantially reduced
the potential for general war. Instead, it is now predicted that violence and conflict, when it erupts, will
increasingly be in peripheral areas: "from a military
viewpoint, the Third World is emerging as the principal
focus of political-military confrontation between the
United States and the Soviet Union."[4] This thesis is now
regularly reiterated by informed policy makers. While
serving as American deputy secretary of state, Kenneth
Rush commented:

> Any survey of the future role of the devel-
> oping world must also note that this area
> will probably be the greatest source of
> violent conflict for the remainder of the

century, as poverty, maldistributed income,
or sectarian and communal differences fuel
internal violence or even pit one nation
against another.[5]

From the vantage point of the West this expectation
of Third World conflict necessarily reflects its own di-
minished influence and domination over these areas.
Whether from internal strife fostered by numerous causes
or from the increased challenge posed by other powers,
U.S. and Western security planners face difficult choices
about how to limit the erosion of their long-standing
domination of the world; although Western goals are rare-
ly stated so bluntly there can be little doubt that Western policy discussions fundamentally center on this objective.

As domestic support for imperial ambitions has dwin-
dled, American policy makers have evolved a multifaceted
holding operation. First there is the general detente
with former foes in the Communist bloc. This has less-
ened the possibility of direct conflict--at least between
the United States and either the Soviet Union or China.
Second, and in many ways as interesting and subtle as detente, is the assistance and encouragement offered to regional powers who will act as proxies to sustain major
Western interests. Samuel Huntington has noted, "Region-
ally dominant powers or 'local Leviathans' have begun to
emerge: Brazil in South America, South Africa in Southern Africa, Israel in the Middle East, Iran in the Persian
Gulf, India on the subcontinent, North Vietnam in Indochina."[6] An interesting perspective emerges: at the very
time that there is an easing of bilateral relations between the great powers, there is simultaneously developing
the possibility of sharpened new competition to enlist regional allies.

It is likely that domestic political resistance to
direct intervention will combine with continued international political competition to push the major powers toward seeking reliable regional allies. Although the demands of these relationships will surely be more flexible
than those operative during the height of the cold war--
if for no other reason than that there may be more com-
petitors--there will still be strong efforts made to distinguish friends from either neutrals or foes. Moreover--
and this is central to the Southern African situation--
those regional powers that are committed to help themselves militarily and to align solidly with one side or

another are not likely to be rejected in an era when intervention will be more difficult and the international system more fluid.

THE NIXON DOCTRINE AND SOUTHERN AFRICA

In the United States, Vietnam was the all-consuming political issue of the 1960s and early 1970s. The exigencies of this conflict forced Nixon and Kissinger to develop the Nixon Doctrine. Enunciated to explain the rationale for American withdrawal from South Vietnam while continuing to supply armaments and air support, the doctrine called for "regional defense arrangements which provide and take advantage of shared responsibilities."[7] Through this the administration called upon its allies and friends to pick up a greater burden of defense expenditures and to supply a greater portion of manpower needs. Financial aid and "security assistance" were promised to those willing to help themselves, but the main purpose was "the reduction of the American share of defense or financial contributions."[8]

On a global scale there is little doubt that the Nixon administration put its doctrine into operation as rapidly as possible. Nixon called for "strengthening regional forces for cooperation and collaboration" in the Middle East;[9] a similar trend is evident in the Persian Gulf where American interest is growing rapidly due to the energy situation. Nixon noted that "two of the largest Gulf states, Iran and Saudi Arabia, have undertaken greater responsibility for helping to enhance the area's stability."[10] It could hardly go unnoticed, however, that U.S. military sales to these two oil-rich states have been vast in recent years--$3.7 billion to Iran alone.[11] The Nixon Doctrine even lies behind the call for a complete reevaluation of the NATO alliance.[12]

If Vietnam had not brought forth the Nixon Doctrine, it could well be argued that South Africa would have produced it for the United States; the doctrine reiterates on a global scale little more than what South Africa has been begging the major Western powers to allow it to do in Southern Africa for more than a decade. South Africa explains its security strategy in terms of Western defense, regional security, and the preservation of stability on behalf of the "Free World."[13] South Africa is eager both to accept Nixon's call for defense to be "assumed by local or regional forces"[14] and for "close

144

regional cooperation . . . in which the more developed African states can share their resources with their African neighbors."[15] (These remarks were all true for Portugal as well, up to the April 1974 coup.)

South Africa lived happily in the rigid bipolar world when its stern anti-Communism always found favor in the United States. But detente, the changed international structure, and the suddenly altered political situation in Southern Africa are all combining to force South Africa to find new ways to stay close to the United States and Western European powers. Issues that lie ahead on the international agenda include access to raw materials, control and distribution of these resources, and the broad question of ocean shipping. On these matters South Africa is playing a disciplined game of enticing major Western powers with its regional strength, geographic importance, and wealth of natural resources. South Africa's hope is that these economic and strategic inducements will override objections to its racial policies and thereby serve in the current era as its link to Western defense support and cooperation.

STRATEGIC APPRAISALS

In recent years there has been a quantitative, if not qualitative, explosion of Western interest in strategic matters relating to Southern Africa. This has been triggered by the persistent growth and increasing successes of the liberation movements, by the movement of the Soviet navy into the southern oceans, and by the crucial expansion of Western economic ties within Southern Africa.

Despite the fact that there are widely different visions about what the world of Southern Africa is and should be, the vast preponderance of strategic literature is at least implicitly supportive of South Africa (as it had also been of Portuguese colonial rule).[16] The arguments are couched in general terms of "protecting the Cape Route" or "guarding against the Soviet naval threat in the Indian Ocean," and in most cases do not show how the Indian Ocean is threatened or why the Cape Route is in need of protection. Nonetheless these arguments are being used to deepen the commitments of Western countries to South Africa despite the racial implications of such choices.

There is much evidence of such pressure. For example in 1970 Lt. Comdr. Beth F. Coye and her associates wrote in the Naval War College Review, "In the light of U.S.

desire to protect U.S. interests in the Indian Ocean . . .
the United States should encourage the nations of the area
to operate their forces in a multinational naval capacity.
The Navy of the Republic of South Africa should be invited
to participate."[17] The Council of the Atlantic Treaty
Association has called for "naval cooperation among the
Allies . . . outside the geographical boundaries of the
Treaty area."[18]

Alan F. Martin, a U.S. career naval officer with considerable firsthand experience on the Bahrein Islands and
in Indian Ocean waters, has taken a similar position in a
study prepared for the U.S. Naval War College. He urges
the United States to "resume naval cooperation and the exchange of information with South Africa, including participation by the United States and Australia in air reconnaissance and surveillance activity, and assistance in the in-
stallation of command and control facilities in South Africa which are compatible with Allied systems."[19]

The ideas raised by Martin have been echoed by far
more important military leaders in the West. The late
Admiral R. G. Colbert, formerly the president of the U.S.
Naval War College and until his death the commander in
chief of Allied forces in Southern Europe, wrote in The
Atlantic Community Quarterly:

> . . . beyond NATO, south of the Tropic of
> Cancer in the Atlantic, and perhaps in the
> Indian Ocean, a navy to navy approach to
> provide for multinational interlocking ar-
> rangements for the protection and control
> of shipping might be feasible. This could
> be one practical answer to insure the via-
> bility of our vital sea lines of communi-
> cation beyond the immediate NATO area.[20]

Throughout this literature the assumption is that
there is a threat that must be countered. In its most
general form the idea is that Soviet naval growth threat-
ens Western shipping lines of communication and that the
proper defense is closer ties with South Africa.

J. E. Spence in two studies has dealt directly with
the issue of Soviet naval expansion and its implications
for Southern Africa.[21] He sees Soviet goals as limited
to the desire for more political influence in an area
where the USSR has historically been excluded, and he
directly challenges the idea that Western ties with South
Africa are an appropriate way to meet any presumed threat

in the area. Inevitably Western military ties with South
Africa will place the West in the unenviable position of
supporting the white minority against the African majority,
and Spence noted wryly that "if the Soviet Union was bent
on a policy of interference with Western shipping . . .
there are areas where this could be done more easily than
round the Cape."[22] Moreover any military context in which
Soviet and Western fleets were in open conflict would rapidly transcend the Cape area, and the area's influence in
the conflict would not likely be important. A few more
ships or helicopters, or augmented communication and intelligence ties with South Africa would have little importance in the event of a major-power conflict; but they
do have a major impact--both militarily and psychologi-
cally--in the context of racial conflict in Southern Africa. It is this dimension of the strategic equation that
is most often ignored.

CURRENT POLICY

The years of the Nixon administration were marked by
the steady drift of American policy toward positions ever
more favorable to the white regimes. This development
flowed naturally from the demands of Nixon's conservative
political constituency and from the political ideas associated with the Nixon Doctrine. The accession to power
of President Ford is not likely to change the direction
of American policy. And Kissinger will no doubt play a
major role in defining Ford's foreign policy.
Insofar as there is any intellectual grounding for
America's current Southern Africa policy, National Security Study Memorandum 39--a frequently leaked document--is
commonly cited.[23] With the presentation of this memorandum, Nixon and Kissinger evidently selected an option of
increased "communication" with Southern African peoples
as their policy orientation. This choice would soon be
associated with an unwillingness of the United States to
be particularly critical of the white regimes and a general playing down of any moral or political differences
with them. It all flows together. Communication--who
could oppose it? Regional self-reliance sounds good too.
The Southern Africa problem is with the whites in power--
they are the ones communicated with, and they are also
the ones who define the shape of regional stability.[24]
There is both military and diplomatic evidence of
increased U.S. ties: the general slippage with regard to

the South African arms embargo; and the fact that planes and goods that previously were denied U.S. export licenses are now getting them. On its own South Africa is taking numerous steps to align itself with Western defense arrangements. Armed Forces Journal International has reported that South Africa has "copied many of the NATO weapons family. . . . The basic shoulder weapon called for is R-1 and is an exact copy of the NATO FN 7.62 assault rifle."[25] A South African government white paper has reported that South Africa has fully computerized its military stores items by the NATO classification system. And a sympathetic American journalist, allowed to visit the new communications complex in Silvermine near Cape Town, has reported that the South Africans are charting ship movements "in an operational area ranging from the Antarctic to North America and from South America to Bangladesh." More important in the context of U.S./South African alignment is the fact that "the sophisticated electronics gear . . . can flash these ship plottings to war rooms in the U.S. and U.K. in seconds."[26]

The Nixon administration also made considerable efforts to help the Portuguese in their African wars prior to the coup. For example Boeing 707s were sold to Portugal for ferrying troops in and out of Africa. And the much discussed Azores agreement of December 1971 was a major U.S. move toward assisting Portugal; it fit with the overall Nixon defense strategy by preserving a base that was already in operation, by supporting an ally that was eager to be befriended, and by fundamentally adhering to a status quo position in both the Atlantic and Southern Africa. In the aftermath of the coup it is still difficult to see how American policy will develop. The situation with regard to the Azores has not altered and the United States apparently supports Portugal's desire to keep the Cape Verde Islands separated from newly independent Guinea-Bissau. Nonetheless the apparent willingness of the new Portuguese government to turn the government of Mozambique over to FRELIMO and to seek a negotiated settlement in Angola will inevitably mean a reevaluation of U.S. policy in the region. It would be valuable to know more about the significance of the visit to Washington of Admiral Hugo Biermann, South African chief of the armed forces, shortly after the Portuguese coup. And it is hoped that the CIA "destabilization" campaign against Chile will not be a model for U.S. behavior against the victorious liberation movements in Portuguese Africa.

Developments within NATO have paralleled U.S. developments. From 1972 onward increasing attention has been paid by the NATO command to developments outside the NATO area. This command has now been given authority to plan for the military protection of European shipping lines in the southern oceans, and to complete a survey of North American and European oil requirements for the next ten years.[27] Inevitably this type of planning must involve South Africa for she possesses much of the information about shipping in the southern oceans. The difficulty with military planning--as the U.S. experience in Vietnam so sadly demonstrated--is that once put into motion it is difficult to halt. Plans can take on a life of their own that lead to new and more dangerous commitments. The contingency planning now under way is informally linking South Africa with the entire structure of Western defense. By so doing the United States and its major NATO partners are taking the unwise step of aligning their own defense needs with those of South Africa's white minority.

CONCLUSIONS

Within Southern Africa the interplay of Western security interests and white Southern African security interests is a rich mixture of subtlety, ambiguity, and hypocrisy. Nonetheless it is not hard to discern what the concepts of bilateral relations, multinational cooperation, or regional security planning mean in the context of Southern Africa. The Nixon Doctrine and the general Western desire for political and economic stability everywhere have in effect given South Africa the go-ahead to make the region "stable" and "secure" in any manner it chooses. This is facilitated by arms sales, by diplomatic protection, and by substantial economic investment from all major Western countries.

The dangers in this are evident: if the Vietnam experience has taught America and the West anything at all, it should have been that little commitments can grow into large ones and that verbal commitments can be as dangerous as written ones. That is where we stand in South Africa today--on the brink of becoming tied to the defense of the white regime; reconsideration is essential if tragedy is to be avoided.

NOTES

1. Henry Kissinger, "The Year of Europe," Department of State Bulletin 68, no. 1768 (May 14, 1973): 593.

2. New York _Times_, March 6, 1972.

3. See Samuel P. Huntington, "After Containment: The Functions of the Military Establishment," _The Annals_ 406 (March 1973): 1-16. Huntington, a Harvard University professor, is an important and well-informed civilian strategic planner. He presented the core of this article to a hearing-symposium before the Subcommittee on National Security Policy and Scientific Developments of the Committee on Foreign Affairs, House of Representatives.

4. Samuel P. Huntington, _National Security Policy and the Changing World Power Alignment_ (Washington: Government Printing Office, 1972), p. 104.

5. Kenneth Rush, "The United States and the Changing World," _Department of State Bulletin_ 68, no. 1763 (April 9, 1973): 420.

6. Huntington, "After Containment: The Functions of the Military Establishment," op. cit., p. 5. A substantial literature on the evolution of regional systems has begun to emerge. On Southern Africa see Larry Bowman, "The Subordinate State System of Southern Africa," _International Studies Quarterly_ 12, no. 3 (September 1968): 231-61; Timothy M. Shaw, "Southern Africa: Dependence, Interdependence and Independence in a Regional Subsystem," workshop on Southern Africa, Dalhousie University, Halifax, Nova Scotia, 1973, mimeographed; and Christian P. Potholm, "The Limits of Systemic Growth: Southern Africa Today," workshop on Southern Africa, Dalhousie University, Halifax, Nova Scotia, 1973, mimeographed. On other regions see _International Studies Quarterly_ (December 1969); Louis J. Cantori and Steven L. Spiegel, _The International Politics of Regions: A Comparative Approach_ (Englewood Cliffs, N.J.: Prentice-Hall, 1970); and William R. Thompson, "The Regional Subsystem: A Conceptual Explication and a Propositional Inventory," _International Studies Quarterly_ 17, no. 1 (March 1973): 89-117.

7. Melvin R. Laird, _Department of Defense Appropriations for 1972_, hearings before a subcommittee of the Committee on Appropriations, House of Representatives (Washington: Government Printing Office, 1971), p. 20.

8. Richard Nixon, _U.S. Foreign Policy for the 1970's: Shaping a Durable Peace_, a report to the Congress (Washington: Government Printing Office, 1973), p. 9.

9. Ibid., p. 140.

10. Ibid., pp. 140-41.

11. New York _Times_, July 29, 1973.

12. Kissinger, "The Year of Europe," op. cit., and New York _Times_, June 16, 1973.

13. See Adm. H. H. Biermann, "Die Politieke en Militer-strategiese rol van die Republiek," Paratus, September 1972, pp. 10-23, 44, and 61 for the most detailed recent South African statement along these lines; see also South Africa in World Strategy (London: South African Embassy, 1969), and Larry Bowman, "Intercontinental Cooperation and Potential Conflict: Portugal and South Africa," in Conflict in World Politics, ed. Steven L. Spiegel and Kenneth N. Waltz (Cambridge, Mass: Winthrop Publishers, 1971).

14. Richard Nixon, U.S. Foreign Policy for the 1970's: The Emerging Structure of Peace, a report to the Congress (Washington: Government Printing Office, 1972), p. 168.

15. New York Times, February 19, 1970.

16. See S. W. B. Menaul, "The Security of the Southern Oceans: Southern Africa the Key," NATO's Fifteen Nations (April-May 1972) and The Cape Route (London: The Royal United Service Institution, 1970).

17. Lt. Comdr. Beth F. Coye, ed., "An Evaluation of U.S. Naval Presence in the Indian Ocean," Naval War College Review 23, no. 2 (October 1970): 46.

18. Atlantic Community News, June 1973, p. 2.

19. Alan F. Martin, "A U.S. Strategy for the Indian Ocean Area in the 1970's," study prepared for U.S. Naval War College, 1972, pp. 125-26.

20. Adm. R. G. Colbert, "The Shifting Balance of Power at Sea," The Atlantic Community Quarterly 10, no. 4 (Winter 1972-1973): 478.

21. J. E. Spence, "Naval Armaments in the Indian Ocean," paper presented to the Cornell University Conference on Problems of Naval Armaments, 1972, pp. 7-17, and J. E. Spence, The Strategic Significance of Southern Africa (London: Royal United Service Institution, 1970), pp. 40-48.

22. Spence, The Strategic Significance of Southern Africa, op. cit., p. 46.

23. See Ross K. Baker, "Towards a New Constituency for a More Active American Foreign Policy for Africa" (Denver: African Studies Association, 1971), mimeographed; John Seiler, "U.S. Foreign Policy Toward Southern Africa: Continuity and Change" (Johannesburg: The South African Institute of International Affairs, 1973); and Richard C. Giardina, "Southern Africa and the United Nations: The State Department Responds," 1971.

24. For an analysis of how "communication" serves the interest of the white regimes by giving them time to increase their military strength and bolster their internal

security forces, see Larry Bowman, "Southern Africa Policy for the Seventies," Issue 1 (Fall 1971): 25-26.

25. Robert Poos, "The South African Army," Armed Forces Journal International (June 1973), p. 29.

26. Ibid., p. 31. In assessing the validity of this report it is important to note that Poos had an opportunity to visit many military and naval installations in South Africa; he interviewed high-ranking military officers and his report is highly supportive of the South African government position.

27. Texts Adopted by the North Atlantic Assembly at its Eighteenth Annual Session (Bonn: North Atlantic Assembly, November 19 to 24, 1972), p. 14.

5

CONFLICTING ECONOMIC
INTERESTS OF AFRICA AND
THE UNITED STATES

Eleanora West

Robert L. West

There is no way that a discussion of African-American economic relations--taking a view of trends leading into the late 1970s and the 1980s--can avoid somber conclusions. Before becoming engulfed in clouds of pessimism, therefore, it may aid our perspective to recall the serendipitous origins of African-American economic relations.

True, there had been the slave trade in West Africa; but the formal inauguration of U.S. economic relations with Africa was the treaty of commerce and amity between Zanzibar and the United States (1833), which provided for trade on most-favored-nation terms, with fixed minimum tariff charges. Within a decade Zanzibari spices were traded for American greycloth--still called "Americani" in East Africa. And so for a century and more the pattern of commerce persisted: tropical foodstuffs, rare spices and oils, latterly with the addition of nonferrous minerals, were traded for American manufactures and cereals-- that unique product of American energy and technology.

This pattern of commerce persisted profitably but did not grow mightily. European hegemony and the logic of shipping costs combined to restrain African-American economic intercourse to modest levels. Africa is not a major trading partner of the United States. (The term "Africa" will be employed in this study to designate the economic region identified by the United Nations as "African developing countries"--the African continent excluding the Republic of South Africa but including

_____

Shukri Ghanem, Michel J. P. Houde, and Ahmed Siddik Osman assisted in the preparation of this study.

Egypt; in statistical data Botswana, Swaziland, and Lesotho are not included.) The European Economic Community (EEC) and Africa's former metropoles far outweigh the United States in Africa's trade, aid, and investment relations. This has sometimes occasioned mild irritation. African statesmen have been known to complain of American "neglect" and American traders to grumble about preferences negotiated with Africa's dominant trading partners. But on balance the fact that Africa is of secondary economic interest to the United States and the United States is of secondary economic interest to Africa has surely contributed more to cordial relations than to irritation.

Of course in important respects the relationship is one-sided. The United States is an industrial giant. Fluctuations in American economic activity, changes in American commercial policy, or instability of the dollar can exercise a significant indirect impact on African economies. The reverse is not true. This is a conventional caveat, traditionally cited in discussion of this subject. But the conventional meaning is not really the important one in this study; the analogy "America sneezes and Africa catches a cold" is not demonstrably the case, and in any event it is less likely to be true in the future when the full economic weight of Europe and Japan is considered. But it is true that the United States, particularly in periods of stress and change, may adopt policies or embark on lines of action to accommodate its own vital interests and those of its primary trading partners--with unconscious or ill-considered damage to African-American economic relations. African states might do the same, but it is perhaps less likely that American expressions of caution about impending damage would not be heard.

It is important to cite a key distinction between the structure of American international economic relations and that of the other countries which make up the community of developed market economies. More than 30 percent of U.S. foreign trade is with developing countries, and more than one-third of American assets abroad are located in the developing world. This is one-and-a-half times as large as the proportions that obtain for other developed market economies (excepting Japan, which in this respect is similar to the United States): there is substantially less concentration of economic relations with other industrialized countries in the case of the United States than for other developed countries. For the United States the relative proportion of African trade is a small percentage of total trade, aid, and investment relations--but relations with other developing areas are very important.

There is an evident symmetry in Africa's relations with developed market economies other than the United States. For Africa the relative proportion of U.S. trade is small (6 or 7 percent of total foreign trade) and the United States is secondary in aid and investment relations, but Africa's relations with other developed countries are very important. More than four-fifths of Africa's foreign trade and virtually all of its aid and foreign investment relations are with developed countries.

It is precisely the existence of this symmetry that underlies the thesis of this paper. In the late 1970s and 1980s, which we believe will be periods of stress and change, there will be important international economic issues in the relations between the United States and the developing countries. Equally important international economic issues will arise in the relations between Africa and the developed market economies. Because African-American bilateral economic ties are of secondary importance to both parties, the resolution of the important issues may result in adoption of policies and in lines of action taken by both parties with unconscious or ill-considered damage to African-American economic relations. In fact the complementary nature of the African and the American economies--which in the past seemed to assure that the commodities exchanged, by the working of comparative advantage, contributed to reciprocal and mutual benefit--make it quite likely that this process will generate economic conflict between Africa and the United States in the years ahead.

In examining this thesis we will first present reasons for noting that change is occurring in the framework of international economic relations between developed and developing countries. We will then describe the profile of African-American economic relations in the recent past and the trends emerging for the future. Finally we will illustrate the character of the conflicting economic interests of Africa and the United States in the coming period by discussing some of the issues involved in the production and trade of key commodities of significance both to Africa and the United States: petroleum, non-ferrous minerals, and food.

THE CHANGING STRUCTURE OF INTERNATIONAL ECONOMIC RELATIONS

One of the foundations of the political and economic order constructed after the Second World War was the

pattern of trade and payments between the industrialized
countries (of Western Europe, North America, and Japan)
and the less developed countries (of Africa, Asia, and
Latin America). For 20 years--from the end of the 1940s,
when wartime restrictions and controls were relaxed, to
the end of the 1960s--a stable framework was based on the
supply of fuels, minerals, and tropical foods by the less
developed countries in exchange for manufactures and
cereals from the industrial countries. Between the two
groups of countries the terms of this exchange altered
only modestly and slowly over the two decades. With respect to each of the major commodity components of the
exchange, trends were relatively fixed and predictable.

The postwar pattern of international payments, investment, and foreign aid was adapted to these trade flows,
which constituted about one-fifth of all international
transactions. The generally stable trends in the terms
of trade among these major commodity groups, and the financial flows adapted to the trade pattern, established
the development prospects, determined the location of
industries, and sustained the fiscal systems of the developing countries. The stability of this framework was
one of the fundamental conditions permitting the orderly
achievement of decolonization, the localization of military conflicts in the Third World, the limitation of East-
West confrontations around the world, progress toward regional economic integration, and other accommodations that
characterized the international relations of the postwar
period.

Within the framework fuels and minerals were produced
by technologically advanced and highly capital-intensive
methods in developing countries; supplies flowing to developed countries were generally adequate, prices were
low, and real earnings per unit slowly declined. Manufactured goods were produced in industrial countries, and
increasingly behind protective walls in urban centers of
less developed countries, utilizing a slow-changing technology adapted to cheap and plentiful energy, minerals,
and food; trade in manufactured goods grew rapidly among
developed countries, but more slowly and at rising real
prices in trade between developed and developing countries.

At the same time tropical food exports to developed
countries grew in volume relatively rapidly but at declining real prices; domestic food production in less developed countries was technologically stagnant, highly
labor-intensive, and progressively insufficient in volume
to meet growing domestic demand. And cereals produced in

a few developed countries by capital and energy-intensive
methods were supplied to developing countries to fill
domestic food gaps on concessional terms.

Minerals, fuels, and tropical foodstuffs exported by
less developed countries financed purchases of consumer
and capital goods manufactured in industrialized countries. Additional manufactured goods required in development programs were financed through foreign direct investment and borrowing abroad by developing countries.
Cereals were provided from developed countries on foreign
aid or other concessional terms. This system was, however,
in increasingly precarious balance; the persisting trends
within the different commodity components of the exchange
--which were responsible for the stability of the system
over two decades--progressively threatened its disruption.

By the beginning of the 1970s there was much evidence
that the system was breaking down, that the distribution
of relative benefits was growing increasingly uneven, and
that the generally stable trends in the terms of trade
among the commodity groups could no longer be sustained.
The accumulated debt burden became a serious impairment for
some developing countries. World food reserves were exhausted and current supplies were inadequate to fill the
domestic gap in less developed countries; instances of
famine and acute hardship could not be accommodated readily. Foreign aid and borrowing terms hardened. Shortages of some nonferrous minerals and changed relations
between producers and consumers of energy resources significantly altered the terms of trade for food, manufactured goods, and minerals-fuels. Changed net earnings
positions threatened the payments and financing pattern.

The construction of a new pattern of trade and payments not only between developed and less developed countries but also among the developing countries is only
beginning. Some of the future trends that must be accommodated by the new pattern seem evident, such as rising
real costs of food and fuels in international transactions and a reversal of capital flows between industrialized and developing countries. But the future policy regarding the management of energy and other resources is
not yet established and would appear to occupy a crucial
position in the reconstruction process.

Petroleum and associated products constitute by far
the most important commodity in trade between developing
countries and industrialized countries, and in trade among
the less developed countries; changes in unit values have
a substantial, if highly uneven, direct impact on individ-

ual country balance-of-payments positions and financing
flows. But the indirect impact is of even greater importance. Existing technology for production of cereals
and manufactured goods was designed for cheap energy in-
puts--for the terms of trade between energy and other
commodity components of the international trade pattern
of the past 20 years. In an important sense the new pattern of trade and payments must adapt to the altered
terms of exchange between fuels (and some critical nonferrous minerals) and the other components of trade between industrialized and developing countries.

The new framework for trade and payments, critically
dependent on international energy and resources policies
still to be established, will alter the development prospects, the location of industries, and the viability of
the fiscal systems of less developed countries; it will
shift the rates of natural resources exploitation and
consequently the effective relative resource endowments
under utilization in each of the developing countries.
The new pattern that will eventually emerge, with its
associated distribution of benefits, will affect the overall structure of international economic, political, and
security relations. And in the intervening period of uncertainty and adjustment the established structures and
procedures of the past 20 years are likely to function
erratically.

PROFILE OF AFRICAN-AMERICAN ECONOMIC RELATIONS

We will summarize in this section some of the significant characteristics of trade, aid, and investment relations of the United States vis-a-vis developing countries
in Africa, and of Africa vis-a-vis developed market economies and the United States. We will describe the structure of these relations as they existed in the 1960s, and
cite evidence of trend changes appearing in the 1970s.

We will distinguish among groups of African countries
classified by reference to their participation in the production and trade of key commodities in Africa's international economic relations. One such group consists of
the seven African exporters of crude petroleum: Algeria,
Angola, Egypt, Gabon, Libya, Nigeria, and Tunisia. By the
early 1970s each of these countries was a net exporter of
mineral fuels and, except for Angola and Egypt, this commodity class constituted the most important source of export earnings. A second group consists of four African

countries--Guinea, Morocco, Zaire, and Zambia--for which minerals, ores, and nonferrous metals represent the most important class of exports. For the rest of the African countries the most important exports are agricultural products. In this regard we will identify two subgroups: the 14 countries that are major exporters--at least $100 million annual export earnings from agricultural products by 1970--and the other African exporters of agricultural products, for which we will present information on 22 countries.

Not all African countries have a high degree of concentration on a single class of exports. Any system of grouping requires the assignment of countries with relatively diversified structures of production and trade. For example in the petroleum group noted above Angola is also a significant exporter of coffee, Nigeria exports a substantial volume of agricultural products, and Egypt is a major supplier of cotton and textiles; in the minerals-ores-nonferrous metals group Morocco and Zaire also have substantial export earnings from agricultural products; and in the agricultural group Liberian iron ore is an important export. In short the classification of countries does not provide a perfect match to the classification of commodities. But the United States and the rest of the world manage their international economic relations by trading with countries, not with groups of commodity producers irrespective of nationality. And there are important differences among the groups of African countries classified in this way, with respect to the content of their economic relations with the United States and the rest of the world.

Trade Shares and Growth Rates. During the period from 1948 to 1971 the shares in total world trade of the United States, the United Kingdom, and the developing market economies, including Africa, all declined. As shown in Appendix Table A.1 of our study, from 1948 to 1971 the U.S. share of total world exports fell from 24 percent to 14 percent; the U.S. share of imports rose slightly from 13.9 percent to 14.7 percent. Africa's share of total world exports declined from 4.3 percent to 3.9 percent; its share of imports fell from 4.7 percent to 3.7 percent. The significant gainers in world trade shares were Japan and the industrial countries of Europe.

For both Africa and the United States there has been an increase in the annual growth rate of trade over the period from 1961 to 1972. Table 4 shows world exports--

TABLE 4

World Exports, by Origin and Destination, 1961-72

Origin of Exports	U.S. $ Billion	World Total	Developed Market Economies	United States*	Developing Market Economies	Africa	Centrally Planned Economies
			Annual Percentage Growth Rates of Exports to Various Destinations, 1961-66				
World	165.2	9.1	10.2	7.3	6.6	6.3	7.7
Developed market economies	112.6	9.8	10.8	9.5	6.3	5.1	13.0
United States	25.1	6.0	6.9	--	5.2	12.5	-19.7
Developing market economies	33.0	7.2	7.5	4.9	5.7	8.9	11.1
Africa	6.7	9.7	9.4	9.9	8.8	12.2	14.6
Centrally planned economies	19.5	8.0	13.7	-20.2	11.8	14.3	5.4
			Annual Percentage Growth Rates of Exports to Various Destinations, 1967-72				
World	298.2	13.6	14.5	13.3	11.6	10.0	11.6
Developed market economies	213.4	14.6	15.3	15.7	12.2	10.3	12.9
United States	40.2	9.4	10.2	--	7.5	8.3	20.3
Developing market economies	52.7	11.0	11.2	7.8	10.3	8.6	11.7
Africa	11.8	12.6	12.8	4.7	11.0	5.6	14.6
Centrally planned economies	32.3	11.2	13.2	9.8	9.9	9.8	11.1
			Annual Percentage of Exports Going to Various Destinations, 1961-66				
World	165.2	100	67.1	11.2	21.0	4.4	11.4
Developed market economies	112.6	100	73.8	10.9	22.0	5.0	3.8
United States	25.1	100	66.1	--	33.1	3.0	0.8
Developing market economies	33.0	100	71.9	18.7	21.3	3.3	5.7
Africa	6.7	100	80.7	7.7	11.9	7.0	6.4
Centrally planned economies	19.5	100	20.5	0.6	14.4	2.7	64.6
			Annual Percentage of Exports Going to Various Destinations, 1967-72				
World	298.2	100	70.5	12.8	18.8	3.8	10.2
Developed market economies	213.4	100	76.7	13.2	19.1	4.2	3.8
United States	40.2	100	69.0	--	30.1	2.1	0.9
Developing market economies	52.7	100	73.6	18.6	19.8	3.1	5.4
Africa	11.8	100	81.6	6.8	10.3	5.5	6.4
Centrally planned economies	32.3	100	24.1	0.7	15.0	3.2	60.7

Source: United Nations, Yearbooks of International Trade Statistics.

*1960-65 and 1965-70.

by origin and destination--for these years. Total exports from Africa grew at an average annual rate of 9.7 percent in 1961-66, and 12.6 percent during 1967-72. For the same periods the U.S. rates of growth were 6.0 percent and 10.2 percent. However, the average annual rate of growth of exports from the United States to Africa declined from 12.5 percent for 1961-66 to 8.3 percent for 1967-72 while in the same periods the growth rate of U.S. exports rose for developed market economies, developing market economies, and the centrally planned countries of Eastern Europe. The rate of growth of Africa's exports to the United States declined from 9.9 percent in 1961-66 to 4.7 percent in 1967-70 despite increased rates of growth in exports from Africa to developed market economies (9.4 percent to 12.8 percent) and developing market economies (8.8 percent to 11.0 percent). The rate of growth of exports among African countries declined significantly from 12.2 percent in 1961-66 to 5.6 percent in 1967-72.

As a consequence of these growth rates both Africa's share of U.S. foreign trade and the U.S. share of Africa's foreign trade fell steadily over the 1961-72 period. In the 1967-72 period only 2.1 percent of U.S. exports went to Africa, and 6.8 percent of African exports went to the United States. In 1972 imports from developing Africa increased sharply but this was almost totally accounted for by imports from the oil-producing countries of Algeria, Libya, and Nigeria.

Appendix Table A.2 shows the dominance of industrial Europe as a market for Africa's exports and as the source of Africa's imports. Since 1960 Africa has increased its trade with Japan, the centrally planned economies of Eastern Europe, and China. While there will doubtless be some shifts of trade to other parts of the world, it is reasonable to assume that the basic directions of African trade will remain essentially unchanged for the foreseeable future. The industrial countries of Europe include the former metropoles and, as indicated above, many of the economic ties established during the colonial era continue.

Appendix Table A.3 gives the value of U.S. trade for the years 1968 to 1972. Again the importance of the markets of developed economies predominates, but more than 30 percent of U.S. foreign trade is with developing countries.

Commodity Structure of Trade. Not only is Africa's trade characterized by concentration in its direction, but it is also marked by high commodity concentration. By the early 1970s half of Africa's export earnings were supplied by fuels and copper. In 1970 five commodities accounted for 61 percent of all exports from Africa--crude petroleum, copper, coffee beans, raw cotton, and cocoa beans. Appendix Table A.4 shows the proportion of total exports from Africa represented by these commodities and their average annual rate of growth for the years 1965 to 1969. The highest rates of growth were for crude petroleum and copper exports; forest products and iron ore also increased at high rates, although their proportion of total export earnings was not large. Five oil- and copper-producing countries--Libya, Zambia, Algeria, Nigeria, and the United Arab Republic (UAR)--accounted for 50.7 percent of Africa's exports in 1969.

Two major products made up 80 percent or more of the exports in each of 11 African countries in 1970; in 9 other countries two major products had a share of 70 to 79 percent. Nearly two-thirds of the countries of Africa received 60 percent or more of their export earnings from only two commodities. The principal examples of single-product export trade in 1970 were Libya (99.9 percent from crude oil), Mauritania (89.5 percent from iron ore), Burundi (84.4 percent from coffee), Mauritius (90.7 percent from sugar), and Zambia (95.3 percent from copper).

The composition of U.S. foreign trade in 1970 by Standard International Trade Classification (SITC) categories is shown in Appendix Table A.5. Of the U.S. total of $815.2 million in imports from Africa, $495.4 million was coffee, tea, cocoa, and spices; and $213 million was inedible crude materials and mineral fuels. U.S. exports to Africa are chiefly machines and transportation equipment ($454.9 million); cereals and cereal preparations ($115.7 million); and basic manufactures ($111.2 million).

Tables 5 and 6 show the commodity structure of African and U.S. foreign trade as well as the areas of concentration of U.S. trade with Africa.

Tropical foods (chiefly coffee and cocoa) represent 62 percent of all of Africa's exports to the United States and, by comparison, 36 percent of Africa's exports to all of the developed market economies. The United States purchases only a small part of its manufactured-goods imports from developing countries in Africa. In other respects U.S. trade with African nations is similar to its trade with all developing countries.

Africa's trade with the United States is similar in structure to its trade with all developed countries,

162

TABLE 5

Exports of African Developing Countries, 1969 and 1970, by Commodity Classes
and Regions of Origin and Destination
(in millions of dollars)

Commodity Class	Total Imports	Food	Other Agricultural Products	Fuel	Raw Minerals and Nonferrous Metals	Manufactures and Others
S.I.T.C.[a]	0-9	0+1+22+4	2 except 22,27,28	3	27+28+68	5+6+7+8+9 except 68
A) Total 1969 Exports of All African Developing Countries						
To world, total	11,320	3,275	1,375	3,510	2,390	770
To developed market economies	9,210	2,465	935	3,230	2,250	330
To developing and central-plan economies	2,110	810	440	280	140	440
B) 1970 Exports to United States*						
From all African developing countries	815	529	81	99	64	41
From crude petroleum exporters	223	85	14	99	15	10
From nonferrous minerals, metals exporters	59	18	13	--	23	6
From agricultural products: major exporters	491	397	52	--	23	18
From agricultural products: other exporters	42	29	2	--	2	8

aStandard International Trade Classification.

*For exports to United States, "Food" contains S.I.T.C. class 0, only; classes 1+22+4 are included with "Other Agricultural Products."

Sources: United Nations and UNCTAD.

TABLE 6

Imports of African Developing Countries, 1969 and 1970, by Commodity Classes
and Regions of Origin and Destination
(in millions of dollars)

Commodity Class	Total Imports	Food	Fuel	Machinery and Transport Equipment	Manufactures and All Other
S.I.T.C.^a	0-9	0+1+22+4	3	7	2+5+6+8+9 except 22
A) Total 1969 Imports of All African Developing Countries					
From world, total	10,030	1,471	670	3,650	4,239
From developed market economies	7,670	903	165	3,290	3,312
From developing and central-plan economies	2,360	568	505	360	927
B) 1970 Imports from the United States*					
By all African developing countries	987	142	14	455	376
By crude petroleum exporters	468	71	6	218	173
By nonferrous minerals, metals exporters	188	36	1	89	62
By agricultural products: major exporters	289	27	6	132	124
By agricultural products: major exporters	42	8	1	16	17

^aStandard International Trade Classification.

*For imports from the United States, "Food" contains S.I.T.C. class 0, only; classes
1+22+4 are included with "All Other."

Sources: United Nations and UNCTAD.

except that Africa imports a higher proportion of foodstuffs and a somewhat smaller proportion of manufactured
goods from the United States, and markets a smaller proportion of fuels and minerals in the United States as compared with its trade with all developed market economies
(see Appendix Tables A.6 and A.7).

The largest proportion of Africa's exports to the
United States comes from its abovementioned 14 major
agricultural exporters and 7 crude petroleum exporting
countries. And more than half of Africa's imports from
the United States are purchased by the 7 crude petroleum
exporting countries.

The role of African food imports from the United
States, and especially of cereals, merits special note in
describing U.S.-African relations; throughout the 1960s
most of these cereal exports from the United States were
financed on concessional terms, and fulfilled a role in
bridging the food gap between domestic demand and production, chiefly in North African countries.

Foreign Economic Assistance to Africa. A major concern
of the African nations is the realization of economic
development along with growth and change in output. The
goals set for Africa's first and second development decades were the implementation of the development and
growth of manufacturing, iron and steel, and chemical industries; increased educational enrollments; increased
electricity production; additions and improvements in
transportation; and the stimulation of tourism. Concomitant with these goals is the need to increase food production and lessen the need to expend export earnings on
foodstuffs. Except in special cases almost all of the
African countries rely on external economic assistance
assistance and private investment for at least a third of
their resources to finance development.

While the United States was, throughout the 1960s,
and remains at present the second largest supplier--after
France--of bilateral assistance to Africa, it is not generally in a dominating position; EEC countries other than
France and the multilateral agencies provide more external
assistance to Africa than does the United States. This
secondary position of the United States as lender and
donor has defined the chief areas of conflict between
Africa and the United States on questions of aid--and defined them somewhat differently from the conflict-areas
in which the United States is engaged elsewhere in the
world. On the whole U.S. bilateral assistance to Africa

has been perceived at home and abroad as more concerned
with support of developmental goals and less with other
objectives, at least as compared with U.S. aid elsewhere
in the world. In general there have been fewer instances
of conflict about the objectives of U.S. external assistance than encountered elsewhere in the world. But there
is continuing disagreement about the magnitude, the inter-
country distribution, the division between bilateral and
multilateral channels, and the terms of U.S. economic
assistance. None of these areas of conflict could be
described as very serious, but none are likely to diminish
in the future.

The direction of U.S. aid to African countries par-
allels the pattern of U.S.-African trade relations (see
Table 7); of the total flow of official U.S. bilateral
economic assistance to Africa for the 1962-72 period,
41.9 percent was received by the seven crude petroleum
exporters, 24 percent by the exporters of nonferrous
minerals and metals, and 22.1 percent by the major exporters of tropical foodstuffs. Assistance from international organizations to Africa (see Table 8) does not
show a similar concentration and in fact 64.5 percent of
assistance from this source was to the agricultural exporting nations. Among bilateral aid givers only the
United States has attempted to distribute assistance to
most African nations, and it is abandoning this role.

Africa's share in the worldwide official net flow of
external resources from developed market economies and
multilateral agencies declined from an average of 30 percent for the first half of the 1960s to 23 percent for
the second half. Twelve of the Development Assistance
Committee (DAC) countries more than doubled their assistance to Africa during the 1960s, as did the multilateral
agencies. However, Belgium, France, the United Kingdom
and the United States decreased their bilateral aid to
Africa (see Appendix Tables A.8 and A.9). Compared with
the world total there has been a significant decline in
the share of aid resources going to North Africa (19.1
percent in 1960 to 5.1 percent in 1970), while the share
of Africa south of the Sahara has remained at about
17-18 percent.

The largest per capita bilateral assistance from the
United States to Africa was to the four-nation group of
exporters of nonferrous minerals and metals ($27.73 per
capita for the period from 1962 to 1972, as compared with
$6.08 for the small agricultural exporters). On the
other hand international organizations provided the

TABLE 7

U.S. Bilateral Official Economic Assistance to African Developing Countries, 1962-72
(obligations and loan authorizations in millions of dollars)

Commodity Class	Total	Official Development Assistance Grants, Loans, and Technical Assistance	Food Aid	Other Official Economic Loans	Percent of Total	Total Per Capita (dollars)
All African developing countries	4,632	2,198	1,862	572	100.0	$14.84
Crude petroleum exporters	1,940	735	1,000	205	41.9	17.26
Nonferrous minerals, metals exporters	1,111	438	530	143	24.0	27.73
Major agricultural exporters	1,322	854	247	221	28.5	11.29
Other agricultural exporters	259	171	86	3	5.6	6.08

Source: U.S. Agency for International Development.

TABLE 8

Assistance from International Organizations to African Developing Countries, 1962-72
(in millions of dollars)

Commodity Class	Total International Organizations*	World Bank	IDA and IFC	UNDP and U.N.	African Development Bank	European Economic Community	Percent of Total	Total Per Capita (dollars)
All African developing countries	4,694	1,571	972	789	60	1,302	100.0	$15.04
Crude petroleum exporters	1,020	599	157	188	15	61	21.7	9.08
Nonferrous minerals, metals exporters	693	378	85	101	4	125	14.8	17.30
Major agricultural exporters	1,838	557	503	268	19	491	39.2	15.70
Other agricultural exporters	1,143	37	226	232	23	625	24.3	26.79

*Excludes $265.4 million in African regional and unallocated aid.

Source: U.S. Agency for International Development.

largest flow of assistance per capita ($26.79) to Africa's
22 small agricultural exporting nations. Between these
two extremes other bilateral donors and lenders provided
assistance to African countries with which they have special economic and historical associations.

Economic assistance from the United States and the
combined multilateral agencies has shifted during the last
half of the 1960s and even more in the 1970s to greater
emphasis on hard loans and less in the form of grants or
soft loans. In the early 1970s the proportion of grants
to loans was declining, the interest rate was rising, and
the grant-element of loans and of total official development assistance from the United States was declining. The
relatively rapid growth of World Bank lending, together
with the higher borrowing rates of interest confronted in
capital markets, account for the hardening of assistance
from international organizations. This may pose future
problems for some African economies as the repayment of
these loans becomes an increasing burden, but debt-burden
difficulties were not widespread among African countries
at the beginning of the 1970s--in part because many very
low-income countries of Africa have not been considered
eligible borrowers in the past.

Private Investment in Africa. Information relating to the
distribution of private investment flows is more limited
than that for trade and aid flows. Private-flow information is relatively complete only for direct investment.
In 1969-70 Africa accounted for about one-fourth of total
net direct private investment flows from all DAC countries
to all developing countries, thus showing a slight increase in Africa's share from the 1965-69 period. Table
9 shows the regional and sectoral distribution of total
direct investment flows from DAC countries to developing
countries. The dominant sector of direct investment,
both for Africa and all developing market economies, is
in the petroleum industry.

By far the largest share of U.S. direct investment
in Africa is concentrated in the petroleum area. At the
end of 1972 (see Appendix Table A.10) the book value of
U.S. total direct investment in Africa was $3,086 million,
of which $2,254 million was in petroleum; $425 million
was in mining and smelting. Only 1.5 percent of U.S.
assets abroad are represented by direct investment in
Africa. Of this one-third is invested in Libya and another one-third is in Nigeria, largely in petroleum. The
United States and the total community of industrialized

TABLE 9

Regional and Sectoral Distribution of Development Assistance Committee's
Total Direct Investment in Developing Countries, 1965-70
(in millions of dollars)

Region	Year	Petroleum*	Mining	Manufacturing	Other	Total
Europe	1965/66	44	10	124	90	268
	1967/68	19	3	130	55	207
	1969/70	60	5	224	59	348
Africa	1965/66	328	85	89	84	586
	1967/68	352	85	80	65	582
	1969/70	487	58	95	99	739
Latin America and Caribbean	1965/66	-57	99	591	292	925
	1967/68	73	180	540	297	1,000
	1969/70	295	-29	643	306	1,215
Middle East	1965/66	374	1	12	5	392
	1967/68	198	--	7	14	219
	1969/70	243	--	24	15	282
Asia and Oceania	1965/66	62	28	129	117	336
	1967/68	92	37	185	99	413
	1969/70	155	104	147	68	474
All regions	1965/66	751	223	945	588	2,507
	1967/68	734	305	942	530	2,511
	1969/70	1,240	138	1,133	547	3,058

*Includes natural gas.

Sources: U.N. Conference on Trade and Development (UNCTAD), and Organization for
Economic Cooperation and Development (OECD).

countries share a predominance of overseas private direct investments in petroleum, but the degree of U.S. concentration is much greater both in Africa and worldwide.

The distributional pattern of aid and investment among African countries, concentrated in the ways described above, is one of marked inequality. Table 10 presents one way of viewing the distribution of grants, loans, and private overseas direct investment among sub-Saharan African countries. Three of these countries, with a total population of 6 million people and a gross national product (GNP) per capita greater than $240, received the largest per capita grants, loans, and private overseas investments. Seventeen of the poorest sub-Saharan countries, with a total population of 163 million people and a per capita GNP of less than $140, received the smallest amount per capita of aid and private investment.

Summary. Tables 11, 12, and 13 summarize the international economic relations of Africa with the United States and the rest of the world. Trade, aid, and private overseas direct investment are shown in value terms, percentages, and value per capita. The countries that receive the largest proportion of their imports from the United States are also the ones that receive the largest per capita amounts of grants, loans, and private direct investment. These patterns are the context within which future economic relations between the United States and Africa are set.

The countries of Africa enter the mid-1970s in a world in which oil prices are sharply increased from past levels and the developed economies are scrambling to insure themselves sufficient supplies of energy and other mineral resources. For Africa population is growing and food production is lagging behind the growing demand for food; at the same time the world surplus stocks of food are exhausted; major grain deficits are expected for the foreseeable future; and development aid is lagging.

If energy products (oil and natural gas) and non-ferrous minerals and metals are available on terms remotely similar to those of the past decade, the developed countries of the world in the years to come will depend increasingly for these products on developing countries. Energy and mineral resources are unevenly distributed on the African continent. About 67 percent of Africa's exports originate in 11 petroleum and mineral exporting countries. However, Africa's fuel and mineral exports to

TABLE 10

Distribution of Aid among Sub-Saharan African Countries--Grants, Loans, and Private Overseas Direct Investment (PODI)

Per Capita Characteristics	Number of Countries	Population (millions)	(1) Cumulative Grants Received 1960-70 ($ million)	(2) Total Debt Outstanding, End of 1971 ($ million)	(3) Book Value PODI, End of 1967 ($ million)	Per Capita Values for Columns (1)	(2)	(3)
Foreign claims $ 50* PODI $ 10 GNP $140	17	163.1	3,020.1	2,089.0	466.2	18.52	12.81	2.86
Foreign claims $ 50 PODI $ 10 GNP $140	5	38.9	2,117.9	763.6	803.2	54.44	19.63	20.65
Foreign claims $ 50 PODI $150 GNP $140 $240	10	32.3	1,889.5	1,547.3	1,175.5	58.50	47.90	36.39
Foreign claims $150 PODI $100 GNP $240	3	6.0	401.5	1,123.6	985.8	66.92	187.27	164.30
	35	240.3	7,429.0	5,523.5	3,430.7	30.92	22.99	14.28

*Amounts in this column are approximate.

Sources: Organization for Economic Cooperation and Development, Development Assistance, 1972 Review, and World Bank.

TABLE 11

African Developing Countries: International Economic Relations
(millions of dollars)

World Relations, Not Including United States

Commodity Class	Exports, 1970	Imports, 1970	Official Grants Received, 1960-70	Official Loans Balance Outstanding, End 1971	Private Overseas Direct Investment, Book Value, End 1967	GNP, 1969	Population, 1969 (in millions)
All African developing countries	12,455	10,667	12,073	9,484	5,557	47,139	312
Crude petroleum exporters	6,104	4,411	4,575	3,503	2,043	20,022	112
Nonferrous minerals, metals exporters	2,318	1,752	1,940	1,639	1,171	6,846	40
Major agricultural exporters	3,372	3,488	3,085	3,474	1,911	16,277	117
Other agricultural exporters.	661	1,016	2,473	867	432	3,994	43

Relations with United States

Commodity Class	Exports, 1970	Imports, 1970	Bilateral Official Grants Received, 1962-72	Bilateral Official Loans Authorized, 1962-72	Private Direct Investment Book Value, End 1972
All African developing countries	815	987	2,183	2,449	3,086
Crude petroleum exporters	223	468	878	1,062	2,296
Nonferrous minerals, metals exporters	59	188	502	609	384
Major agricultural exporters	491	289	586	736	375
Other agricultural exporters	42	42	218	42	30

Sources: U.N. Conference on Trade and Development, Organization for Economic Cooperation and Development, and U.S. Agency for International Development.

172

TABLE 12

African Developing Countries: International Economic Relations
(percentages)

World Relations, Not Including United States

Commodity Class	Exports, 1970	Imports, 1970	Official Grants Received, 1960-70	Official Loans Balance Outstanding, End 1971	Private Overseas Direct Investment, Book Value, End 1967	GNP, 1969	Population, 1969 (in millions)
All African developing countries	100.0	100.0	100.0	100.0	100.0	100.0	100.0
Crude petroleum exporters	49.0	41.4	37.9	36.9	36.8	42.5	36.0
Nonferrous minerals, metals exporters	18.6	16.4	16.1	17.3	21.1	14.5	12.8
Major agricultural exporters	27.1	32.7	25.6	36.6	34.4	34.5	37.5
Other agricultural exporters	5.3	9.5	20.4	9.2	7.8	8.5	13.7

Relations with United States

Commodity Class	Exports, 1970	Imports, 1970	Bilateral Official Grants Received, 1960-70	Bilateral Official Loans Authorized, 1962-72	Private Direct Investment, Book Value, End 1972
All African developing countries	100.0	100.0	100.0	100.0	100.0
Crude petroleum exporters	27.4	47.4	40.2	43.4	74.4
Nonferrous minerals, metals exporters	7.2	19.0	23.0	24.9	12.4
Major agricultural exporters	60.2	29.3	26.8	30.1	12.2
Other agricultural exporters	5.2	4.3	10.0	1.7	1.0

Sources: UNCTAD, OECD, U.S. Agency for International Development.

TABLE 13

African Developing Countries: International Economic Relations
(per capita dollars)

| | World Relations, Not Including United States | | | | | |
Commodity Class	Exports, 1970	Imports, 1970	Official Grants Received, 1960-70	Official Loans Balance Outstanding, End 1971	Private Overseas Direct Investment, Book Value, End 1967	GNP, 1969
All African developing countries	39.90	34.17	38.67	30.38	17.80	151.00
Crude petroleum exporters	54.32	39.26	40.72	31.18	18.18	178.19
Nonferrous minerals, metals exporters	57.83	43.71	48.40	40.89	29.22	170.81
Major agricultural exporters	28.80	29.79	26.35	29.68	16.32	139.04
Other agricultural exporters	15.49	23.81	57.95	20.32	10.12	93.59

| | Relations with United States | | | | |
	Exports, 1970	Imports, 1970	Bilateral Official Grants Received, 1962-72	Bilateral Official Loans Authorized, 1962-72	Private Direct Investment, Book Value, End 1972
All African developing countries	2.61	3.16	6.99	7.84	9.89
Crude petroleum exporters	1.98	4.17	7.81	9.45	20.43
Nonferrous minerals, metals exporters	1.47	4.69	12.52	15.19	9.58
Major agricultural exporters	4.19	2.47	5.01	6.29	3.20
Other agricultural exporters	.98	.98	5.11	.98	.70

Sources: UNCTAD, OECD, U.S. Agency for International Development.

174

the United States are a very small proportion of the American imports of these commodities. The United States imports its foreign supplies of oil primarily from Latin America and secondarily from the Middle East. Also the United States imports the greater portion of its foreign mineral needs from other less developed areas. Thus Africa is neither a major provider of these key resources for the United States nor a significant outlet for American exports.

The African-American relationship is not altogether symmetrical however. While it is true that the relative U.S. share of Africa's imports is not greatly significant in dollar or quantity terms, the quality of America's exports to Africa does make a difference. Most African countries, including the oil and mineral exporting countries, are food deficit areas. The key means of meeting this deficit is by importing cereals and cereal products. As American cereal surpluses are exhausted, and the two other major cereal exporters no longer have surpluses, the lack of American cereal exports and higher prices can cause increasing hardship for African countries. In the past the United States has provided cereals to African countries through its foreign assistance programs on concessional terms; in the 1960s American cereal exports made up critical African food deficits at low prices and often under grant or soft-loan terms.

African nations have become increasingly concerned with the goal of completing independence by expanding their control over their own economic destinies. This has often taken the form of public policies for enlarged control over exploitation of natural resources. These resources are viewed as critical national assets, the exploitation of which should not be controlled by foreigners. These critical areas of natural resources are the very ones in which U.S. private direct investment is concentrated. African countries are generally not in a position to establish yardstick operations in these extractive industries to provide means of assessing and controlling foreign performance. More often African nations have decided to nationalize the assets of foreign corporations in petroleum and minerals.

American corporations are in an unfavorable position to adjust to these moves. The bulk of U.S. overseas investments are in equity holdings. Alternative techniques of investing, through loans, are not likely to develop as a large-scale substitute for equity holdings because a well-organized international loan market does not exist

in the United States. American corporations have also
been slow to develop such alternative means as technical
and service contract capability. Rigidities in American
corporate responses to African moves toward economic independence often lead to pressures on the U.S. government
to react accordingly. There is a tendency to translate
control and restriction of corporate activity into questions of high politics and national morality. Congress
may be urged to cut off aid, limit trade, and stop critical food exports. Adding to these tendencies in American
reactions is the fact that many U.S. corporations are
worldwide in operations, and are concerned about the effect of yielding in one country on potential actions by
other countries where the stakes for the U.S. corporation
may be much higher. In the past few years--largely as a
derivative of American relations with developing countries outside Africa, especially in Latin America and the
Middle East--there has been a hardening of both American
corporate attitudes and American government reactions.

AREAS OF POTENTIAL AFRICAN-AMERICAN
INTEREST CONFLICT

In African-American economic relations during the
1960s there were certain instances in which the pursuit
of U.S. interests in importing Africa's coffee and cocoa,
investing in production of African fuels and minerals,
and accommodating American economic assistance to these
objectives were tending toward conflict with African interests in development, independence, and distributional
equity. At the close of the 1960s the potential for increasing conflict was visible with respect to the terms
of trade at which African-American exchange of goods took
place; the mechanism of commodity price determination;
the concentration of American investment in exploitation
of natural resources; the amount, terms, channels, and
distribution of economic assistance; and such particulars
of commercial policy as the employment of preferences,
participation in commodity agreements, and reservation of
sectors and activities for preferred access by nationals
or exploitation by the state. It is important to note
that most of these areas were showing increased potential
for conflict as a result of the persisting trends--with
respect to concentration, relative price movements, and
the established division of economic activities--that
gave the framework of trade and payments its appearance
of stability and durability in the 1950s and 1960s.

176

If the trends had continued into the later 1970s
the nature and even the scenarios of African-American
conflict would be largely predictable. The conflicts
would themselves constitute the evidence of stress in
the pattern of trade and payments and the difficulties,
particularly for many of the African states, of obtaining
satisfaction of their national interests within that
framework.

Instead the stress produced an interruption of
certain trends. Through alterations in the price-
determination mechanism, intervention in the planned expansion of supply, and precipitation of a series of direct actions to reduce private foreign ownership and
control of exploration and exploitation, the stable
trends of the 1950s and 1960s in international trade,
investment, and relative price of mineral fuels have been
sharply changed by oil-producing countries--mostly outside Africa. There is widespread speculation, if only
limited evidence, that similar efforts to alter past
trends and structures may follow with respect to nonferrous minerals and some tropical foodstuffs. Among
the developed market economy countries, reactive policies
and adjustments are as yet undecided. In these circumstances any predictions of the nature and scenarios of
African-American interest conflicts in the future are
extremely hazardous. Advocates and options abound; the
possibilities range from all-out economic warfare to
American autarky.

The forecasting is not made easier by taking account
of the fact that the United States is a larger producer
of petroleum, minerals, and foodstuffs than is Africa,
with the technological capacity in time--if for reasons
of politics or ideology the United States decides to bear
the economic costs--to free itself of dependence on Africa as a source of supply and indeed to enter the export
field as a competitor in some lines of African export
earnings. Any variant of this course of action would
not be precipitated by the direct conflict of American
and African interests--which are simply too limited to
induce American reactions of this magnitude. But something of this kind might result from American conflict
with other developing countries, with exactly the same
consequences for African-American relations.

Equally dreadful is the possible ruin of African-
American economic relations as a consequence of actions
by African states--if for reasons of politics or ideology
such states decide to bear the economic costs--to free

themselves of dependence on industrialized countries.
Though it is unlikely that any such course would be precipitated by a direct conflict of American and African
interests, such conflict might result from African conflict with other developed countries, with exactly the
same effect on African-American relations.

Probably cooler heads will prevail on all sides.
But no one knows; the magnitude of changes in institutions
and economic relationships are currently unpredictable;
and speculation in the face of such profound uncertainty
is of limited value.

It may help to narrow the range of speculation, however, by identifying the magnitudes of potential changes
from past trends with respect to some of the key commodities of mutual interest to Africa and the United States.

Petroleum. Before the events of the last quarter of 1973
the declining trend of real prices for petroleum had been
reversed. Still, at perhaps $4.00 a barrel, the projected
demand for petroleum from developing country sources for
industrial Europe, Japan, and the United States was of
awesome proportions for the late 1970s and through the
1980s. So was the scale of the financing outflow from
developed countries, even after allowing for anticipated
increases in dividends and other return flows of the companies involved in overseas energy operations.

The form by which an additional $3.00 a barrel was
added to the price of crude petroleum in the latter part
of 1973--including evidence of determination to confirm
the higher real price in the longer run by production
limitation and cartel solidarity--contributed to the
urgency of implementing programs for demand compression
and development of alternate energy sources justified by
the higher relative price of petroleum. The extent to
which the United States will be able to insulate itself
from making very large payments to developing countries
for imported oil can only be guessed; it depends critically on public policy decisions not yet made, the determination to see through the costs of those policies, and
technological advances applied to large-scale production
that are only pilot-tested or yet to appear. But it does
seem very unlikely that the domestic cost of energy, including petroleum, can be expected to decline much or soon
from the level established by the price at which crude oil
will be sold in Arabia and the Persian Gulf.

A reasonable prospect for the balance of the 1970s
may be for increased energy costs in the United States at

a scale of $3.00 a barrel for crude oil above 1973 prices. The net balance-of-payments effect for the United States is very difficult to predict for the same period.

For Africa the direct effect of higher crude petroleum prices in the 1970s may be projected on assumptions similar to those discussed for the United States. African petroleum is marketed chiefly in Europe, which is unlikely to be able to insulate itself from very substantial dependency on imported crude oil in the 1970s. Based on the assumption of an increase of $3.00 a barrel for crude oil above 1973 prices the following figures show the direct balance-of-payments effects on African countries for the 1971 level of trade in petroleum, including crude and products. (The $3.00 per barrel increase in the price of crude is assumed to result in an average $4.50 a barrel increase in the price of the products, at the mix which obtains in Africa. All countries in the first group noted and all but two in each of the next two groups have refinery capacity, and nine are net product exporters; none of the countries in the last group have refineries.)

	In $ Million	As Percent of Export Earnings
All African developing countries	5,406	47.0
Crude petroleum exporters	5,704	105.9
Minerals, metals producers	-82	-3.6
Major agricultural exporters	-174	-5.5
Other agricultural exporters	-42	-6.7

Using the existing level of petroleum consumption, this measures the balance-of-payments effect of the higher petroleum prices--a very substantial net gain for the petroleum exporters and a net loss of about $300 million a year for the other African countries, with significantly higher proportional losses for the exporters of agricultural products.

The higher prices of petroleum will doubtless lead to substitution of energy sources and efforts to restrain demand, including the gradual adoption of technologies with lower energy-input coefficients. Until the effects of such changes can be felt the growth of output and demand for energy may be assumed to retain the same pattern

in the future as in the early 1970s. Growth, by raising
petroleum consumption, will require higher imports of
crude and either reduce domestically produced crude or
divert it from export. The following figures show the
direct balance-of-payments effect of the increased price
of petroleum with respect to future growth (a 1 percent
rise in consumption):

	In $ Million	As Percent of Export Earnings
All African developing countries	-8.4	-.073
Crude petroleum exporters	-4.4	-.081
Minerals, metals producers	-1.0	-.042
Major agricultural exporters	-2.7	-.083
Other agricultural exporters	-.4	-.068

Thus the balance-of-payments impact on Africa (as a
whole) of the changed trend in petroleum prices is likely
to be a doubling of export earnings for the seven crude
petroleum exporters and an initial 3.5-6.5 percent export-
earnings cost for the other African economies. If Africa
achieves its goal of a 6 percent growth rate for the 1970s
it will incur an additional cumulative annual cost of
about $50 million, or less than one-half of 1 percent of
its export receipts prior to the petroleum price rise.

These losses for nonproducers of petroleum in Africa
are not negligible, but they are not ruinous. Compensa-
tion schemes presently under consideration among developing countries and through the intermediation of the World
Bank and the International Monetary Fund may be able to
offset losses of this magnitude. There does not appear
to be substantial reason to expect greatly increased
African demands on the United States for compensating
aid, trade, or financial concessions. The focus of U.S.
resentment for its higher domestic energy costs--possible
balance-of-payments losses--cannot extend beyond the
three African crude petroleum producers with sufficient
exports to be visible in the American view of the market.
Nonetheless American initiation of or participation in
sanctions directed against oil-producing countries elsewhere in the developing world could damage relations with
some African countries.

The potential for really serious African-American
conflict lies elsewhere: in food and in minerals.

Food. Africa's need for food imports provides an example
of the indirect effects of the changed trends in petroleum, and of how adjustments to the altered terms of trade
may lead to a wide divergence in African and American
interests.

In the early 1970s African imports of foodstuffs
from the developed market economies exceeded $1 billion
a year. About half of this was in the form of cereals.
With agricultural productivity rising less than population
growth, and per capita incomes increasing, African dependence on imported food is expected to increase until the
1980s. The rate of increased dependence could be dramatic
if either programs for improved productivity have delayed
effects or natural disasters such as the Sahelian drought
recur. For a modest rate of increased food imports about
one-half are expected to be in cereals; if higher rates
are required the cereals component could rise sharply,
other acceptable forms of foodstuffs being in even less
adequate state of availability.

The United States, Canada, and Australia are the
residual sources of supply for cereals. They are the
only producers likely to be able to meet increased demand
at least in the 1970s. The factors we will discuss in
terms of the United States apply generally to both Canada
and Australia.

Cereals production in the United States is highly
productive per acre and per man-hour. But it is highly
energy-consuming; fossil fuel is the chief input in U.S.
cereals production. Expressed in gasoline equivalents,
each bushel of corn requires inputs of energy equivalent
to a gallon of gasoline. The extent to which increased
U.S. domestic energy costs are passed on to the costs of
cereals production will depend on energy policy decisions
not yet determined. But on assumptions already described
in the discussion of petroleum above, the higher price of
crude oil would result in an increased corn production
cost of $4.22 per metric ton. (Each increase in average
American energy costs equivalent to ten cents a gallon of
gasoline will raise the cost of corn production by $4.22
per metric ton.)

For Africa's 1970 imports of cereals, some 5.6 million tons, this indirect impact of higher petroleum
prices, passed on to the importer, would cost African
countries some $24 million, or about .2 percent of export

earnings. This is a small increase but about 5 percent
of the 1970 cost of the cereals imports.   If American
domestic energy policy results in higher gasoline-
equivalent energy prices, each ten cents a gallon added
to American domestic prices will add another 5 percent
to Africa's cereals import costs.

The incidence of this increased cost of cereals imports is very uneven among groups of African countries;
the balance-of-payments impact on the small African
agricultural-products exporters is more than double that
for crude petroleum exporters and for major agricultural
exporters (all expressed in terms of export earnings),
and the impact is nearly four times as great as for minerals producers.

Thus lies the potential for conflicting interests between the poorest African nations and the United States.
American domestic policy to counteract dependence on foreign sources of energy may result in very high rates of
pass-through to higher food production costs--a reaction
to U.S. perception of conflict of interest with developing
countries outside Africa. But the consequent higher costs
for imports of foodstuffs, and deterioration in terms of
trade, will fall most heavily on African countries least
capable of absorbing or offsetting the cost.

Nor is there an evident solution in attempting to
avoid the food deficit by a major acceleration of agricultural productivity-improving programs. The available
technology for rapid increases in food production, largely
derived from American methods and designed for a world of
cheap and plentiful energy resources, requires greatly
increased energy consumption to achieve higher yields.
The critical bottleneck is nitrogen fertilizer, requiring
very large quantities of energy to produce. In American
cereals production the nitrogen fertilizer input alone
requires half a gallon of gasoline per bushel.

In summary American response to the changed trend in
the terms of trade among fuels and other commodities of
importance to African-American economic relations may be
policies that have the effect of passing on higher costs
to groups of African countries least capable of bearing
them. The indirect impact on the balance of payments of
African countries will appear in some degree in higher
costs for virtually all imports; the case of American
cereals exports to Africa is a case with particularly unfavorable distributional results among African countries.
Of greater importance, however, is the poor adaptation of
American-derived technology to the conditions of high

energy costs. The United States will be less capable in
the future of contributing an appropriate technology to
efforts of African countries to adapt to the changed
trends in international trade relations.

Minerals. Potential conflicting interests may also be
found in the nonferrous minerals sector; some major African minerals exporters have explored ways of improving
their position by combining with other producers to influence supply and price of exports. Chile, Peru, Zambia,
and Zaire produce about 80 percent of world copper output
and have formed a producers' organization to address
problems of copper marketing and pricing.

There is an excited speculation in the United States
that this constitutes a threat to American interests from
developing countries. Producers of a long list of nonferrous minerals and metals are visualized as prepared
and capable of adapting the tactics of members of the
Organization of Petroleum Exporting Countries (OPEC), of
withholding vital commodities, of unilaterally driving
up the prices of their products, and of otherwise extract-
ing concessions from the United States and other industrialized countries.[1]

The prospects of such a strategy by minerals producers are extremely dubious. The narrow range of prices
within which copper producers, for example, can feel
secure from the threat of technological substitution with
unpredictable and lagged consequences for copper demand
is an entirely different order of magnitude from the prospects associated with petroleum. The long-term goals of
copper producers as compared with members of OPEC are
entirely different; the former want to sustain their share
of metals demand while the latter want to conserve their
resource. The requirement for vertical integration to
secure market control is central for copper but unimportant for petroleum--and so on.

But these considerations are much less important than
the perception of such a danger by an excited and sullen
public and its harassed government. Preventive sanctions,
protection, politicization of economic relations, reduced
foreign assistance authorizations, formation of consumers'
cartels--all are considered when the danger is perceived
and widely publicized.

Adoption of such measures may be judged improbable,
but African producers of both agricultural and mineral
primary commodities cited in discussion of these measures
can scarcely be reassured by the atmosphere. Meanwhile

their food and fuels import costs are rising. While
minerals terms of trade generally improved through the
1960s, they are historically unstable and highly dependent
on output growth in industrial uses. The problem of earnings stabilization remains; efforts to address the problem are subject to suspicions of imminent realization of
the threat from the Third World.

Perhaps these are questions of public psychology
rather than of economics, but the aura of impending conflict can itself make much more difficult the adjustments
required by the concentration of American direct investment in the exploitation of African natural resources.
We have described earlier the strong and established trend
toward national control over the development of these resources, and the generally limited range of flexibility
in American accommodation to this trend. In a period of
change and uncertainty in the 1970s and 1980s, while a
new framework of trade and payments linking developing
and developed countries is constructed, the greatest
danger of perceived conflicting interests between Africa
and the United States may derive from the fear of change
itself.

NOTE

1. See C. Fred Bergsten, "The Threat From the Third
World," <u>Foreign Policy</u>, no. 11, Summer 1973, pp. 102-24.

The analysis of African and U.S. economic interests by Eleanora West and Robert West falls into two distinct parts. The first, a survey of the state of African-U.S. economic relations, is a very useful summary of the data on trade, aid, and investment. It illustrates in detail the one overriding fact about African-U.S. economic ties: that they are of extremely limited significance for both areas. The second part of the authors' analysis consists of the aggregate figures assembled, which give an exaggerated impression of the extent of African-U.S. trade flows, in the sense that these figures rest heavily on trade and investment in petroleum products. When these are removed from the data the magnitude of African-U.S. trade and investment flows shrinks drastically. This means that the economic connections between the United States and Africa are not only small overall, but are mainly significant for the petroleum-producing countries--notably Libya and Nigeria.

Despite these limited economic relations the authors see conflict and tensions ahead, not in direct or exclusive African-U.S. confrontation, but rather as part of a larger set of conflicts between less developed countries (LDC) and more developed countries (MDC). It is in this wider framework that the African-U.S. economic relationship must be considered.

DIFFICULTIES FOR THE INTERNATIONAL ECONOMY

Not even the most pollyannaish of observers can deny that serious difficulties are likely in the international economy during the next few years. The authors give some of the main factors at work. First is the necessity for both consuming and producing countries to adjust to the consequences of higher levels of crude oil prices, particularly the need for oil-importing economies to adapt to the massive balance-of-payments deficits generated by the recent quadrupling of crude oil prices. Second, declining stocks of food grains, lagging productions, sharply rising food prices, and rising fertilizer and energy costs create a special set of tensions and dangers. These include devastatingly higher LDC import bills for food-

stuffs, with resulting pressures on balances of payments;
reallocation of public expenditures away from development
purposes to the satisfaction of emergency current expenditure needs; and the possibility of hunger and even famine
on a scale unknown in recent years. All of this, the
Wests note, must also be placed in the context of sustained population growth at relatively high rates in LDCs,
though this presumably is a longer-term aspect of the
problem. Third, there is an apparent decline in development assistance in the face of severely adverse conditions
in the foreign accounts of donor countries--economic slow-
downs coupled with inflation and a shrinking pro-aid political base in donor countries, this deriving in part
from resentments in the MDCs over rising prices in crude
oil and other commodities. Fourth, there is the intensifying demand in the LDCs that local natural resources be
controlled by local governments and people, and the related demands for both a higher level of prices for LDC
raw material exports, based on the oil model, and a redistribution of the benefits of raw material production
in favor of the LDCs. And finally, there is a restruc-
turing of the world monetary system related to the generalized floating of exchange rates and the decline of the
dollar as a key currency.

THE IDEOLOGICAL FACTOR

In addition to these factors there are several others
that are less directly or frequently stressed but that
seem important nonetheless. The first is ideological.
The classical theories of international trade and investment tend to stress harmony of interests and mutual benefits between trading partners or between foreign investors
and host countries. These theories have been for this
reason under attack for a long time on the grounds that
they are biased in favor of the more developed members of
the world economic community. The critics have indeed
succeeded--at least in the LDCs--in making the classical
arguments disreputable and even villainous. Intellec-
tuals, statesmen, and economists from the LDCs nowadays
tend to focus on the conflict element in economic relationships. They tend to perceive of trade and investment
as basically exploitative. The old-fashioned idea that
in most cases everybody's income is higher with trade and
investment than without it is either neglected, rejected
outright, or said to be true and relevant only in the
short run.

Related to this is the more recent transformation of the ideological and intellectual environment whereby growth of income and output is given markedly lower priority as a social objective, while more equitable income distribution and "economic independence" are stressed more. The extreme expressions of these views emphasize the limits to overall growth, the virtual impossibility for most poor countries to reach--in any reasonable time horizon--a standard of living approaching that in the MDCs, and the critical importance of relative incomes as against absolute income levels.

All of these ideas nourish propensities toward inward-looking, autarkic growth strategies--propensities that are strong everywhere but particularly in LDCs. They exacerbate the schizophrenia that characterizes attitudes toward foreign investment in much of the world--desiring to have the capital, technology, skills, markets, and other benefits that usually accompany foreign investment while at the same time fearing and distrusting it. They strengthen the forces within LDCs that most urgently push for aggressive and high-risk policies toward commodity exports or foreign investment.

THE PSYCHOLOGICAL FACTOR

The second factor is more psychological than ideological, though the lines are not entirely clear. The oil crisis had massive effects in shaking up traditional attitudes in both more and less developed countries. On the one side there were awakened primitive sentiments of national economic self-interest--for example all the heated talk in the United States about economic self-sufficiency, or self-sufficiency in crude oil by 1980, the clamping of embargoes on key exports, and the resentment against Japanese investments in the United States. On the LDC side the successful cartelization by the oil producers stimulated some similar effort and much talk among many other raw material producers.

The strong fears and passions generated in the advanced countries by the oil crisis and by threats of comparable developments in other raw materials have already subsided from their peaks. But there remains some danger that attitudes deriving from a sense of vulnerability and intense economic dependence--the psychological inheritance of the oil crisis--will have long-term consequences harmful to the expansion of the international economy. The

most obvious is the possibility, even likelihood, that
vast new investments will be made in research and development of raw material substitutes, and in the discovery
of domestic or politically "safer" sources of supply.
Higher prices alone would have had this effect, but
threats of politicization of trade and of cartelization
of other raw materials surely intensify it.

SOME POSITIVE FACTORS

Amidst all these elements of gloom there can be found
a few positive factors in the economic outlook for the
LDCs, and particularly for African countries. First, the
effects on LDCs of higher crude oil prices are not entirely negative, at least not for all LDCs. Petroleum products are basic inputs in the production of most synthetics,
which are the main substitutes and hence competitors for
natural raw materials. The prices of all manner of synthetics have thus been rising sharply, and not only have
prices of natural products risen in sympathy, but the competitive position of naturals has been much improved.
Moreover it is not likely that this shift in favor of
natural commodities is a transient or short-term phenomenon.
Similarly the pervading pessimism about commodity
prices, which led many to believe that export-based development strategies were infeasible, now seems less justifi-
able than ever. A shift in relative prices has taken
place in favor of primary products, and this is not likely
to be a passing thing either. The world has become more
Ricardian in the sense of being characterized by a search
for primary products that are more remote, more difficult
to exploit, and hence more expensive.
A third positive factor, rather less important, is
the preoccupation with pollution and related problems in
the industrial countries, which increases the propensity
of advanced country investors (including multinationals)
to invest in industry in the LDCs. It can be anticipated
that in the next few decades a significantly greater share
of new capacity in some lines of industry (oil refining,
chemicals, pulp and paper, metal refining, and similar
"dirty" industries) will be built in poor countries than
is now the case.
Finally, and specifically with respect to Africa, a
far-reaching change has taken place in the aid environment in the United States. It has become apparent that
new and important political forces are at work in aid

matters. For the first time an African aid constituency
has come into being, based on an alliance between liberals and blacks and forged mainly in response to the urgent
needs arising from the problems of the drought-afflicted
areas in Africa. This is what explains the recent high
levels of U.S. assistance to the Sahel countries. More
broadly it helps explain why the flow of economic assistance to Africa has not declined in recent years, as it
has in other parts of the less developed world.

These optimistic notes are probably insufficient in
number and strength to alter the bleak theme mapped out
by the Wests. But they do suggest that there are at least
a few compensating forces at work, forces tending to maintain and even increase the flow of aid, trade, and investment, and that these may be particularly significant with
respect to Africa.

One of the important contributions of the analysis
presented by Eleanora West and Robert West is the comprehensive set of statistics on African-U.S. trade that they
have assembled in such a convenient form. Up-to-date
statistics on African trade and other economic activity
are, for understandable reasons, often spotty and not
readily available. The statistical sections of the study
done by West and West are therefore most useful and wel-
come. Especially important as well is their analysis of
African-American relations and the areas of potential conflict.

The conclusions of their study are predicated on the
premise that African-U.S. trading relations are so marginal to the partners that direct conflict of economic
interest may actually be discounted. On the other hand,
the study maintains, such conflict of interest may emerge
as part of a larger confrontation between the developed
and developing countries over the access to primary products held by the latter. While for a static view of economic relations this premise of the marginal nature of
African-U.S. trade relations is acceptable, it cannot be
tenable for a long-term dynamic analysis of international
economic relations.

Only two decades ago economists were arguing that
Western trade with Eastern Europe was of marginal importance and could be ignored in the interest of maintaining
the cold war. Yet today American corporations are scrambling for footholds in the vast Soviet market. Twenty
years ago America's economic interest in Africa was concentrated in Southern Africa, primarily in South Africa
and Rhodesia. Currently the aggregate of U.S. investment
in the rest of Africa is at least double that in the Republic of South Africa. It can be argued that this trend
is likely to continue as the situation in Southern Africa
reaches its inevitable denouement, with African majorities eventually replacing the racist white-minority regimes in the area. The events of 1974 in Portugal and
the Portuguese African territories suggest that this
outcome may be closer than the most optimistic observers
could have imagined a year ago.

TABLE 14

African Strategic Minerals, 1968-69
(percentages)

Mineral	Africa's Share of World Production	U.S. Imports from Africa as Share of Total U.S. Consumption	Africa's Share of Known World Reserves
Antimony	30.0	40.0	30.0
Chromite	37.0	30.0	96.0
Cobalt	64.0	56.0	40.0
Copper	22.0	4.9	16.5
Gold	71.0	0	60.0
Manganese ore	25.0	43.0	NA*
Platinum	27.0	31.0	47.0
Uranium	20.0	45.0	NA*

*NA = not available.

Source: Frederick S. Arkhurst, African Diplomacy: Its Evolution and Future, paper commissioned by Carnegie Endowment for International Peace for its seminar on diplomacy, November 1973.

A FINITE WORLD WITH LIMITED RESOURCES

The central fact that has been overlooked in the enthusiasm over the exploitation of the world's resources
is that the earth is a finite planet with limited resources; thus America, like other countries, will have to
begin to be concerned about the availability and limits
of natural resources wherever they may be: "Shortages of
supply have replaced shortages of demand as the dominant
force in world economics for the first time in almost
fifty years, and the power position of suppliers and consumers has thus changed drastically."[1]

In this sense American interest in African resources
and trade is bound to increase. This of course does not
necessarily postulate conflicts of economic interest between Africa and the United States. One would hope that
the spectre of inevitable and universal scarcities that
some economists, ecologists, and population experts are
predicting will result in a more enlightened view of the
human condition to enable the conservation, judicious exploitation, and equitable distribution of the world's resources as the only basis of maintaining a tolerable existence on this planet.

AFRICAN OUTPUT OF MAJOR WORLD COMMODITIES

In specific terms the fact that Africa produces significant proportions of total world output of certain key
minerals and agricultural commodities would suggest that
its trade with the United States will increase in the
future, particularly when other sources of supply begin
to decline for various reasons. For instance of eight
major strategic minerals Africa produced an average of
37 percent of total world output in 1968/69; for two of
these minerals--cobalt and gold--African output was 64
percent and 71 percent, respectively, of world production.
Africa's share of known world reserves of various minerals is equally impressive (see Table 14).

Figures for 1971 are equally notable; of total world
production of major minerals and selected agricultural
products, Africa's share (in percentages) was as follows:[2]

Cobalt	72.0	Cocoa	72.5
Beryl	25.0	Palm kernels	65.2
Tantalum and		Palm oil	54.8
niobium	20.0	Ground nuts	
Aluminum	15.7	(peanuts)	24.7
Manganese ore	13.2	Wood and lumber	20.9

This evidence seems to point to the probability of increasing trade between Africa and the United States, particularly since there are indications that most African countries are anxious to diversify their trading relations and thus break away from the traditional patterns of trade that have locked them into a closed circuit with the former metropole countries. This trend will continue even if the negotiations for association between the European Economic Community (EEC) and 44 African, Caribbean, and Asian countries are successful.

It seems reasonable to suggest that the high price of oil, which is not likely to be relieved in the foreseeable future, will make U.S. manufactures more competitive than those of Europe; and this fact will not be lost on the African countries. Worldwide inflationary pressures, which are higher among America's competitors, are also likely to accentuate this trend. Thus on several considerations one can postulate an increase in economic relations between Africa and the United States.

THE TERMS OF TRADE

West and West claim that from the end of the 1940s to the end of the 1960s the terms of trade between primary products and manufactures "altered only modestly and slowly" and that "trends were relatively fixed and predictable." What this overlooks is the fact that the "fixed and predictable" terms of trade were adverse to primary producers in Asia, Latin America, and Africa.

While the pent-up demand for primary products built up during the war years led to increases in the prices of primary products immediately after World War II, the available evidence points to a secular deterioration, over the two decades, in the terms of trade for primary producers, except in the cases of crude oil and some non-fuel minerals.[3] Even with fuels and minerals, West and West concede that "supplies to developed countries were generally adequate, prices were low, and real earnings per unit slowly declined." They add that trade in manufactured goods grew rapidly among developed countries but more slowly, and at rising real prices, between developed and developing countries. The adverse terms of trade against primary producers have persisted until the early 1970s when there appears to have been the beginning of one of the cyclical upswings in the prices of raw materials. It is likely that this strengthening of the prices

of primary products will be sustained by the high price of
oil, which should make synthetic products less competitive
than natural products such as fibers, timber, etc. The
increasing awareness of the limits to the availability of
world resources, coupled with the possibility of other
primary producers following the example of the OPEC countries and organizing to maintain prices, may accentuate
this trend.[4]

INTERNATIONAL INVESTMENTS AND SOVEREIGNTY
OVER NATIONAL RESOURCES

As West and West rightly suggest, the most likely
conflict of economic interest between Africa and the United States is in the confrontation between American investments in Africa and the right of African countries to
exercise complete sovereignty over their natural resources.
There is no doubt that the exploitation of African resources under colonialism was an outright rip-off. Even
after independence most African countries are conscious
of the threat of neocolonialism. In spite of this nationalization and threats of the take-over of foreign investments have been rare in Africa. Rather the tendency
has been the acquisition of a company's major stockhold-
ings by the national government after necessary compensa-
tion has been mutually agreed upon. The exception of
course is Libya where U.S. oil companies were nationalized
outright.
The indications are that the exploitation of African
resources will increasingly be undertaken in joint partnership between foreign investors and either national governments or private citizens, with the major stockholding
always being in indigenous hands. Equally clear is the
fact that African governments will control the activities
of foreign corporations to ensure that they are consistent with national aspirations and national policy. West
and West make the point that there is "a tendency [by U.S.
investors] to translate control and restriction of corporate activity into questions of high politics and national morality. Congress may be urged to cut off aid,
limit trade, and stop critical food exports" This kind
of over-reaction has not been very common in the African
situation; but this is not to argue that forceful diplomatic pressure has not often been applied. At any rate
the developing pattern of investment partnership among
African governments, entrepreneurs, and foreign private

investors should go a long way to avoid the suspicion that leads to control and restriction and to the adversary involvement of foreign governments.

The role and influence of multinational corporations in developing countries is pertinent in this connection. It is very doubtful that multinational corporations will be given a free hand in Africa as in the past. The current debate on multinational corporations is bound to influence the attitude of developing countries toward the kind of license that these corporations are allowed to exercise.[5] The exposure of the kind of political intervention in the host country, both by the multinational corporation and its home government, as exemplified in the case of Chile, will tend to make host governments even more cautious.

FOREIGN AID

It is difficult to visualize a conflict of interest between Africa and the United States over the decline or even outright cessation of U.S. foreign aid. In the first place foreign aid is a grant, albeit not without some strings or at least some self-interest motivation on the part of the donor; consequently the recipients really do not have any right to complain about aid withdrawal. Second, U.S. aid to Africa has been marginal even in the case of those countries where American aid has been concentrated. This is not to suggest that emergency stop-gap aid such as in the case of the Sahelian drought is not of great importance. But increasingly there has been growing skepticism about the role of foreign assistance in national development. For instance a great deal has been made of the French as the premier aid donor to Africa, but one has to search for the contribution of such aid to the development of French-speaking Africa. The fact is that a large portion of foreign aid tends to flow back to its source:

> The level of aid is stagnant and debt servicing of some LDCs [less developed countries] has reached the point where they are now net exporters of capital to the industrialized world. The quality of aid is declining as most terms harden; tying alone reduces the real value of aid by 10 to 30 percent of its nominal value. . . .

> The United States is the least responsive
> to Third World needs of any industrialized
> country at this time. U.S. help is small
> and getting smaller. Its quality is de-
> clining. It often runs directly counter
> to the central objectives of LDCs.[6]

There is a spreading disenchantment among both donors
and recipients of foreign aid because of the failure of
aid in the majority of cases to meet respective expectations; and there is no doubt that the next decades will
see the eclipse of the concept of foreign aid as a mechanism to engender development. The growing reservations
regarding the role of foreign aid, however, derive from
more fundamental considerations. In the first place there
is the question of the goals of development, which may not
have coincidence for donors and recipients. Furthermore
current analysis of development has been almost exclusively concerned with instrumentalities and has given scant
attention to normative questions about the quality of
life, the nature of society, and the optimum world order
that real development should insure. In the absence of
considerations such as these it is easy to assume that
foreign aid, by providing the necessary mechanisms, can
bring about development. After one-and-a-half development decades the fallacy of these assumptions needs no
emphasis.

Foreign aid is addictive and carries the risk of
creating or perpetuating a relationship of dependency between donor and recipient, which cannot be conducive to
true development. For the central issue in development
"is the difference between being the agent of one's development as defined in one's own terms, and being a mere
beneficiary of development as defined by someone else."[7]
Excessive dependence on foreign aid can also introduce
distortions into the development process. Development
will demand drastic readjustments in African society,
great effort and sacrifice, and the total mobilization of
the energies of the African people toward clearly defined
and endogenously determined goals, geared to the improvement of the quality of life of the people. Foreign aid
that generates complacency could delay the assumption of
these responsibilities and blunt the incentives to change.[8]

The decline of foreign aid as an alleged instrument
of development will not end in inevitable disaster for
most African countries, and should not lead to conflicts
of interest between Africa and the United States. The

possibility of serious conflict of interest will be political rather than economic and will arise over the situation in Southern Africa, and particularly South Africa. The dramatic events in Portugal in April 1974 and their repercussions in the Portuguese African territories may bring such a confrontation nearer.

NOTES

1. C. Fred Bergsten, *Foreign Policy*, no. 14 (Spring 1974), p. 85.

2. *West Africa*, August 5, 1974, p. 964.

3. Reginald H. Green and Ann Lerdman, *Unity or Poverty: The Economics of Pan-Africanism* (London: Penguin African Library, 1968), p. 42.

4. C. Fred Bergsten, "The Threat from the Third World"; Zuhayr Mikdashi, "Collusion Could Work"; Stephen D. Krasner, "Oil is the Exception," and C. Fred Bergsten, "The Threat is Real," in *Foreign Policy*, nos. 11 and 14 (Summer 1973 and Spring 1974). See also Benson Varon and Kanji Takenchi, "Developing Countries and Non-Fuel Minerals," in *Foreign Affairs* (April 1974), pp. 497-510.

5. *Foreign Policy*, nos. 11, 12, 13, and 15 (Summer, Fall, and Winter 1973, Spring 1974).

6. C. Fred Bergsten, *Foreign Policy*, no. 11 (Summer 1973), p. 104.

7. Denis Goulet and Michael Hudson, *The Myth of Aid* (New York: Orbis Books, 1971), p. 19.

8. Frederick S. Arkhurst, ed., *Africa in the Seventies and Eighties: Issues in Development* (New York: Praeger Publishers, 1970), p. 191.

CONFLICTING POLITICAL
INTERESTS OF AFRICA AND
THE UNITED STATES
W. B. Ofuatey-Kodjoe

African leaders lamenting the political division of
Africa have often referred to the African continent as
"Balkanized." There is another sense in which this apt
association of Africa with the Balkans might have ominous
consequences not only for Africa but for the entire world.
It may be that Africa is to the world today what the Balkans were for the European system before the First World
War. Africa certainly features some of the same interpenetration of such factors as governmental instability,
economic insufficiency, ethnic and racial animosities,
and conflicting ideologies that characterized the Balkans
during the latter part of the nineteenth century.

First, the continent of Africa is peopled by poor,
newly established states, straining their meager resources
in a sometimes futile effort to modernize. Second, these
states are characterized by boundaries that cut across a
multiplicity of linguistic and ethnic communities, filled
with animosities that sometimes render problematic the
very existence of the states. Third, Africa is just wit-
nessing the beginning of its final and most intensive onslaught of blacks against the most entrenched and intransigent remnants of white domination. Most important however is the fact that similar to the relationship between
the Balkans and the European international system, the
African subsystem is linked to the world system because
of the client-patron relationship that exists between the
white-supremacist protagonists in the African struggle
and the United States--one of the great powers in an essentially bipolar world of avowedly antagonistic ideologies.

In this regard perhaps the most crucial danger in the
present situation is the potential that the Africans have

198

for soliciting the aid of Asians and perhaps the "socialist powers" in their struggle against the existing combination of the so-called white redoubt and the Western
powers. It is this confrontation of antagonistic alliances that could involve extra-African powers in an African conflict that is bound to have racial connotations.
It is for this reason that the investigation of the relations between the African states and the United States--
leader of the Western alliance and a deeply involved ally
of the white redoubt--is not only intellectually stimulating but also pragmatically necessary.

Accounts of both the evolution and the present nature
of U.S. relations with Africa have been presented by many
writers and in varying detail.[1] This study will suggest
some reliable explanations for the dynamic relationships
between the causes that underlie these relations. It
will examine not only the national interests of the African states but the values and priorities that form the
bases of these interests. Basically four questions will
be studied: what is the interest of the United States in
Africa; what is the interest of the African states; what
are the actual and potential areas of conflict or coincidence between these interests; and what does the relationship between these interests imply for the future of Africa, the United States, and the world.

Foreign policy is primarily strategy by which a
state attempts to deal with other states in order to
achieve the goals that its national interest demands.
Therefore in attempting to discern the national interest
of the states under consideration in this study it will
be necessary to discuss, though not in detail, their foreign policies. This is due in part to the desirability
of avoiding the repetition of available material, especially with regard to U.S. foreign policy. And more important it is due to the theoretically valid reason that
it is not the analysis of foreign policy in itself that
is likely to yield the reality of a state's national interest as perceived and pursued by its national leaders,
but the analysis of the application of that policy as it
is manifested in the actual behavior of the state.[2]
Therefore this study will try to discover patterns in the
actual behavior of the states in their foreign relations,
and attempt to infer from these patterns the state's conception of its national interest.

U.S. INTEREST IN AFRICA

With the exception of Liberia and Ethiopia, the United States had no direct relations with black Africa until 1955. However, the first decade after World War II is very important in the analysis of U.S. interest in Africa, for it was during this period that the United States established an interest in Africa that has remained constant up to the present time. The nature of this interest may be discerned in those aspects of the behavior of the United States toward the colonial powers that have some bearing on African issues.

A look at the relevant U.S. activities during this period cannot fail to reveal the emergence of a certain pattern. For instance through the Marshall Plan the United States consciously supported the deployment of substantial portions of U.S. military and economic aid to the African territories of the aid-receiving countries in order to consolidate their colonial ties.[3] In the case of France the United States went so far as to become a substantial arms supplier and financier for the colonial war in Algeria.[4] At the same time the United States kept up the consistent practice of voting with the colonial powers to ward off attempts to terminate colonialism through various organs of the United Nations.[5] The pattern that these activities suggest is one of consistent and vigorous U.S. support for the maintenance of Africa under colonial control.

As time went on this pro-colonial policy of the United States came under increased pressure due to the rise of African nationalist movements and the increasing vociferousness of their demands for independence. The dilemma that faced U.S. officials was how to reconcile their pro-colonial policies with the reputation which the United States had developed during the war as a champion of anti-colonialism. This issue was not merely moral; it involved a political problem of some importance. It was important for the United States to maintain its anticolonial reputation for the benefit of the African nationalists, because if their countries were to become independent it was clear that the United States would have to depend on their goodwill in order to safeguard its strategic interests in that area.

The United States responded to this dilemma by attempting to accomplish the difficult task of simultaneously inhibiting the progress of the nationalist movements and retaining the friendship of the nationalist leaders.

The strategy for this goal was to make general statements of support for the principle of self-determination, tempered by constant references to the dangers of "premature independence,"[6] and at the same time to help the colonial powers to hold off the anticolonial onslaught as long as possible by continuing the policy of giving them economic and military assistance as well as voting support in the United Nations.

When this pattern of activity is analyzed in the light of U.S. policies and interests around the world a conception of U.S. interest in Africa emerges that has two distinct but related aspects. First, the United States has defense or strategic interests in Africa that are derived from the overall policy of trying to contain international communism. And second is what might be called a U.S. cultural interest in Africa. The cultural aspect of U.S. interest in Africa is related to U.S. conceptions of world order and to U.S. conceptions of how the world should be organized in order to insure the safety and integrity of the American way of life. As such the presence of the cultural aspect is not as compelling as defense interests in times of anxiety over national security, and it is therefore less apparent to the eye. However, it is always an aspect, and sometimes an extremely potent one, of the determinants of foreign policy.[7]

The strategic interests of the United States in Africa have had several elements. By far the most important of these was U.S. interest in Africa as a link in the ring of alliances designed to "contain" international communism. The colonial powers in NATO and South Africa were both part of this elaborate system of alliances. The fact that black Africa was under the colonial control of the NATO allies insured that a gap in the alliance chain that might have existed from Gibraltar to the Zambezi River was effectively sealed. In effect the African colonies were an extension of NATO, a sort of African equivalent of the Central Treaty Organization (CENTO). Therefore the existence of colonial rule in Africa was seen as serving the strategic interests of the United States. It is not surprising that George McGhee, then assistant secretary of state for Near Eastern, South Asian, and African affairs reported in May 1950 that he was pleased by the fact that he could describe Africa as a relatively stable and secure region "in which no significant inroads have been made by Communists."[8]

Under these circumstances the strategic interest of the United States was seen to lie in denying Africa to communist military or ideological inroads, and this interest was seen as requiring a policy of opposition to the "precipitous" dismantling of the colonial empires in Africa. In addition to the requirements of the containment policy the United States had two other strategic interests in Africa, which could be served by keeping Africa in the hands of its European allies. First, with Africa in friendly hands the United States would have much less trouble getting access to African strategic raw materials being mined there. Second, due to the proximity of West Africa to the continental United States it was considered important that the control of the sea-lanes off the West African coast and around the Cape of Good Hope into the South Indian Ocean be in the hands of the United States or its friends.[9] Both of these interests could be safeguarded by the maintenance of the colonial empires.

The pattern of U.S. behavior cannot be explained in terms of only strategic or geopolitical considerations. A fully satisfactory explanation has to take into consideration the abovementioned cultural aspect of the U.S. national interest in Africa. It has frequently been suggested that the U.S. policy of pro-colonialism was only adopted in order to support the colonial powers out of loyalty to them as alliance partners and to strengthen the Western alliance in the face of the communist threat. In rebuttal to this it may legitimately be argued that in fact continued colonial expenditures were a serious drain on the strength of the Western alliance and that furthermore the stake of the colonial powers in the alliance was so high that U.S. opposition to colonialism would not have caused them to leave it. The most important argument against that position however is that the pattern of U.S. activities simply does not lead to that conclusion.

The often repeated grave concern of the United States over the dangerous, retrogressive, and destructive nature of premature independence; the pattern of infrastructural aid to the colonies in which the colonial powers served as conduits; the demonstrated willingness to help keep the colonies by force if necessary; and the preference of the United States for assimilating its own overseas dependencies--all these show a tenacity that was lacking in the attitude of at least some of the colonial powers. This suggests that the U.S. policy of maintaining control over colonial territories was not only in the interest of the other colonial powers, but was seen as being directly in the interest of the United States itself. For instance it seems that even after reluctantly accepting the inevi-

tability of eventual decolonization the United States was
more alarmed than the British by the speed with which that
process finally happened, and was more reluctant to accept
it. As Vernon McKay has noted: "By the time Britain took
the crucial, precedent-setting step of giving independence
to Ghana on March 6, 1957, it was obvious to even the most
conservative officials that the United States could not be
more royalist than the Queen."[10]

The anxiety of U.S. officials about the speed of decolonization arises from their concern over their judgment
that "premature independence" could mean the incompletion
of the process of assimilating these territories into
Western culture and thus creating a multitude of states
whose orientations could jeopardize the survival of the
American way of life. This idea is based on a concept
expressed by Gabriel Almond: ". . . the survival of Western culture is dependent upon its assimilation in significant measure in the modernizing societies of Asia, Africa
and Latin America. . . ."[11] Therefore it would be in the
national interest of the United States to play "a cooperative role with the administering powers"[12] in the
task of "affecting the course of cultural change" in the
African territories.[13] And if this national interest was
to be served, what was needed was a "period of grace to
further the development within Africa of healthy political, economic and social institutions . . .,"[14] or in
other words more time to give the colonial administrations
a chance to complete their civilizing mission of assimilating the African territories into Western culture.

As noted previously, during the first decade after
World War II the United States generally had no direct relations with the colonial territories in Africa. Nevertheless the pattern of U.S. relations with the colonial
powers in and out of the United Nations supports the conclusion that U.S. leaders had a conception of a U.S. national interest in Africa, which they tried to achieve.
This conception of the national interest had two necessary and complementary aspects. The strategic aspect was
concerned with the defense of the republic and the "free
world," and the cultural aspect was concerned with creating the kind of "free world" that would be compatible with
the long-term survival of American culture. When applied
to Africa this meant that the United States had an interest in using Africa as part of its network of global strategic defense against communism and at the same time an
interest in assimilating the African territories into
Western culture. During the period under consideration

both these aspects of the U.S. national interest provided the rationale for U.S. policy, although the strategic aspect was probably uppermost in the minds of U.S. leaders due to the intensity of the heat of the cold war. The subsequent evolution of U.S. policy in Africa may be seen as a manifestation of the dynamic relationship between these conceptions of the national interest as they impinge on the consciousness of policy makers, as well as of successive attempts to cope with new situational challenges and exigencies in order to meet the national goals that these conceptions of the national interest call into being.

As expected, the first new challenge to face U.S. policy was the granting of independence to the African territories. Between 1955 and 1964 practically all the African territories north of the Zambezi acquired statehood. As they became independent they joined the other territories and whatever allies they could acquire in an extremely vigorous attempt to press a wide range of political and economic goals. Although the division is quite arbitrary, this discussion will be limited to only the political aspects of U.S. reactions to the new reality of African interests. In the main, confrontations between the United States and the African states occurred in the United Nations, although there have also been a few bilateral interactions between the United States and individual African states that are of some significance for this study.

The main political goals of African diplomacy at the United Nations have been the eradication of colonialism and racial discrimination and the promotion of human rights in general. Reserved for Africa's most intensive energies have been the specific goals of eliminating Portuguese colonialism in Africa and destroying white-minority rule in Southern Africa. In this effort Africa's adversaries were the colonial powers, including the United States. In both the U.N. General Assembly and Security Council the voting record of the United States has always shown a very high level of consistency with the other colonial powers. The main difference between the United States and the other powers is that while most of the others have given up any pretense with regard to their colonialist attitudes the United States still feels the need to attempt to cover up the impact of its actions by making the most sweeping and emphatic anticolonial statements.

Since about 1964 the anticolonial offensive in the United Nations has concentrated on the territories

continuing under Portuguese control and the white-minority
regimes of Rhodesia, South Africa, and Namibia. In the
face of the refusal of these regimes to heed any U.N.
resolutions directed at them the anticolonial forces have
been turning increasingly to demands that the United Nations use more forceful methods to eradicate white-
minority rule in Southern Africa.

At the same time the United States, in response to
this increase in anticolonial pressure, has begun to move
from the previous policy of abstaining on colonial issues
to voting affirmatively on resolutions condemning the activities of its allies in Southern Africa. In the case
of Portuguese colonialism the United States broke rank
with France and Britain quite early. By June 1961 the
United States was voting with the majority for a resolution condemning the use of repressive measures by the
Portuguese in Angola. In the case of South Africa the
United States began as early as 1958 to vote with the
majority on resolutions showing "mild regret" or "great
concern" over South African events. However, the real
breakthrough did not come until June of 1964 when the
United States supported the Security Council resolution
to create a special committee of experts to undertake a
technical study of measures that might be used against
the regime in South Africa. Finally on October 27, 1966,
the United States supported the General Assembly resolution terminating the South African mandate over Namibia.
In all these cases however the United States has scrupulously avoided making any commitments that might have led
to taking any actions to force Portugal or South Africa
to comply with U.N. resolutions. Thus in spite of this
small change in voting pattern the United States finds
itself still in the colonialist camp. According to one
observer:

> It appeared that no sooner had the United
> States moved to a point where it could,
> in good conscience, vote for a mildly con-
> demnatory resolution, than the majority of
> world opinion took another long stride
> ahead, leaving the U.S. again in the minor-
> ity, along with the "colonialist" nations.[15]

With regard to Rhodesia the United States has consistently
backed Britain against all efforts by the United Nations
to press for decisive action against the Smith regime.
When the United States finally voted in the Security

Council's Resolution 232 (December 1966) for the adoption of mandatory sanctions, it did so at the instigation of the British government.[16]

The consistent support that the United States has given the white redoubt in the United Nations has been reinforced by the U.S. response to sanctions that have been voted agsinst the redoubt. The United States has consistently refused to comply with U.N. sanctions against these countries--even sanctions that the United States has itself supported. For instance U.S. officials refused to comply with the Security Council resolution of July 1963 calling on members not to supply military equipment to Portugal for use in its overseas territories on the grounds that the United States had already had a policy of not selling to Portugal arms for use in those territories, in spite of the admission by the United States that "arms supplied to Portugal for other purposes [could be] used in its overseas territories."[17] In August of 1963 U.S. officials explained U.S. refusal to comply with the Security Council ban on the sale of weapons to South Africa by insisting that the United States already had such a policy, with the exception of "existing contracts which provide for limited quantities of strategic equipment for defense against external threats," which the United States had to honor, and that in any case the ban under consideration was purely voluntary.[18] The most blatant of these actions was the passage of Section 503 (the Byrd Amendment) of the Military Procurement Act in the U.S. Senate, making it legal for the United States to ignore the mandatory sanctions against Rhodesia that the United States itself had voted for.

Waldemar Nielsen described the policy of the United States as one "of straddling the fence, with an ear to the ground, an eye to the future, and a finger in the dyke."[19] The United States may indeed have its "finger in the dyke," but to characterize its behavior as "straddling the fence" completely misses the point of U.S. policy. The only conclusion that the facts of the case will allow is that U.S. policy has been consistently anti-African. Supporting one side with arms while attempting to mollify the other with rhetoric cannot possibly be described as straddling. Despite differences in the styles of various U.S. administrations the pattern has been of consistent support of the colonialists and the white redoubt. And this pattern is consistent with the conceptions of U.S. national interest that have always motivated U.S. policy toward Africa.

It is clear that apart from considerations of general alliance cohesion U.S. strategic interests are served by maintaining friendly relations with Portugal and South Africa. Continued Portuguese presence in the NATO alliance; access to the Portuguese base in the Azores, the U.S. space tracking station, and the Simonstown naval base in South Africa; and the control of the South Indian Ocean especially after the closing of the Suez Canal—all of these no doubt have some utility for U.S. strategic interests. However, the strategic importance of these gains has receded in the light of the changing situation. Although the U.S. facilities in South Africa are obviously important they are not indispensable. As for Portugal, in the light of its meager contributions it may be an understatement to say that Portugal's loss to NATO may not be entirely disastrous to the alliance. Viewed against what the support of the white redoubt has and will continue to cost the United States in its relations with the African states, the strategic gains outlined above seem really insignificant. It would seem therefore that the strategic interest is not enough to explain the U.S. policy of supporting the white redoubt against black Africa, and that the interest of the United States in the survival of Western culture has been increasingly brought into play as the motivation and rationale for U.S. policy in that area.

This cultural factor came to the forefront in a form that was particularly uncomfortable for the United States and Britain—the form of racism. But uncomfortable as this might have been it was virtually impossible for the United States and Britain to rebut the African contention that the basis of Anglo-American action had been that "the blood of white Rhodesian rebels is too sacred to be shed in the interests of African majority rule,"[20] especially in light of the fact that neither the United States nor Britain had been so shy about intervening elsewhere to safeguard their colonial or security interests, as in Aden, Guiana, Egypt, and the Dominican Republic, or to support whites as in Stanleyville.

As noted above, U.S. officials have interpreted the U.S. interest in the survival of Western culture to require the assimilation of the African territories. Due to the multiracial character of the societies in Southern Africa the formulation of a policy to achieve the basic U.S. interest has been rendered more complicated. The preferred U.S. model for multiracial societies has been the more respectable one of maintaining white supremacy in an integrationist/assimilationist context as is the

case of the United States itself. Therefore U.S. policy
has been based on the judgment of U.S. officials that the
same pattern represents the best guarantor of the survival of Western culture in Southern Africa. However, in
the face of the increasing determination of the Africans
to achieve majority rule in their own homeland the whites
in Southern Africa feel, with varying depths of conviction, that nothing short of explicit white superiority
can "save Western culture." The insistence of the white
redoubt on white supremacist rule has caused the United
States some discomfort. For U.S. officials are acutely
aware of the fact that the explicit position of white
superiority adopted by the whites of Southern Africa is
infamous for its diametrical opposition to contemporary
norms of self-determination and human rights. They are
also aware of the fact that if the whites in the redoubt
were to retreat from their position and to adopt the more
internationally accepted integrationist/assimilationist
model of white superiority advocated by the United States
they could avoid all the international censure and also
make their alliance more consistent with the U.S. position
as leader of the "free world." However, the white regimes
in Southern Africa continue to be adamant on the issue of
white supremacy, thus transforming the U.S. cultural interest in Africa into a racial interest. For without any
choice as to what form of Western culture to support in
that area except that presented in the form of white supremacist regimes, the U.S. position has been that it
cannot afford to echo the words of Winston Churchill--to
preside over the demise of Western culture in Africa--and
therefore it must support the white regimes. It is clear
that the American and especially the British public would
not have supported the use of force against the Smith regime.

THE UNITED STATES IN AFRICA

Vigorous U.S. involvement in Africa began with the
Congo crisis of 1960. Since that time the United States
has had several occasions to deal directly with African
states. A cursory examination of the pattern of U.S. intervention in Africa reveals that the same consistent conceptions of U.S. national interest that have operated in
U.S. action in the United Nations are also operating in
the direct relations between the United States and the
African states.

In 1960 the United States helped to establish order
and stability in the Congo while working under the aus-
pices of the United Nations and in cooperation with several African states. This action was praised by most of
the African states. Four years later the United States
came under the sharp verbal attack of almost all the African states for its part in the infamous Stanleyville airlift. In 1967 the United States intervened in the Congo
again, this time on the side of a Congolese government
that had increasingly come to be recognized as a client
state.

The strategic U.S. interest is discernible in these
apparently different types of action. For instance according to Adlai Stevenson, then U.S. representative to
the United Nations, the United States backed U.N. action
in the 1960 Congo crisis because it was "the only instrument by which the end of the Western system of colonialism
can be prevented from opening the doors to the new imperialism of the East."[21]

In relation to the independent states the same rationale of attempting to forestall communist regimes in
Africa was responsible for a U.S. tendency to support conservative regimes such as in Ethiopia and the Congo (Kinshasa) with military and economic aid. A spectacular example of this is the alacrity with which the U.S. government recognized the Ankrah military government in Ghana
after the ouster of Kwame Nkrumah, and offered the new
government a loan that had just been refused to Nkrumah.[22]
Similarly the rationale for U.S. aid programs has frequently been based on the idea that "all of the African
countries are going to require some consideration to keep
out the Communist influence."[23]

Also operating as a persistent rationale for U.S.
actions in Africa was the cultural aspect of U.S. national
interest. The incident that most typifies this is the
abovementioned Stanleyville airlift. It is clear that
there were no economic or strategic considerations involved in this action nor did U.S. officials claim any.
The only claim made by U.S. officials, based on humanitarian grounds, is generally recognized to be at best inconsistent with U.S. actions elsewhere and possibly quite
groundless.[24] Even without discounting strategic considerations completely, it is difficult not to notice the
difference between the great sensitivity that the U.S.
government showed for the lives of the white hostages and
the callousness with which it disregarded the lives of
the tens of thousands of Africans shot down by the white

mercenaries on their way to Stanleyville in an operation
highly coordinated, by design or coincidence, with the
U.S. airlift. It may be that the frenzied comment by the
New York _Times_ about "dazed and ignorant savages"[25] is in-
advertent testimony to the deep-seated cultural and racial
attitudes that gave birth to U.S. action. Another situation exhibiting the effect of cultural attitudes on U.S.
foreign policy is the Nigerian Civil War. When hostilities broke out in Nigeria the U.S. government refused to
sell arms to the Nigerian government while being officially opposed to secession, in full knowledge of the fact
that Biafra was receiving a relatively unrestricted flow
of arms from unauthorized international arms dealers,
some of whom were American.[26] This attitude of the U.S.
government toward Nigeria was due at least in part to the
widespread acceptance in the United States of the skill-
fully cultivated conception of the Ibos as a highly tal-
ented, industrious, Westernized, and above all Christian
people.

In all its political dealings with Africa the United
States has exhibited three consistent patterns: support
for colonialism in dependent African territories; support
of white-minority rule in Southern Africa; and selective
intervention in independent African states in favor of
conservative regimes. This pattern has its roots in the
U.S. government's conception of U.S. interest in Africa.
One aspect of this conception of national interest is
based on the perception of Africa as a tool in the fight
against international communism. The policy to achieve
this interest of denying Africa to communist intrusion
was designed initially to perpetuate or prolong colonialism and later on for selective intervention. Although
economic relations are not the concern of this study, it
is notable that U.S. economic policy in Africa has been
entirely consistent with this national interest, as is
amply demonstrated by the 1963 report of the Clay Committee and by the pattern of U.S. aid to Africa in general.[27]
There is however another aspect of the U.S. national interest in Africa, derived from the belief among U.S. officials that the survival of the American way of life is
contingent on the development of Western culture in the
underdeveloped world including Africa. This aspect of
U.S. interest was also operative in its desire to prolong
colonialism and in its more racial manifestations--its
tenacious support of white-minority regimes in Southern
Africa. Of course this aspect of the U.S. national interest is less openly acknowledged due to the fact that

it is based more or less explicitly on a doctrine of white superiority inconsistent with current international norms concerning human rights and equality. Nevertheless it has always coexisted with the strategic aspects of U.S. national interest and has become a more prominent consideration as the strategic considerations have faded further back in the consciousness of U.S. decision makers.

In much the same way as the U.S. interest in Africa, the African interest in the United States is part of the African leaders' conception of a wider global interest. The African leaders have certain perceptions of what they need to do individually and collectively to meet the internal needs of their fledgling states and to advance their political interests in the bipolar world; and their interest in the United States is derived from this general orientation. Therefore in order to understand the African interest in the United States it is necessary to understand the overall global interests of the African states.

As in the case of the United States the national interests of the African states may be inferred from the pattern of their diplomatic practice. But in contrast to the United States the establishment of the pattern of African diplomatic practice is perhaps less difficult to accomplish; for in their diplomatic practice the African states have been less subject to great inconsistencies and wide discrepancies between actions and rhetoric. On becoming independent the African states have evolved a two-tier system of diplomatic practice. One level of this system is the diplomatic interaction among the African states and the other level is the relations between African and non-African states. In both of these interdependent arenas there have been disagreements and sometimes deep rifts between the African states. However, an examination of the diplomacy of these states does yield a consensual core of policy goals that represent what we might call the "African interest."

INTER-AFRICAN DIPLOMATIC PRACTICE

Modern interstate relations in Africa began with the First Conference of Independent African States, held in Accra in April 1958. Since then there have been many bilateral and multilateral contacts between the African states, the high point of which was the formation of the Organization of African Unity (OAU) in 1963. The history

211

of African diplomacy has been studded with ideological
and personal rivalries. The full story of the factionalism that was initially submerged by and later resurfaced
within the OAU has often been told.[28] The notable point
about it is that throughout this stormy history the African leaders have always recognized the need for an organi-
zational framework within which they could pursue their
individual interests as well as Africa's collective goals.
The creation and continued existence of the OAU is testimony to this recognition. Thus the OAU represents the
creation of an African community of a type where all the
leaders could agree, at least for the present, with the
group's norms, principles, goals, and problem-solving
capability. In the OAU's charter (Article 2, Section 1)
can be found the formal statement of the goals of the organization:

1. to promote the unity and solidarity of the African states;
2. to coordinate and intensify their cooperation
   and efforts to achieve a better life for the
   peoples of Africa;
3. to defend their sovereignty, their territorial
   integrity and independence;
4. to eradicate all forms of colonialism from
   Africa; and
5. to promote international cooperation, having due
   regard for the Charter of the United Nations and
   the Universal Declaration of Human Rights.

Taking into added consideration the principles of "absolute dedication to the total emancipation of the African
territories which are still dependent" and the "affirma-
tion of a policy of non-alignment with regard to all
blocs," as expressed in Article 3 of the OAU Charter, it
is clear that the OAU was fashioned as an instrument for
achieving economic and political modernization of Africa;
African unity and nonalignment; and total liberation of
Africa. The actions of the African states have been consistent with these goals.
     The fact that African unity and nonalignment have
been two of the most important and controversial issues
in the diplomatic life of contemporary Africa is well
known. Yet in spite of the disagreements between the advocates of "union" government and of "alliance and cooperation," and between the proponents of step-by-step
union and of immediate union, and despite the widely

discrepant interpretations of nonalignment the African
states have consistently shown a determination to resolve
conflicts among African states within the confines of the
contenent and a corresponding disapproval of intervention
in African conflicts by outside powers.[29] This policy
was evident in the OAU's treatment of the 1963 border dispute between Algeria and Morocco, and in the substitution
of African troops for the British troops that had initially been invited to put down the mutiny of the Tanganyika
Rifles in 1964. It was also evident in the Congo crisis
of 1964 where, in spite of the complications introduced
by the issue of internal subversion and by the split over
the extent of a communist threat in the rebellion, the
OAU Council of Ministers adopted a six-point resolution
urging among other things that the Congolese government
discontinue the use of mercenaries, and appealing to foreign powers to refrain from interfering in the internal
affairs of the Congo. All these and many other instances
support the conclusion that whatever disagreements exist
among the African states with regard to the interpretations of African unity and nonalignment, they have a deeply felt shared interest in maintaining in Africa a system
of exclusive jurisdiction that precludes the intervention
of outside powers in African conflicts.

There is no single issue on which the African states
share fundamental agreement more than the issue of the
liberation of all the remaining colonial territories in
Africa. This was enshrined in the charter of the OAU not
only as a purpose but also as a principle to which members, as noted above, pledged "absolute dedication."
Furthermore it was the subject of a special resolution of
the conference of African heads of state adopted immediately after the adoption of the OAU Charter in 1963--a
resolution which declared that the African leaders were
"unanimously convinced of the imperious and urgent necessity of coordinating and intensifying their efforts to
accelerate the unconditional attainment of national independence by all African territories still under foreign
domination." In the same resolution the African heads of
state pledged themselves to coordinate their efforts in
supporting the liberation movements in the dependent territories and established a coordinating committee, which
later became the African Liberation Committee, to be "responsible for harmonizing the assistance from African
States and for managing the Special Fund to be set up for
the purpose."

The committee has run into a host of difficult problems, confronted as it has been with the difficult task

213

of trying to coordinate the struggle in the face of the
intransigence of the white redoubt, the factionalism
within the liberation movements themselves, and the dis-
pleasure of the more impatient wing among the African
states.[30] However, the willingness of members of all the
factions within the African states to serve on the liberation committee and the willingness of all African states
to submit to mandatory assessment for the liberation fund
is evidence of their complete agreement on the fundamental
issue of liberation. Even the dismal failure of the OAU
to take decisive action with regard to UDI is due more to
tactical disagreements under conditions of relative power-
lessness than to any disagreement on the basic point of
the interest of all African states in the total independence of all African territories from colonial and white
supremacist rule.[31]

AFRICA AT THE UNITED NATIONS

Given their limited diplomatic activity in pursuit
of their interests, the African states have made the United Nations the focus of their individual and collective
diplomatic offensive. Therefore their activities at the
United Nations provide additional information on the interests of the African states. An examination of the
U.N. diplomacy employed by the African states shows even
more coherent evidence of the same collective commitment
to decolonization and development that is demonstrated
in their activities in the OAU and in their intra-African
diplomacy.

David Kay's analysis of all U.N. speeches made by
the African states and their allies in plenary and main
committee sessions between 1960 and 1966 shows that the
leading issues, in rank order, were decolonization,
South Africa/human rights, economic aid and development,
and disarmament.[32] For example during the Sixteenth Session of the General Assembly there were 1,131 speeches
made on the twin issues of decolonization and South Africa, exceeding the combined total of speeches on the
next eight key issues by about 35 percent.[33] This demonstration of concern for these two issues was not limited
to speeches alone; it is even more emphatically demonstrated in the pattern of voting activity of the African
states. As Benjamin Meyers showed in his study of the
voting behavior of the African states during the Eighteenth Session of the General Assembly, out of 32 roll

214

calls on the subjects of decolonization, self-determination, apartheid, and greater African representation at the United Nations, there was total agreement on all African votes.[34]

In both their intra-African and extra-African diplomatic practice the African states have shown varying patterns of consensus and disagreement. As noted above, they showed remarkable agreement on the issues of decolonization, respect for the principle of human rights, African unity, and African development. On these issues therefore it is accurate to note the existence of an African interest. As might be expected, the fact that the African leaders agree on a common interest has led to great similarity in their foreign policies. The political aspects of these foreign policies may be enumerated in their broadest outlines as the total liberation of the African continent from white supremacist and colonial rule, the unification of Africa, and the maintenance of a posture of nonalignment regarding other blocs. In terms of actual operation these broad lines of policy in the contemporary context have called for two specific efforts: maintaining exclusive jurisdiction and control of events within the continent and allowing as little intervention as possible from outside Africa; and moving against the white redoubt.

Underlying all this is a conception of the interest of Africa that is shared by these African leaders more or less with fervor. This interest is perceived to be the need for the African states to collectively achieve power and dignity and equality. In a fundamental sense this interest represents the same continuing effort toward the fulfillment of the goals of African nationalism. Having suffered under colonialism that was justified on the grounds of white superiority, many African leaders are committed in varying degrees to the assertion of black dignity through the achievement of black sovereign equality.[35] The first step was obviously the removal of white political domination--hence the advocacy of the total liberation of Africa. After that has to come the attainment of black equality, through the increased power that will be attained by political unification and nonalignment. It is this fundamental interest in redressing the distribution of international power in favor of Africa--which is born of the concept of the indivisibility of African dignity--that informs the remarkable agreement of the African states in their opposition to the white redoubt and therefore their opposition to the United States.

CONFLICTING INTERESTS BETWEEN THE
UNITED STATES AND AFRICA

With the African interest as outlined above, it is
not surprising that the prestige that the United States
enjoyed in Africa at the time of the independence of
Ghana has subsequently suffered serious erosion. Since
that time the African states have had numerous occasions
to observe the policies of the United States and, with
very few exceptions, they have found the actions of the
United States to be consistently opposed to African interests. To put it simply the United States and the African states have had conflicting political interests and
these conflicting interests have given rise to mutually
antagonistic policies.

The interests of the African states in increasing
their power and their dignity has given rise to the two
policy imperatives noted above: the destruction of the
white supremacist regimes in Southern Africa; and the
maintenance of exclusive jurisdiction over African affairs. The interests of the United States in denying
Africa to communist military or ideological intrusion,
and keeping it in the hands of the protectors of Western
culture has given rise to different policies. Originally
U.S. policy makers held the view that this interest could
be safeguarded by the perpetuation of colonialism in Africa. However, the independence of the African states
frustrated this objective. Since that time the U.S. interest, as noted previously, has given rise to two political imperatives: alliance with the white supremacist regimes in Southern Africa; and selective intervention in
Africa to sustain conservative regimes.

The juxtaposition of these two sets of policies reveals the basic nature and the depth of the conflict between the United States and the African states. First,
the U.S. policy of intervention--which was demonstrated
in its attitude toward the ouster of Nkrumah and most
graphically in the Stanleyville "rescue mission"--and its
support of the client regimes in Liberia, Ethiopia, and
the Congo (Kinshasa) is in contravention of the African
commitment to continental jurisdiction. For several reasons however this conflict of interests is not impossible
to reconcile. In the first place the way in which the
policy of nonalignment is interpreted by the African
states is not uniform. At the present time most of the
African states are pro-West and are therefore more likely
to condone U.S. intervention in African issues (as opposed

to Chinese intervention for example), provided the intervention is within one state, favors a conservative incum-
bent regime (or is discreet if it favors an opposition),
and does not involve a racial issue. Furthermore the regimes that benefit from such intervention are not likely
to deplore such activity, as was the case in the Congo in
1964 and 1967.

In relation to the issue of Southern Africa the conflict of interest between the United States and Africa is
total, intransigent, and completely irreconcilable. The
United States for strategic and cultural reasons is committed to the survival of the white supremacist regimes,
preferably in some form of assimilationist society. However, the United States has shown that if it must, it is
prepared to support the white redoubt in its present form.
The commitment of the African states to the destruction
of those regimes is no less strong. Although, as we have
seen, there is some disagreement among the African states
with regard to many other issues, including some aspects
of the tactics for furthering liberation, they all agree
on one thing: the continued existence of white supremacist
rule on African soil is unacceptably incompatible with African dignity.

There is yet another respect in which the African
states and the United States have a conflict of interests.
This is related to fundamental differences in the U.S. and
African conceptions of world order.

In a fundamental sense the interest of the African
states that manifests itself in the policy of nonalignment
goes far beyond the mere exclusion of major-power intervention in Africa; it represents the role that the Africans would like to play in the world system and their conception of world order. Although many African policy
makers found that they were in a position of heightened
maneuverability during the intense period of the cold
war, they later recognized their infinitely more important interest in keeping the world from being destroyed.
As Nkrumah noted:

> For Africans especially there is a particu-
> lar tragedy in the risk of thermonuclear
> destruction. Our continent has come but
> lately to the threshold of the modern world.
> The opportunities for health and education
> and wider vision which other nations take
> for granted are barely within the reach of
> our people. And now they see the risk that

217

all this richness of opportunity may be
snatched away by destructive war. . . .[36]

Therefore all the African states have a genuine interest
in international peace, especially among the great powers.
To the extent that they feel they have a contribution to
make toward peace they have attempted to play that role.
However, the African conception of world order also holds
that this international peace and security should be maintained in a way consistent with the principles of self-
determination and respect for human rights and dignity.[37]
Africans are committed to the vindication of these principles in general and particularly as they relate to Africa.

In this sense the African states are fundamentally
revisionist: they are motivated by a deep and unrelent-
ing desire to increase their power, prestige, and wealth
in relation to non-Africans. The African leaders are af-
flicted by a pervasive and intensely distressing feeling
of being the lowest on the totem pole and they are determined to redress this situation by establishing some
kind of juridical and actual equality with the rest of
the international community. So far the Africans have
been trying to revise the distribution of international
power by peaceful change so as not to violate their interest in international peace. However when faced with
the necessity of making a choice between the principle of
human dignity and the principle of international peace,
the response of the African states is likely to be the
choice of human dignity over peace.[38]

Contrary to the African states the U.S. conception
of world order is based on the principles of international
peace and security, anticommunism and the assimilation of
non-Western cultures to the norms and values of Western
society. On several occasions, beginning with the intervention of U.S. troops in the Soviet Union immediately
after the Bolshevik Revolution, the United States has
been eager to press its anticommunistic sentiment far
enough to destroy international peace. In the face of
the growth of Soviet power however the United States has
accepted the bipolarity of the contemporary international
system. As a result the U.S. conception of world order
has led to a policy of settling down to a "protracted
conflict" against communism that the United States hopes
to win by propagating the American way of combining "individual freedom and mass welfare of a primarily material
kind."[39]

On the basis of this conception of world order the
United States has always been suspicious of the principle

of nonalignment to which most of the African states have
committed themselves. This distrust was most blatantly
articulated by John Foster Dulles who considered nonalignment immoral. John Kennedy was credited with deviating
from this policy, but on closer scrutiny his policy
amounted to no more than patronizing conditional toler-
ance.[40] Since his administration U.S. policy has re-
verted back to the position of explicit distrust of any
government that will not profess to join it in the cru-
sade against what it considers to be the world's greatest
evil. The United States is a power with a very strong
status quo orientation, the foreign policy of which is
based on "resistance to Communist expansion by economic,
diplomatic, propaganda, and, if necessary, military means,
and the establishment of a peaceful and legal international order in which American material and security interests would be protected."[41]

In addition to the specific areas of conflict already
cited there exists a potential conflict of interest between the United States and the African states on the
basis of the different principles they stress within their
conceptions of world order. While they both have a theoretical commitment to international peace and security the
United States also stresses anticommunism as a concomitant
interest while the African states stress human equality
and dignity. Barring unforeseen circumstances, the present detente between the USSR and the United States suggests that the chance that the anticommunism of the United
States would lead to widespread war will remain slim.
However, the chance that the commitment of the African
states to liberation would lead to widespread war seems to
be increasing. Although the African states have exhausted
every peaceful method of liberating Southern Africa their
determination has not decreased. With the beginning of
systematic guerrilla operations legitimized by OAU, by
U.N. resolutions, and by the material support of the independent African states, the Africans seem to have settled
into a protracted conflict of their own with the white redoubt. In this regard the conflict of interest between
the African states and the United States hinges on the
seemingly unbreakable alliance between the United States
and the white supremacist regimes. The extent to which
this conflict of interest is reconcilable depends on the
possibility of changing either the African commitment to
their dignity or the U.S. commitment to the support of
the white redoubt.

FUTURE TRENDS IN U.S. AND AFRICAN RELATIONS

National interests, as has been noted previously, "are neither more nor less than what the duly constituted decision-makers conceive them to be."[42] Put another way, the national interest is the policy maker's conception of what goals he should pursue in the international arena in order to meet what he considers to be the resource, cultural, and security needs of his society. Of course the way in which he interprets these needs is the result of the way in which the interplay of political forces impinges itself on his consciousness and the ideological framework within which he is operating.[43] In an important sense this ideological framework and the political interplay are the roots of the national interest and therefore any attempt to forecast the trends in the substance of the national interest cannot be made without careful examination of these forces and their possible future configurations.

The roots of U.S. foreign policy goals are deeply established in "a general ideological consensus in the United States in which the mass of the population and its leadership generally share."[44] This consensus involves elements of anticommunism and what we might call "Anglo-Saxonism." The anticommunist aspect of this consensus and its effects on U.S. conceptions of the U.S. national interest have been massively documented in other studies.[45] The "Anglo-Saxonism" that underpins the cultural aspect of the U.S. national interest is based on the alleged superiority of Anglo-Saxon culture and institutions, and is responsible for the "melting-pot" notion of assimilating various ethnic groups into the mainstream of Anglo-Saxon America. With regard to racial minorities this "Anglo-Saxonism" is the basis of the tacit assumption of white superiority that sustains the integrationist/assimilationist model of multi-racialism. This "Anglo-Saxonism" is responsible for the fact that the United States is a white racist society, as the Kerner Commission has documented.[46] Since one of the goals of the foreign policy of a country is to safeguard the institutional and cultural integrity of the society, it is clear that it is the racist nature of American society that accounts for the racial aspect of conception of the U.S. national interest, which in turn leads to the policy of natural alliance with South Africa and support of Southern Rhodesia and Portugal. As James Rosenau has pointed out, the emanation of racist foreign policies from a racist society is entirely to be expected. For the same motivations condition the perspectives of the attentive public and the foreign policy decision makers, in both domestic

and foreign affairs, provided the same issue is involved.
Rosenau noted as an example: "An American who defines
himself as a civil libertarian is likely to feel obliged
to be as attentive to incidents of racial strife in South
Africa as to those in Mississippi."[47] Of course the same
can be said of those who support white supremacy. In fact
in the United States it is the white supremacists, like
Allen Ellender, Strom Thurmond, and Reverend Karl McIntyre,
who have been most vocal in their support of the white redoubt.[48] The fact that such "respectable" figures as Dean
Acheson, George Ball, General Marshall, and William Buckley
have expressed some support for the white supremacist regimes in South Africa should attest to the widespread nature of this support and dispel any notion that the support
is coming from any rabid fringe.[49]

If U.S. policy in Africa is going to change there
must first be a fundamental change in the racist character of American society. Such a fundamental change seems
extremely unlikely at the present time. It is true that
as black Americans have gained more electoral power in the
American political system they have shown an inclination
to attempt to influence U.S. policy toward Africa through
such organizations as the American Negro Leadership Conference on Africa and the Black Congressional Caucus.
However, they have met with minimal success and the prospect of their strongly influencing the U.S. government in
any consistent manner is rather dim. On the contrary
what seems to be growing is the influence of the advocates of "law and order," anticommunism, and racism in
both the United States and Southern Africa along with the
strength of organizations like the American-Affairs Association and the American-Southern African Council that
these forces have created.[50]

If this trend continues the United States will remain the symbol of the entrenchment of international white
power in Southern Africa and the main prop of the determination of international white power not to yield to the
rising demands by blacks for power redistribution, freedom,
and justice.[51] Any suggested changes in U.S. foreign policy that do not take this racial factor into consideration
have no chance of being successful.[52]

The conception of national interest held by African
leaders is also rooted in racial considerations.[53] Given
the nature of the African states, considerations of foreign policy are almost exclusively the concern of the government elite, and their conception of the national interest emanates from their ideological response to colonialism.[54] Colonialism was justified on the basis of the

ideology that whites had a mission to civilize Africans because of inherent white superiority. The demand for self-determination had to be justified on grounds that la mission civilisatrice was inadmissible because of the fact of the equality and dignity of African culture. To a greater or lesser degree African leaders share this basic antagonism toward the doctrine of white supremacy. However, there are differences in the completeness with which African leaders have rejected the white supremacist basis of colonialism and these differences account for the well-known division of Africans into moderates and radicals. Those leaders who are more emphatic in their rejection of the legitimacy of la mission civilisatrice have shown a tendency to be more distrustful of the former metropolitan powers as being neocolonialist, and have been more assertive in their commitment to Pan-Africanism and nonalignment. On the other hand those African leaders who are more ambivalent toward the legitimacy of colonial rule have been more susceptible to the assimilationist ideology, more pro-West and less nonaligned in their foreign policy orientation, and less committed to Pan-Africanism.[55] These two tendencies coexist in each of the African states. However, due to the fact that, after learning their lesson in the case of Ghana, the colonial powers granted independence to the colonial territories while the nationalist movements were still in the hands of the "moderates," the majority of the African states at present espouse the pro-West variant of nonalignment.

The type of nonalignment likely to prevail in Africa will of course be influenced by the course of the cold war and other changes that might occur in the international system. However, it seems that the majority of the African states will move further away from the European orbit toward a more aggressive type of nonalignment and the creation of a more truly nonaligned subsystem with a distinct culture. After several reversals the radical African states seem to be winning more followers toward a more radical commitment to the redistribution of international power. Furthermore there are forces within the African states that are pushing them toward a more radical stance. One of these forces is the increasing politicization of the African masses leading to increased race consciousness on their part. These factors combined suggest that the African states do not seem to be moving toward an accommodation with the doctrine of white supremacy. On the contrary the indication seems to be that they are moving in the direction of more long-term, concerted, and sustained activity designed to increase their power. The most crucial area of concern is of course Southern Africa. As noted previously, this is the one issue on which all African governments agree, for as Julius Nyerere noted: "The issue in Southern Africa is one of principle. It does not allow for compromise, because compromise on a matter of human rights is a denial of those rights."[56] This statement probably represents the views of an increasing number of Africans.

Due to the fundamentally irreconcilable nature of the conflict of political interests between the United States and Africa, and the projection that these conflicts are likely to worsen, the prognosis not only for future relations between the United States and the African states but for the peace of the world is very pessimistic. After several years of trying all available peaceful methods the expectation of the African states and the liberation movements is that the white redoubt cannot be toppled except by major, forceful, and extended revolutionary activity. They are also convinced that they cannot sustain such an effort without substantial outside help. The logical source of such support is the Asian and Communist states. At the present time many of the African states are still cautious about receiving military supplies and equipment from Communist sources. However, the longer the conflict continues, the more bitter and openly racist it will become, and even the moderates will be forced by their highly racially aroused constituencies to take a more militant posture, and accept Communist aid.[57] In such an event the spectre of a race war and possible world war will hang heavy over the world. The suggestion that the United States would stand aside from the ensuing conflict is as unrealistic as it is undesirable. The responsibility of the United States for letting the situation develop to this point is unescapable. Beyond that, as Chester Bowles noted: "The most powerful country in the world, which asserts that it is leading a global coalition for freedom, cannot declare itself to be nonparticipant in the affairs of a continent boiling with change, without abdicating its position of leadership."[58]

It seems inevitable that the United States would be drawn into the conflict that is now shaping up in Southern Africa. The question is whose side it would be on. Would the United States diffuse the intrusion of the cold war in this situation as it had once done successfully in the Congo in 1960 or would it precipitate a "worse Vietnam" by backing the whites in Southern Africa and thus inviting

the Communists to back the blacks in the North? Unfor-
tunately in view of the racist nature of American society
the latter possibility is the more probable.

NOTES

1. See for instance Rupert Emerson, Africa and
United States Policy (Englewood Cliffs, N.J.: Prentice-
Hall, 1967); Waldemar Nielsen, The Great Powers and Africa (New York: Praeger, 1969).
2. James Rosenau, The Scientific Study of Foreign
Policy (New York: Free Press, 1971).
3. Andrew M. Karmack, The Economics of African Development (New York: Praeger, 1967), p. 201.
4. Nielsen, op. cit., p. 253.
5. See C. Good, "The United States and the Colonial
Debate," in Alliance Policy in the Cold War, ed. Arnold
Wolfers (Baltimore: Johns Hopkins Press, 1959), pp. 224-
70; Thomas Hovet, Jr., Bloc Politics in the United Nations
(Cambridge: Harvard University Press, 1960).
6. See for instance the speech by Assistant Secretary of State Henry A. Byroade, U.S. Department of State,
Press Release, no. 605, October 30, 1953.
7. George Shepherd, Jr. and Tilden LeMelle, eds.,
Race Among Nations (Lexington: D. C. Heath & Co., 1970),
p. 2.
8. U.S. Department of State, Bulletin 22 (June 19,
1950): 999-1002.
9. Hans Morgenthau, "United States Policy Towards
Africa," in Africa in the Modern World, ed. Calvin W.
Stillman (Chicago: University of Chicago Press, 1955),
p. 318.
10. Vernon McKay, Africa in World Politics (New York:
Harper, 1963), pp. 322-23.
11. Gabriel Almond, The American People and Foreign
Policy (New York: Praeger, 1960), p. 30.
12. Speech by George McGhee, U.S. Department of State
Bulletin 22, no. 572 (June 19, 1950): 999-1003.
13. Almond, loc. cit.
14. McGhee, op. cit.
15. Quoted in Emerson, op. cit., p. 90.
16. U.N. Security Council, Resolution 232, December
16, 1966.
17. U.S. Department of State, Bulletin (August 19,
1963), p. 308.
18. U.S. Department of State, Bulletin (August 26,
1963), pp. 337-38.

19. Nielsen, op. cit., p. 297.

20. Statement by Alex Quaison-Sackey, U.N., Monthly Chronicle 2, no. 2 (December 1965): 14-26.

21. U.S. Department of State, Bulletin (July 10, 1961), pp. 67-71.

22. Nielsen, op. cit., p. 314.

23. Ibid., p. 290.

24. George Shepherd, Jr., Non-Aligned Black Africa (Lexington: D. C. Heath & Co., 1970), p. 48.

25. New York Times, December 4, 1964.

26. Nielsen, op. cit., p. 323.

27. See ibid., p. 390.

28. See the insightful account in Immanuel Wallerstein, Africa: The Politics of Unity (New York: Vintage Books, 1967).

29. Ali Mazrui, Towards a Pax Africana (Chicago: University of Chicago Press, 1967).

30. For a full account of this issue see Wallerstein, op. cit., pp. 152, 175.

31. Nora McKeon, "The African States and the OAU," in Alliances: Latent War Communities in the Contemporary World, ed. Francis A. Beer (New York: Holt, Rinehart and Winston, 1970), p. 278.

32. David Kay, The New Nations in the United Nations 1960-1967 (New York: Columbia University Press, 1970), pp. 45-50.

33. Ibid., p. 45.

34. Benjamin D. Meyers, "African Voting in the United Nations General Assembly," The Journal of Modern African Studies 4, no. 2 (1966): 217.

35. See Mazrui, op. cit., pp. 21-41.

36. Kwame Nkrumah, "African Prospect," in Africa: A Foreign Affairs Reader, ed. Philip W. Quigg (New York: Praeger, 1964), p. 277.

37. Mazrui, op. cit., p. 64.

38. Ibid., p. 135.

39. Almond, op. cit., p. 159.

40. Shepherd, op. cit., p. 107.

41. Almond, op. cit., p. 159.

42. Rosenau, op. cit., p. 259.

43. F. S. Northedge, ed., The Foreign Policies of the Powers (New York: Praeger, 1968), p. 21.

44. Almond, op. cit., p. 158.

45. For a critical examination of this theme see Bernard S. Morris, International Communism and American Policy (New York: Atherton Press, 1966), pp. 117-32.

46. See Report of the National Advisory Commission on Civil Disorders (New York: Bantam Books, 1968), p. 203.

47. James Rosenau, "Foreign Policy as an Issue-Area," in Domestic Sources of Foreign Policy, ed. James Rosenau (New York: Free Press, 1967), p. 36. For a full discussion of the influence of race on international politics see Rosenau, "Race in International Politics: A Dialogue in Five Parts," in Race Among Nations, ed. Shepherd and LeMelle, op. cit., pp. 61-122.

48. Vernon McKay, "Southern Africa and American Policy," in Southern Africa and the United States, ed. William Hance (New York: Columbia University Press, 1968), p. 21.

49. Nielsen, op. cit., p. 318.

50. See McKay, op. cit., pp. 19-25.

51. Locksley Edmondson, "Africa and the Diaspora: The Years Ahead," in Africa in World Affairs, ed. Ali Mazrui and Hasu Patel (New York: The Third Press, 1973), pp. 11-18.

52. For a discussion of some proposals see Nielsen, op. cit., pp. 337-78.

53. Shepherd, op. cit., p. 20.

54. L. Gray Cowan, "Political Determinants," in African Diplomacy, ed. Vernon McKay (New York: Praeger, 1963), p. 128.

55. This discussion is developed more fully in W. B. Ofuatey-Kodjoe, "Pan Africanism and African Unity: The Role of Ideology in the Politics of African Unity" (unpublished, 1968).

56. Julius Nyerere, "South Africa: Peace or War," Pan-African Journal 4, no. 1 (Winter 1971): 54.

57. Shepherd, op. cit., p. 74.

58. Chester Bowles, Africa's Challenge to the United States (Berkeley: University of California Press, 1956), pp. 96-97.

In 1960 Gabriel Almond noted:

> the climate of hostility in which the
> United States has to operate has become
> even more widespread and intense. The
> negative emotions and hysterias unleashed
> by the disruptive changes and the new na-
> tionalisms of the non-Western world seem
> to require a target, and the United States
> as the most powerful Western nation must
> bear the burden of memories of colonialism,
> as well as the burden of leadership, with-
> out permitting these violent moods and ex-
> pressions of hate to deflect it from a
> steady and vigorous course.[1]

These comments, which came at a time when the cold
war was still a factor in international relations despite
signs of a slight thaw, are pertinent especially as regards Africa. Much of the criticism of U.S. policy vis-a-
vis Africa has in fact derived from the seeming contradiction between continued American verbal support for the
traditional Wilsonian doctrine of self-determination as a
basic element of foreign policy, on the one hand, and on
the other the emphasis and support that the United States
gives to nonviolent, evolutionary progress toward independence, which works in practice for the maintenance of existing white-dominated regimes in Southern Africa.

The dichotomy in these policies has never been satis-
factorily explained. Observers appear to agree that it
is due in part to the rather low priority that strategic
defense and economic interests in Africa hold in the
U.S. view of world areas considered important, if not
vital, to U.S. policy considerations. Ofuatey-Kodjoe,
however, has discerned from his study of the application
of U.S. foreign policy as regards Africa a "consistent
and vigorous U.S. support for the maintenance of Africa
under colonial rule," underlying a U.S. policy that, in
present as well as past manifestations, is both anti-
African and racist. The official attitudes and actions
affecting Africa are said by Ofuatey-Kodjoe to flow from
U.S. defense and strategic concepts for the control of

international communism and the cultural requirements for
the maintenance of a world order that will ensure the survival of the American way of life.

While it is a generally accepted--and usually sound--
view that U.S. actions and policies in specific areas are
linked to pertinent strategic, economic, or defense factors, the introduction of race as a motivation for U.S.
foreign policy has received a new, if not entirely original, emphasis in Ofuatey-Kodjoe's study. A careful examination of U.S. policies and actions in Africa reveals
little basis for his theory or in fact for most of the
current interpretations of U.S. attitudes in and toward
the African continent.

U.S. INTERESTS IN AFRICA

In comparison with Europe, Asia, the Middle East, and
Latin America, U.S. interests in Africa, with few exceptions, are marginal. It is obvious that the United States
has continued interest in maintaining access to African
raw materials and in trade with and investment in various
countries of the continent, especially North Africa,
Nigeria, the Congo, and South Africa. As Andrew Kamarck
noted:

> The absolute figures on our trade with
> Africa look fairly impressive but are rela-
> tively not very important. The commodities
> we get from Africa are, of course, very
> useful and even indispensable for some pur-
> poses but it would be possible for the Ameri-
> can economy to get along without them. . . .
> The loss of American imports from Africa
> would undoubtedly cause hardships to some
> industries, raise costs somewhat in others
> . . . but one can scarcely claim that Africa
> is economically vital to us at present. We
> could get along without African commodities
> and African markets with an imperceptible
> ripple in our standard of living.[2]

There is of course a movement toward more extensive
investments in certain areas and territories of Africa,
with Zaire, South Africa, and, especially, Nigeria being
the more important recipients, although the Portuguese
territory of Angola has received some prominence due to

228

its petroleum resources in Cabinda. With the exception
of Nigeria, however, it is little likely that these increased investments will affect significantly the comparative importance of U.S. trade and investments in Africa
as compared with some other areas of the world. There is
the possibility that petroleum from Nigeria, which is assuming increasing importance as a supplier to the United
States, may bring about a greater interest in Africa on
the part of the United States and compel a greater appreciation of the need to cultivate African goodwill in the
political issues currently facing the African continent.
However, over the next few years this does not appear as
a likely possibility. Thus far Nigeria has displayed
little interest in utilizing its petroleum resources to
pressure the United States on policies and actions
directed to other areas and countries of Africa. Moreover it should be kept in mind that U.S. dependence on
Arab petroleum did not affect initial U.S. support for
Israel in the Middle East imbroglio, although it was an
important factor in U.S. determination to exert an all-
out effort to find a basis for Arab-Israeli reconciliation
on a ceasefire as the prelude to peace negotiations. At
the same time the adverse effects of the Arab embargo on
petroleum to the United States have caused us to launch a
search for means of developing new energy sources to re-
lieve American dependence on foreign sources of energy.
Such an effort, however, even if successful, will take
years. Hence unless in the unlikely event that Arab nations and Nigeria join in utilizing the oil weapon to
force more favorable actions on the part of the United
States as regards Southern Africa, U.S. policy as regards
this area will continue along its cautious way.

U.S. defense and security arrangements as they per-
tain to Africa appear to be of even less significance
than U.S. economic interests in the area; maintenance of
sea-lanes in the hands of friendly states and the availability of port facilities relate far more to economic
activities than to defense considerations, and it is difficult to imagine that such facilities would be denied to
the United States except perhaps in a war situation.
Even in such a situation, however, alternative arrangements would not be difficult to put into operation.

It would appear then that U.S. strategic interests
in Africa in terms of defense, trade, and investments,
as forming the basis of U.S. foreign policy, are not very
significant in relation to U.S. interests in other areas.
U.S. foreign policy vis-a-vis Africa in fact shows in one

sense a lack of interest as compared with Europe, Asia,
and Latin America. It is this lack of interest that con-
tributes in part to the application of policies regarded
by African leaders as inimical to the continent.

THE CULTURAL ASPECT OF U.S. POLICY

As noted above, Ofuatey-Kodjoe has put forward the
interesting idea that the most important of U.S. strategic interests as concerns Africa is to be found in the
American emphasis on the assimilation of Africa into Western culture as necessary for the survival of the American
way of life. In the context of earlier U.S. policies of
Communist containment and, later, competition with the
Communist powers in an atmosphere of detente, this idea
has some validity. It is doubtful however that it was
the paramount consideration underlying U.S. hesitancy during the preindependence period in Africa to give more substance than rhetoric to oft-proclaimed traditional U.S.
policy of self-determination, while alleging the prior
need for progress toward the construction of healthy political, economic, and social institutions; nor in the
present Southern African situation does it have much relevance to particular African problems confronting U.S.
policy, including what is widely regarded as U.S. support
for the maintenance of the white redoubt.

There can be little doubt that in the competition between the Marxist-Leninist approach of the Soviet-Communist
variety and the West, the survival of Western culture will
in the long run be "dependent on its assimilation in significant measure in the modernizing societies of Asia,
Africa, and Latin America."[3] It is hardly conceivable
that Western culture as we know it could survive in isolation in a world otherwise dominated by Soviet and/or
Chinese Communist cultural institutions and values. The
hesitancy by the United States to take a more forthcoming
view of the African liberation movement was due in part
to ignorance of the extent to which the process of acculturation had gone on among indigenous elites in the French
and British territories. After independence the United
States lent its support to British and French efforts to
maintain the closest ties possible with their former de-
pendencies in the continuation of this process. As Robert
A. Lystad has noted:

> The process of acculturation that went on
> for centuries among some African groups

has rapidly accelerated since the end of
the colonial period. The recent spurt is
a product in part of new forces, in part
of the "snowball effect" of accumulating
acculturation during the entire colonial
period. Its effects may be seen in the
widespread, though by no means universal,
assimilation into African cultures of many
items of material culture . . . and of certain social institutions and standards.

The most important effects, from the
standpoint of foreign policy analysis,
however, are the acceptance by the African
elites of the concepts of modern science
and technology and of the nation-state as
the most effective instrument for organizing and administering large numbers of
people.[4]

There is almost no available evidence to support the
idea that considerations of Western culture have guided
the application of U.S. foreign policy in specific situations with which it has been confronted in Africa. To
the contrary, U.S. actions have generally been based on
much more obvious and visible factors including, among
others, developments in other parts of the world having
greater priority than events in Africa, positions taken
by the Soviet and Chinese policy makers, U.S. interest in
the maintenance of political stability and the status quo
in an area of lesser concern to the United States, and
the requirements of the NATO alliance. This has been particularly true in view of the fact that African orientation outside its own cultural traditions has generally
been toward Western norms.

The concept of "African socialism" that at one time
caused some concern to U.S. policy makers because of its
implicit relationships to Marxism-Leninism has turned out
to be rather harmless in terms of U.S. and Western European interests even in Sekou Toure's Guinea and Boumedi-
enne's Algeria where the "revolutionary" ideology has had
its greatest development. The "African socialism" preached
by Leopold Senghor has so much reflected Western capitalism
and cultural values that Stanislas Adotevi, the Dahomean
Marxist intellectual, has dubbed African socialism an im-
poster.[5] Moreover common acceptance by all African states,
radical and moderate alike, of the concept of nonalignment
has removed much of the fear of extensive Soviet and Chinese Communist cultural inroads into the Western cultural

"preserve" in Africa. As Donald Rothchild has noted:
"The inherited economic ties of colonial times remain
largely intact, and political structures and cultural patterns have changed much less than anticipated."[6] As a
consequence the United States has turned toward a status
quo outlook in keeping with its marginal interests in
Africa and its increasingly limited capabilities.

U.S. policy with regard to Rhodesia, South Africa,
and the Portuguese territories has been fully examined
in the comments on Houser's study (see comments by Ngwabi
M. B. Bhebe and Larry Bowman). The idea of "white superiority" certainly has wide internal acceptance in the
United States and creates limited sympathies for the South
African, Rhodesian, and Portuguese regimes in the white
redoubt. Moreover U.S. policies in the area have and will
be governed by power relationships and the prevailing international situation as well as by the extent to which
the "black majority" in Southern Africa through its own
efforts--and even perhaps with the help of Soviet and Communist arms supplies--can bring about a redressment of the
situation.

POINTS OF CONFLICTING U.S. AND AFRICAN VIEWS

The conflict between U.S. policies as applied to
Africa and the interests shared in common by all African
states has been severe in the area of the African drive
for the total liberation of the continent from colonial
and minority regimes. This has been a consistent conflict
in the postwar period. Successive U.S. positions, first
opposing postwar independence claims, then accepting them
reluctantly in following British and French leads, and
finally giving only lip service to the decolonization of
Southern Africa, have lent some credence to the charge
that U.S. policies have been essentially anti-African and
diametrically opposed to the traditional U.S. posture in
favor of self-determination.

From the U.S. point of view, however, there was a
certain validity in standing back from espousals of African independence at a time when the United States was
burdened with the task of drawing Western Europe out of
the morass of the war years and organizing it to confront
Soviet pressures in the cold war. Moreover the United
States genuinely believed that strong African political,
economic, and social institutions were not yet in place,
and that the emphasis therefore had to be placed on

evolutionary rather than revolutionary transitions from dependence to independence.

The U.S. military support given to the French in an attempt to stem the Algerian independence movement reflected the continuance of an even more disastrous adventure in the Indochina war. And the economic aid given to the various Western European colonial powers for economic development, while designed to strengthen colonial positions in their dependent areas, did nevertheless give the latter a start on the modernizing goals that are currently indispensable to the progress of the various African states.

Similarly in Rhodesia the United States has followed the lead of its British ally. The United States gave its approval to the 1966 U.N. resolutions calling for selective mandatory sanctions against Rhodesia. However, as Robert C. Good has pointed out:

> Many officials in Washington, on the other hand, continued to have the most serious reservations about the efficacy of sanctions, not to mention the wisdom of using for the first time the mandatory provisions of Chapter VII [of the U.N. Charter] under circumstances making their enforcement virtually impossible. It was an irresponsible use of the Council's august powers, and an open invitation to Afro-Asian states to revile the inconsistency of Britain and its associates. Yet, having come this far down the road, it was difficult to identify a preferred alternative. So Washington followed the British lead--with reluctance and scepticism.[7]

Since that time the United States has refused to go any further than its British ally in moving against Rhodesia, even to the point of joining Britain in the veto of the U.N. African-Asian resolution of March 1970 condemning Britain's refusal to use force in its breakaway territory. However, the Byrd Amendment of 1971, violating U.S. obligations under the U.N. sanctions resolution, appears to be an aberration resulting from U.S. domestic politics and from a parochial economic interest rather than an expression of public support for Rhodesia, although it has had that effect.

U.S. Congressman Charles Diggs, Chairman of the House Foreign Affairs Subcommittee on Africa, has noted:

> Continued U.S. violation of Rhodesian sanc-
> tions can only sharpen the awareness of
> American complicity in supporting the Smith
> regime at a time of growing and sustained
> challenge to white rule by the African
> majority. Thus, the U.S. will be increas-
> ingly viewed as contributing to the already
> violent conflict in Zimbabwe by lending
> moral and economic support to Rhodesian
> whites.[8]

Repeal of the Byrd Amendment having already been voted by the Senate, there is every possibility that this deroga-tion from U.S. international obligations will soon be cor-rected. However, sanctions are unlikely to bring an early solution to the Rhodesian problem in terms of the stated British policy of "No Independence Before Majority Rule" (NIBMAR).[9] Such could be accomplished only by force that from all indications would call for financial and military sacrifices, along with political risks, that no British government is likely to take.

The United States cannot be looked to to go any fur-ther than Britain despite stepped up pressures from the African states, including force in Rhodesia against whites and the rescue operation in Stanleyville in 1964. While African bitterness is understandable this charge is some-what spurious in terms of the exceedingly small investment of U.S. military equipment and manpower in the Stanley-ville operation.

While it would certainly be a potent factor in im-proving the U.S. image in Africa if sanctions could be voted against South Africa, such an action is illusory for the foreseeable future. South Africa currently is the most highly organized industrial state in Africa and possesses a relatively formidable army. Moreover U.S., British, and other Western investments in that country are such as to make any strong action dealing with the apartheid system in favor of the overwhelming black major-ity a most unlikely prospect. Again this situation is due to no U.S. racist alliance with South Africa in the inter-est of maintaining Western culture, but rather to very pragmatic reasons that condemn all possibilities of eco-nomic or military actions on the part of the United States to rectify a most flagrant denial of human rights, equal-ity, and black dignity.

Progress toward the liberation of Southern Africa
will depend on the efforts of the Africans themselves.
While progress has and is being made by the African nationalist liberation movements, except for Guinea-Bissau
there is still a long way to go. As William B. Young and
Richard Pyle have noted:

> Decolonization is one issue on which the
> radical-moderate cleavage still divides
> the OAU. The split is obvious in the Af-
> rican Liberation Committee (ALC), estab-
> lished in 1963 to solicit support for lib-
> eration movements and, more importantly, to
> encourage unity among rival organizations.
> The OAU's moderate but realistic approach
> to decolonization is illustrated by the
> failure of Guinea's attempt to get the Af-
> rican states to commit a specific percent-
> age of their budgets to African liberation
> and by the OAU's reluctance to form an
> African Liberation Army. Even voluntary
> payments to liberation movements through
> the ALC have been sporadic. In 1969 the
> ALC reported that only 13 of the OAU's 41
> members had made contributions, an indica-
> tion of the priority which African states
> afford the decolonization issue when weighed
> against other obligations on scarce budget-
> ary resources. Communist powers--not the
> OAU--are the main source of military sup-
> port for the liberation struggle.[10]

Thus a much more concerted effort on the part of the African states will be necessary to move forward more rapidly toward the achievement of their objectives.
     In the 1960s incidents of U.S. intervention in Africa
brought U.S. policies into conflict with the claims of
some African states to exclusive jurisdiction over African
affairs. This was particularly true in the matter of the
Stanleyville paratroop drop of 1964, although this intervention was assailed primarily on the basis of its racial
overtones. On the other hand earlier policies in 1960
for the reestablishment of order in the Congo generally
had the support of the African states. Thus African attitudes toward American intervention in Africa are not even.
When the United States officially stayed aloof in the
Nigerian crisis this act of nonintervention was vigorous-
ly disapproved by certain African states.

Outside intervention as viewed by the African states, as well as by some expert opinion, appears to be rather vague. To describe U.S. reaction to the ouster of Nkrumah as the application of a U.S. policy of intervention is certainly far-fetched. That the United States at the time recognized the successor government in Ghana and granted it a loan that had earlier been denied to Nkrumah reflected the U.S. desire to assist the Ghana government in facing up to the desperate financial situation in which it found it- self due to Nkrumah's policies, rather than reflecting any desire to intervene in a purely domestic problem. It is also rather difficult to consider U.S. support for so- called client regimes as a form of intervention, in view of the fact that there is no evidence as to what U.S. pol- icy would be regarding a successor government. It is curious that Ofuatey-Kodjoe suggests that U.S. prestige in Africa has completely deteriorated while at the same time holding to the view that at the present time most African states are pro-West, and "are, therefore, more likely to condone U.S. intervention in African issues" under certain circumstances.

    In at least one respect a former source of conflict between the United States and African states has to all intents and purposes disappeared: U.S. suspicion of the African policy of nonalignment has generally been removed and nonalignment now receives general acceptance. Such acceptance, within the context of the U.S.-Soviet detente, has permitted the United States an even freer hand in con- centrating its attentions elsewhere, and at the same time has given the African states greater maneuverability in following their goals, especially in international organi- zations such as the United Nations.

                          STUMBLING BLOCK

    The chief stumbling block to more harmonious U.S.- African relationships will continue to be the divergence in policies as regards Southern Africa. There is no pos- sibility that the African states will surrender their goal of complete liberation of the area. At the same time there is little expectation that the United States, anxious to avoid involvement in another area, will shift away from current policies that indirectly afford some support to the maintenance of Portuguese, South African, and Rho- desian positions. As noted above, the burden of making further progress toward the total decolonization of the continent will have to be assumed by the Africans themselves.

I do not share the views expressed by many experts on African affairs that the deterioration of the Southern African situation through stepped-up violence on the part of the liberation movements could lead to a world conflagration involving the great power blocs. While the so-called "balkanization" of Africa through inherited boundaries has created a multiplicity of states cutting across ethnic lines, this aspect of African territorial organization does not lend itself to power struggles, at least from the outside. Unlike the Balkan situation in the pre-1914 days, there are no contiguous great powers competing for hegemony in Africa. The general absence of basic interests and the distance separating the great power centers from Africa are likely to ensure that that continent will not become in the foreseeable future the focus of world struggle.

NOTES

1. Gabriel Almond, The American People and Foreign Policy (New York: Praeger, 1960), p. 28.

2. Andrew Kamarck, "The African Economy and International Trade," in The United States and Africa, ed. Walter Goldschmidt (New York: Praeger, 1965), pp. 157-58.

3. Almond, op. cit., p. 29.

4. Robert Lystad, "Cultural and Psychological Factors," in African Diplomacy: Studies in the Determinants of Foreign Policy, ed. Vernon McKay (New York: Praeger, 1967), p. 111.

5. Stanislas Adotevi, Negritude et Negrologues (Paris: Union generale d'editions, 1972), p. 132.

6. Donald Rothchild, "Engagement vs. Disengagement in Africa: The Choices for America," in U.S. Foreign Policy in a Changing World, ed. Alan Jones, Jr. (New York: David McKay Co., 1973), p. 216.

7. Robert C. Good, UDI: The International Politics of the Rhodesian Rebellion (Princeton: Princeton University Press, 1973), p. 205.

8. Statement of Congressman Charles Diggs, Chairman House Foreign Affairs Subcommittee on Africa, February 27, 1974, p. 2.

9. For a detailed discussion of British policy regarding NIBMAR see Good, op. cit., chap. 7.

10. William B. Young and Richard Pyle, "The OAU: Ten Years Older and Getting Stronger" (Paper presented at the International Studies Association Panel on Comparative Regional and Global Systems, St. Louis, March 22, 1974), p. 12.

TABLE A.1

Developing Africa's Trade with Main Trading Areas
(percentages)

Area	Exports		Imports	
	1960-64	1965-69	1960-64	1965-69
European Economic Community	45.9	45.8	40.2	35.6
European Free Trade Area	20.7	18.4	18.7	16.1
North America	8.7	7.8	10.9	9.8
Japan	1.8	3.5	5.3	8.1
Centrally planned economies of Eastern Europe and China	6.2	6.6	6.0	8.8
Developing Asia	4.6	3.6	7.1	7.1
Developing Africa	6.3	6.4	5.6	6.8
Rest of the World	5.8	7.9	6.8	7.7
Total	100	100	100	100

Source: Survey of Economic Conditions in Africa in
1970, United Nations, New York, 1971, p. 100.

TABLE A.2

U.S. Trade
(millions of dollars)

| Area | Exports | | | | |
	1968	1969	1970	1971	1972
Developed areas	26,330.5	29,463.1	33,357.8	33,890.5	37,972.1
Less developed areas	10,808.9	11,265.5	12,975.4	13,398.3	14,574.4
Algeria	52.8	63.8	61.8	82.2	97.8
Zaire	50.7	43.8	62.0	84.2	37.2
Ethiopia	46.3	21.5	25.7	26.1	24.1
Ghana	56.0	62.1	58.9	54.8	43.5
Ivory Coast	12.4	19.9	36.3	21.6	22.4
Kenya	19.8	19.1	34.3	40.5	27.1
Liberia	38.4	43.9	46.3	42.7	41.4
Libya	114.9	134.1	104.4	77.7	84.8
Nigeria	56.2	72.3	128.7	168.4	114.6
Other Africa	746.4	797.4	913.0	985.7	865.0

| | Imports | | | | |
	1968	1969	1970	1971	1972
Developed areas	33,027.6	28,417.3	31,357.3	35,989.5	43,677.0
Less developed areas	8,892.4	9,394.7	10,468.0	11,586.5	14,393.8
Algeria	5.2	2.2	9.5	19.8	104.2
Zaire	42.0	34.9	40.6	44.5	43.2
Ethiopia	46.3	44.5	67.2	60.9	57.4
Ghana	78.1	68.5	90.7	105.6	79.7
Ivory Coast	79.0	53.6	92.1	82.5	91.8
Kenya	19.7	15.6	22.8	25.6	27.1
Liberia	51.0	60.2	50.9	49.0	52.4
Libya	89.7	110.6	39.0	51.1	116.1
Nigeria	36.2	70.8	71.2	130.1	271.0
Other Africa	828.1	757.3	792.4	925.6	1,243.0

Source: Direction of Trade, International Monetary Fund-
World Bank, annual, 1968-72, pp. 100-101.

TABLE A.3

Exports of Major Primary Products from Developing Africa
(percentages of total)

Product	1960	1965	1966	1967	1968	1969	Average Growth Rate 1965/69 (percent per year)
Crude petroleum	3.8	17.5	19.8	23.1	26.7	28.3	22.6
Copper and ore	9.8	9.1	11.5	10.8	11.2	13.0	21.1
Raw cotton	12.1	7.9	7.4	7.0	6.1	5.7	2.3
Coffee beans	6.7	7.1	7.8	7.3	6.9	5.6	4.5
Cocoa beans	7.4	5.4	4.1	5.3	5.1	4.9	8.0
Groundnuts	3.0	2.7	2.9	2.4	2.0	1.5	4.2
Wood and timber	2.8	2.7	2.4	2.4	2.4	2.7	11.0
Iron ore	1.8	2.6	2.5	2.6	2.4	2.8	12.7
Diamonds	2.7	2.3	2.3	2.3	2.1	1.9	7.2
Crude phosphate	2.1	2.1	2.0	1.9	1.6	1.4	0.2
Total	52.8	59.2	62.7	65.1	66.7	66.7	

Source: Survey of Economic Conditions in Africa, 1970, part 1, United Nations, pp. 301-302.

241

TABLE A.4

U.S. Imports and Exports, by Category, 1970
(millions of dollars)

| | Imports | | |
	World	All Developing Economies	Africa's Developing Economies
Food and live animals	5,378.9	3,435.5	529.2
Coffee, tea, cocoa, spice	(1,602.7)	(1,516.2)	(495.4)
Beverages and tobacco	855.0	90.4	1.6
Crude materials (excluding fuels)	3,311.3	1,115.0	113.8
Mineral fuel	3,080.8	1,924.9	99.2
Animal, vegetable oil, fat	159.6	121.0	9.0
Chemicals	1,450.3	192.5	5.1
Basic manufactures	8,438.3	1,314.6	44.2
Machines, transportation equipment	11,171.3	562.1	.7
Miscellaneous manufactured goods	4,843.9	1,341.6	2.5
Goods not classified by kind	1,273.8	266.4	9.7
Total	39,963.2	10,435.5	815.2

| | Exports | | |
	World	All Developing Economies	Africa's Developing Economies
Food and live animals	4,349.2	1,567.6	142.0
Cereals and preparations	(2,588.0)	(1,125.5)	(115.7)
Beverages and tobacco	701.7	191.5	21.9
Crude materials (excluding fuels)	4,608.5	797.0	29.3
Mineral fuels	1,594.1	289.6	13.8
Animal, vegetable oil, fat	493.0	287.2	55.1
Chemicals	3,826.1	1,282.5	56.3
Basic manufactures	5,067.0	1,604.5	111.2
Machines, transportation equipment	17,875.4	4,938.4	454.9
Miscellaneous manufactured goods	2,597.7	672.7	36.7
Goods not classified by kind	1,480.6	305.0	17.9
		(767.6)	
Total	42,593.3	12,603.6	986.5

Source: U.N. Commodity Trade Statistics, 1970.

Commodity Composition of Exports and Imports among All Developing Countries
and African Developing Countries, 1960 and 1969
(millions of dollars)

All Developing Countries	1960			1969			S.I.T.C. Categories
	World	Developed Market Economies	U.S.	World	Developed Market Economies	U.S.	
Exports, total	27,390	19,780	5,960	49,640	36,270	9,230	
Agricultural products	14,170	10,550	3,184	16,835	13,120	3,575	except 27,28 0+1+2+4
Raw minerals	1,540	1,420	485	2,685	2,440	555	27 + 28
Fuels	7,650	5,170	1,470	16,260	12,420	1,970	3
Chemical, iron, steel	388	224	92	1,195	520	170	5 + 67
Nonferrous metals	1,350	1,240	305	3,420	3,150	515	68
Manufactured goods	2,140	1,140	395	7,185	4,665	2,405	6+7+8 67,68
Other	152	36	29	2,060	45	40	
Imports, total	29,300	21,800	7,090	52,230	37,460	11,130	
Agricultural products	6,630	3,794	1,820	9,740	5,258	2,267	
Raw minerals	177	104	50	380	252	123	
Fuels	2,900	530	210	4,350	550	240	
Chemical, iron, steel	3,820	3,530	1,340	7,250	6,250	2,575	
Nonferrous metals	365	270	53	800	550	150	
Manufactured goods	14,130	12,550	3,386	27,720	23,400	5,965	
Other	1,278	1,022	231	10	1,200	190	
Africa							
Exports, total	5,310	4,200	420	11,320	9,210	690	
Agricultural products	3,620	2,816	330	4,650	3,400	438	
Raw minerals	428	398	32	670	610	52	
Fuels	245	200	2	3,510	3,230	165	
Chemical, iron, steel	66	44	5	158	67	2	
Nonferrous metals	620	560	32	1,720	1,640	21	
Manufactured goods	269	178	21	752	391	27	
Other	62	4	-2	-140	-128	-15	
Imports, total	6,470	5,310	490	10,030	7,670	860	
Agricultural products	1,346	944	196	1,731	1,031	196	
Raw minerals	19	15	1	49	29	4	
Fuels	510	215	19	670	165	11	
Chemical, iron, steel	745	695	26	1,350	1,210	88	
Nonferrous metals	45	37	--	98	74	4	
Manufactured goods	3,590	3,260	234	5,962	5,046	529	
Other	215	144	14	170	115	28	

Source: UNCTAD, Handbook of International Trade and Development Statistics 1972,
Tables 3.1-3.11.

TABLE A.6

Commodity Structure of Trade among Developing Countries, 1969
(percentages)

	Exports		Imports		S.I.T.C. Categories
	All Developed Market Economies	U.S.	All Developed Market Economies	U.S.	
All Developing Countries					
Agricultural products	36.2	38.9	14.5	20.0	0+1+2-27-28+4
Crude minerals and nonferrous metals	15.4	11.6	2.2	2.4	27 + 28 + 68
Fuels	34.2	21.4	1.5	2.1	3
Manufactures	14.3	28.0	81.8	75.5	5+6-68+7+8
Total	100.0	100.0	100.0	100.0	
African Developing Countries					
Agricultural products	36.4	62.1	13.6	23.6	
Crude minerals and nonferrous metals	24.1	10.4	1.4	1.0	
Fuels	34.5	23.4	2.2	1.3	
Manufactures	4.9	4.1	82.8	74.2	
Total	100.0	100.0	100.0	100.0	

Source: U.N. Conference on Trade and Development (UNCTAD), Handbook of International Trade and Development Statistics, 1972, part 3.

TABLE A.7

Total Official Net Flow of External Resources to
Developing Regions from Development Assistance
Committee (DAC) Member Countries and
Multilateral Agencies: Annual Averages
(millions of dollars)

Region and Period		Bilateral	Multilateral	Total
Africa,	1960-66	1,500.00	168.91	1,669.01
	1967-69	1,354.70	254.06	1,608.76
	1968-70	1,346.54	322.57	1,669.11
Europe,	1960-66	419.09	33.57	452.66
	1967-69	324.35	106.99	431.34
	1968-70	336.40	118.90	455.30
Latin America,	1960-66	739.10	143.06	882.16
	1967-69	956.35	299.43	1,255.78
	1968-70	984.43	395.64	1,380.07
Asia,	1960-66	1,869.56	232.72	2,701.27
	1967-69	3,197.00	351.97	3,548.97
	1968-70	3,208.18	331.77	--
Oceania,	1960-66	105.07	0.76	105.83
	1967-69	190.02	3.32	193.34
	1968-70	228.06	4.69	232.75
Total	1960-66	5,419.92	598.89*	6,013.81
(unallocated	1967-69	6,318.81	1,035.17	7,353.99
aid included)	1968-70	6,381.52	1,196.12	7,577.64

*Totals exclude figures for African and Asian Development Banks.

Note: Bilateral flows are net of loan repayments; multilateral flows are net of loan repayments, grants and capital subscriptions, and net official purchases of bonds by developing countries.

Source: UNCTAD and Organization of Economic Cooperation and Development (OECD).

TABLE A.8

Geographical Distribution of Official Bilateral (DAC Member Countries)
and Multilateral Flows to Developing Countries: 1960-70
(percentages of total net disbursements)

	1960	1961	1962	1963	1964	1965	1966	1967	1968	1969	1970
Africa*	35.5	34.1	33.5	28.6	30.4	27.4	25.0	23.2	23.0	23.5	23.8
North of Sahara	19.1	16.5	14.6	11.8	11.5	7.6	5.5	4.4	4.9	4.2	5.1
South of Sahara	16.4	17.5	18.8	16.7	18.6	19.3	19.0	18.4	17.6	13.7	18.2
America*	6.9	15.8	16.1	18.9	17.1	16.0	18.6	17.1	18.9	18.3	20.7
North and Central	2.9	3.4	3.2	4.5	3.4	5.3	7.3	7.1	7.8	6.5	8.2
South	3.0	11.4	11.5	12.6	10.7	8.8	11.5	9.6	10.5	11.5	12.0
Asia*	53.7	45.5	44.9	47.1	49.0	51.3	50.3	53.4	50.2	50.1	48.8
Middle East	6.7	8.1	6.1	4.9	4.1	4.9	4.3	3.7	4.0	4.2	4.0
South	26.9	20.8	22.6	27.4	31.4	30.8	27.8	29.5	24.1	19.8	18.7
Far East	20.1	16.6	15.9	14.4	13.1	15.2	17.9	19.9	21.8	25.7	26.0
Oceania	0.6	0.5	0.8	0.7	0.7	2.3	2.4	2.4	2.8	3.2	3.8
Total*	100.0	100.0	100.0	100.0	100.0	100.0	100.0	100.0	100.0	100.0	100.0
Total (millions of dollars)	4,176.3	4,857.8	5,303.5	5,817.2	5,799.4	6,212.6	6,358.9	6,896.3	6,869.8	7,000.7	7,501.0

*Includes unallocated disbursements.

Source: U.N. Economic and Social Council, Document E/CN.14/UNCTAD III/3, Table 5, Annex Table 7, TD/118/Suppl. 2.

TABLE A.9

U.S. International Investment Position at the Year End 1972
(billions of dollars)

	Total	Developed Countries	Developing Countries	International Organization and Unallocated
U.S. assets abroad	199,286	114	64	21
Nonliquid assets	180,932	110	63	8
Private, long term	128,360	89	32	7
Direct investment abroad	94,031	64	25	5

Source: U.S. Department of Commerce, Survey of Current Business, August 1973, p. 21, Table 3.

TABLE A.10

Book Value of U.S. Direct Investment Abroad, Year End 1972
(millions of dollars)

	Mining and Smelting	Petroleum	Manufacturing	Other Industrial	Total
All areas	7,131	26,399	39,478	26,024	94,031
Developed countries	4,420	14,200	32,825	12,669	64,114
Developing countries	2,712	9,878	6,652	5,944	25,186
"Other Africa"	425	2,254	124	284	3,086
Liberia	61	--	2	148	209
Libya	--	1,123	--	22	1,145
Other	364	1,131	122	114	1,732
International organizations and unallocated	--	2,321	--	2,413	4,733

Source: U.S. Department of Commerce, Survey of Current Business, September 1973, p. 27, Table 8A.

TABLE A.11

Estimates of Plant and Equipment Expenditures by
U.S. Corporations' Foreign Affiliates: 1971

(millions of dollars)

	Mining and Smelting	Petroleum	Manufacturing	Other Industrial	Total
All areas	1,735	4,865	6,837	1,507	14,844
Developed countries	1,374	2,585	5,878	1,046	10,883
Developing countries	361	1,678	959	461	3,459
(Other Africa)	(50)	(324)	(46)	(25)	(445)
International shipping	--	503	--	--	503

Source: U.S. Department of Commerce, Survey of Current Business, November 1973, pp. 46-49, Tables 1, 2, 3.

TABLE A.12

African Imports and Exports of Various Agricultural Products, 1965 and 1968

(millions of dollars)

Product	Imports 1965	Imports 1968	Exports 1965	Exports 1968	Balance 1965	Balance 1968
All cereals	433.3	488.5	100.7	181.9	-332.6	-306.6
Rice	95.2	106.3	45.4	118.9	-49.8	12.6
Maize	30.4	15.9	17.6	39.2	-12.8	23.3
Wheat	295.7	434.3	19.0	9.9	-276.7	-425.4
Barley	3.8	5.0	1.4	0.9	-2.4	-4.1
Dairy products	135.5	129.0	9.8	6.2	-125.7	-122.8

Note: Data exclude South Africa.

Source: Survey of Economic Conditions in Africa, 1970, part 1, United Nations, pp. 50-51.

TABLE A.13

Africa's Share of World Mineral Production
(percentages)

Mineral	1965	1968
Bauxite	6.1	6.0
Antimony ore	24.5*	28.8*
Beryl	15.8*	26.9*
Chrome ore	32.3	32.6
Cobalt ore	72.2	68.6
Columbium-tantalum	43.0	19.4
Copper ore	22.5	22.4
Gold	78.3*	81.0*
Iron ore	6.3	7.5
Lead ore	9.2	6.2
Manganese ore	26.3	25.9
Tin ore	11.5*	11.0*
Vanadium ore	28.9	27.5
Zinc ore	6.7	5.2
Platinum-group metals	25.1	26.9
Asbestos	14.1*	10.5*
Diamonds	84.8*	74.4*
Phosphate rock	25.9	24.0
Crude petroleum	7.0	10.0
Uranium	12.0	14.3

*Excludes certain producers, particularly the USSR.

Source: Survey of Economic Conditions in Africa,
1970, part 1, United Nations, p. 52.

249

118; economic and social conditions, 98; US investments and trade, 110-12; US military aid, 88, 112-13 (see also Azores)

race war, 94, 131, 223
racism, 40-41, 47, 207, 208, 209-10, 220-21, 223-24
Rand Currency Area, 63
Rhodesia, 18, 31, 64, 82, 95, 105-6, 135, 139; diplomatic relations, 95, 119
Roosevelt, Theodore, 41
Russia (see USSR)

Sahel, the, 58, 71, 189
sanctions, economic and military, 138-39; Portugal, 206; Rhodesia, 64, 95-96, 105, 205-6, 233-34; South Africa, 107-9, 206 (see also arms embargo)
Saudi Arabia, 144
Scali, John, 106
self-determination, 18, 63, 92, 125, 201, 208, 215, 218, 222
settlers, white (see White Settlers)
Sihanouk, Prince, 60
slavery, 41
Smith, Ian, 64
Somalia, 66
South Africa, 35, 39, 40, 79-81, 90-91, 92, 94, 96-105, 107-10, 113-15, 118-23, 124-26, 131-33, 136-37, 139, 141, 143, 144, 145, 146, 147, 148, 149; economic conditions, 99-105; labor, 101-2, 136-37; military, 99, 107-10; racial situation, 60-62, 99-101, 234; relations

with African States, 100-101, 217; U.S. investments in, 103-4, 234; U.S. relations with, 39-40, 46, 48-49, 60-62, 76-78, 79-80, 88-93, 119-24, 208, 217 (see also apartheid, dialogue, sanctions, OAU)
Southern Africa, 29, 34, 35, 42, 45-46, 61-64, 76, 78-79, 81, 82, 88-94, 99, 106, 119, 120-21, 123, 125, 126, 128, 129, 131, 133, 135-37, 138, 139-40, 141, 143-44, 235; Manifesto on, 102
Southern African Customs Union, 63
Southern Rhodesia (see Rhodesia, Zimbabwe)
South West Africa (see Namibia)
South West African Convention, 96
South West African Peoples' Organization (see SWAPO)
Soviet Union (see USSR)
Sudan, 67
Suharto, 33
Sukarno, 33
SWAPO, 96
Swaziland, 63

Tanzania, 32, 65, 118
third world, 60, 70, 125-27, 142-43
Thurmond, Strom, 221
Toure, Sekou, 33, 44
trade, 29, 153-56, 159-61; Portuguese territories, 107; South Africa, 103-4, 107-9; U.S.-Africa, 68, 83, 153-54 (see also commodities)
Tshombe, Moise, 27
Tunisia, 67

254

UDI, 31, 119, 214
Uganda, 64–65
UNCTAD, 68
United Kingdom (see Britain)
United Nations, Africans in, 91, 121, 204, 214–15; colonial issues, 17, 18, 19, 115–16; Congo crisis, 26–27, 209; Namibia, 96–97, 105; Rhodesia, 105 (see also U.S., United Nations votes)
United States: Africa, 14–15, 16–17, 18–19, 24–28, 42–44, 56, 83, 88–92, 107–15, 119–29, 200–211, 216, 217, 230ff; aid (see aid, United States); Algeria, 17, 19, 67; Congo, 25–28, 30–31, 208, 209; economic policy, 20–21, 67–71, 103–4; foreign policy, 62–63, 144–49, 203–4, 218–19; intervention in Africa, 25–28, 30–31, 208, 209, 216–17; national interests, 202, 206–7, 209; Rhodesia (see Rhodesia, U.S. policy); South Africa (see South Africa-U.S. relations); United Nations votes, 18, 91, 92, 123, 205, 208
USSR, 29, 21–32, 34, 142,

143, 145, 218 (see also detente)

Vietnam, 29, 142, 144
Vorster, Balthazar, 99

Waldheim, Kurt, 121
war, race (see race war)
war, world, 217, 219, 223
West Africa, 58–60
white minorities, 63–64, 93, 99, 123, 129, 131, 132, 204, 205
white settlers, 15, 32, 97, 208
white supremacy, 207, 208, 216, 217, 221, 232 (see also racism)
Williams, G. Mcnen, 18
Wilson, Woodrow, 41
World Bank, 168
world economy, 12–13, 27, 34
world trade (see trade, world)

Yazid Mihamed, 19

Zaire, 25–28, 30, 32, 34, 35, 59–60 (see also Congo, Lumumba)
Zambia, 35, 65
Zimbabwe, 35 (see also Rhodesia)

FREDERICK S. ARKHURST is visiting professor of polit-
ical science at Queens College, City University of New
York, and former Vice President of the Phelps-Stokes Fund.
He was also director of African programs at the Adlai
Stevenson Institute of International Affairs in Chicago
and former faculty fellow of the Center for International
Affairs at Harvard University in Cambridge, Massachusetts.
During a long diplomatic career he served as head of the
Ghana Foreign Service and as ambassador and permanent rep-
resentative of Ghana to the United Nations. He has also
edited Africa in the Seventies and Eighties: Issues in
Development (Praeger, 1970), Arms and African Development
(Praeger, 1972); and contributed "Africa: Exploration
and Settlement," to Encyclopaedia Britannica III (1974).

ELLIOT J. BERG is professor of economics and director
of the Center for Research on Economic Development at the
University of Michigan. He has also taught at Harvard
University and was an adviser on economic development to
several African governments. His publications include
"Structural Transformation vs. Gradualism: Recent Economic Developments in Ghana and the Ivory Coast" in Patterns of Modernization in Ghana and the Ivory Coast (University of Chicago Press, 1971); "Wages and Employment in
Less Developed Countries" in The Challenge of Unemployment
to Development and the Role of Training and Research In-
stitutes of Development (OECD, 1971); and "The Character
and Potential of African Economics" in The United States
and Africa (Praeger, 1964).

NGWABI M. B. BHEBE is professor of history at Fourah
Bay College, University of Sierra Leone, and has taught
at the University of Rhodesia and at Princeton University.
His publications also include "Missionary Activity Among
the Ndebele and Kalanga 1900-1923: A Survey," in Chris-
tianity South of the Zambezi (Mambo Press, 1973); and
"Ndebele Trade in the Nineteenth Century," in Journal of
African Studies (UCLA, 1974).

LARRY W. BOWMAN is assistant professor of political
science at the Graduate School of the University of Con-
necticut Research Foundation and has also taught at the

University of Rhodesia and at Brandeis University. He
has traveled extensively in Southern Africa. His publications also include "A Background to White Politics in
Rhodesia," in Rhodesian Perspective (Michael Joseph,
1967); "South Africa's Outward Strategy: A Foreign Policy
Dilemma for the United States," in Papers in International
Studies (Ohio University Center for International Studies,
1971); "Southern Africa and the Indian Ocean," in The
Indian Ocean: Its Political, Economic and Military Importance (Praeger, 1972); and Politics in Rhodesia: White
Power in an African State (Harvard University Press, 1973).

JOHN A. DAVIS is professor of political science at
City College, City University of New York. He has also
taught at Lincoln University in Lincoln, Pennsylvania and
at Ohio State University. He has served as consultant to
various civic and private agencies. He has also edited
African Forum and Journal of Contemporary Affairs, and
been coeditor of Southern Africa in Transition (Praeger,
1966). He is the author of Regional Organization of the
Social Security Administration (Columbia University Press,
1951 and 1967), and "Non-Discrimination in the Federal
Services," in Annals of the American Academy of Political
and Social Sciences (Spring 1944).

GEORGE M. HOUSER has been executive director of The
American Committee on Africa since 1955, and is vice
president of the International Defense and Aid Fund. He
was also one of the founders of the Congress of Racial
Equality in 1947. He has traveled extensively in Africa
and has the most prolific contacts of any American with
the leadership of the African liberation movements. His
publications also include "Non-Violent Revolution in
South Africa," "The South African Crisis and U.S. Policy,"
and "Nationalist Organizations in Angola," in Southern
Africa in Transition (Praeger, 1966).

CLINTON E. KNOX, a distinguished diplomat and scholar,
taught international relations at the School of Advanced
International Studies at Johns Hopkins University. He was
U.S. ambassador to the Republic of Dahomey and later U.S.
ambassador to the Republic of Haiti.

WENTWORTH B. OFUATEY-KODJOE is professor of political
science and director of the Africana Studies and Research
Institute at Queens College, City University of New York.
He is vice president of INTERFUTURE; has been associate

director of Peace Corps Training Projects for Africa at
Columbia University Teachers College; and was formerly
associate editor of the Journal of International Affairs.
His publications also include "Kwame Nkrumah and the For-
eign Policy of Pan-Africanism," in Pan African Journal
(Spring 1974); "Principles and Techniques of Ntumpan
(Talking) Drumming," in Columbia Essays on International
Affairs (Columbia University Press, 1967), and "The Afri-
can Community and Border Disputes," in Visa (February
1964).

GEORGE W. SHEPHERD is professor of international relations and former director of the Center on International
Race Relations at the University of Denver. He has also
taught at the University of Minnesota and at Brooklyn College, City University of New York. He has traveled extensively in Africa. His publications also include Racial
Influences on American Foreign Policy (Basic Books, 1971);
Race Among Nations: A Conceptual Approach (D. C. Heath,
1970); Nonaligned Black Africa (D. C. Heath, 1970); The
Politics of African Nationalism (Praeger, 1962); "South
Africa, the New Debate," in Africa Today (Winter 1973);
and (with Tilden J. LeMelle) "The Future of Race in International Relations," in Journal of International Affairs
(September, 1971).

HERBERT J. SPIRO is a member of the Policy Planning
Staff of the U.S. Department of State. He was professor
of political science at the University of Pennsylvania,
and has also taught at Harvard University, Princeton Uni-
versity, Amherst College, Stanford University, and the
University of Chicago. His publications also include
Politics as the Master Science: From Plato to Mao
(Harper & Row, 1970); Responsibility in Government:
Theory and Practice (Van Nostrand-Reinhold, 1969); and
World Politics: The Global System (Dorsey Press, 1966).
He has also edited Patterns of African Development: Five
Comparisons (Prentice-Hall, 1967); and Africa: The Pri-
macy of Politics (Random House, 1966).

IMMANUEL WALLERSTEIN is professor of sociology at
McGill University in Toronto and former professor of
sociology at Columbia University. His publications include Africa: The Politics of Independence (Vintage,
1961); The Road to Independence: Ghana and the Ivory
Coast (Mouton, 1964); Africa: The Politics of Unity
(Random House, 1967); University in Turmoil: The Politics

of Change (Atheneum, 1969); and The Modern World System: Capitalist Agriculture and the Origins of the European World Economy in the Sixteenth Century (Academic Press, 1974). He has also edited Social Change: The Colonial Situation (Wiley, 1966).

ELEANORA WEST is an economist and free-lance writer, a former researcher at Yale and Columbia Universities, and has also served on various civic committees.

ROBERT L. WEST is professor of international economics and chairman of the International Development Studies Program at the Fletcher School of Law and Diplomacy. He has also taught at Yale University, with the United States Agency for International Development, and at the Massachusetts Institute of Technology. His publications include "An Estimated Balance of Payments for Kenya," in East African Economic Review (July 1956); "Prospects for Congolese Economic Stability," in Emerging Africa (Washington Public Affairs Press, 1963); and "Impact of the Adjustment Process on Developing Countries," in Maintaining and Restoring Balance in International Payments (Princeton University Press, 1966).

FRANKLIN H. WILLIAMS is president of the Phelps-Stokes Fund as well as chairman of the New York State Commission of the U.S. Commission on Civil Rights and a member of the New York, California, and U.S. Supreme Court Bars. He has been assistant attorney general of the State of California, U.S. representative to the United Nations Economic and Social Council, and U.S. ambassador to Ghana.

259

RELATED TITLES
Published by
Praeger Special Studies

AID TO AFRICA: A Policy Outline for the 1970s
                        Paul Streeten

CHINA'S AFRICAN POLICY: A Study of Tanzania
                        George T. Yu

SOVIET POLICY TOWARD BLACK AFRICA: The Focus
on National Integration
                        Helen Desfosses Cohn

THE UNITED STATES AND WORLD DEVELOPMENT:
Agenda for Action 1975*
                        edited by James W. Howe
                        and the Staff of the
                        Overseas Development
                        Council

———————————

    *Also available in paperback as a Praeger Special
Studies Student Edition.